AFTER
MACPHERSON

Policing after the
Stephen Lawrence Inquiry

Edited by
Alan Marlow and Barry Loveday

Russell House Publishing

First published in 2000 by:
Russell House Publishing Ltd.
4 St. George's House
Uplyme Road
Lyme Regis
Dorset DT7 3LS

Tel: 01297-443948
Fax: 01297-442722
e-mail: help@russellhouse.co.uk

British Library cataloguing-in-publication data:
A catalogue record for this book is available from the British Library.

ISBN: 1-898924-71-6

Typeset by The Hallamshire Press Limited, Sheffield

Printed by Cromwell Press, Trowbridge

Russell House Publishing

Is a group of social work, probation, education and youth and community
work practitioners and academics working in collaboration with a
professional publishing team. Our aim is to work closely with the field to
produce innovative and valuable materials to help managers, trainers,
practitioners and students. We are keen to receive feedback on
publications and new ideas for future projects.

AFTER MACPHERSON

Contents

The Contributors

John Alderson CBE
Formerly Chief Constable of Devon and
Cornwall, Assistant Commissioner, Metropolitan
Police and Commandant, Police Staff College,
Bramshill

Lana Burroughs
Senior Lecturer in Social Work, Department of
Applied Social Studies, University of Luton

Robin Fletcher
Superintendent, Metropolitan Police and
Associate Lecturer, Middlesex University

Stephen Hallam
Sergeant, Bedfordshire Police and Associate
Lecturer, Vauxhall Centre for the Study of Crime,
University of Luton

Peter Kennison
Researcher/Lecturer, Middlesex University

Anita Kalunta-Crumpton
Lecturer, Institute of Criminal Justice Studies,
University of Portsmouth

Barry Loveday
Principal Lecturer and Deputy Director, Institute
of Criminal Justice Studies, University of
Portsmouth

Alan Marlow
Senior Development Fellow, Vauxhall Centre for
the Study of Crime, University of Luton

Jayne Mooney
Senior Lecturer, Researcher, Institute of
Criminology, Middlesex University

Michael O'Byrne
Chief Constable, Bedfordshire Police

Eli B. Silverman
Professor of Criminal Justice, John Jay College of
Criminal Justice, City University of New York,
USA. Author of *NYPD Battles Crime*, Boston:
North Eastern University Press.

Gurchand Singh
Senior Lecturer, Department of Social Studies,
University of Luton

Jock Young
Professor of Sociology and Head of Department,
Institute of Criminology, Middlesex University

Race, Policing and the Need for Leadership

Alan Marlow and Barry Loveday

The Macpherson Report was published in February, 1999, and, despite the passing of a year, the police service, and indeed other public services are still coming to terms with its implications. Commentators, reflecting on the anniversary of its publication, concurred that it had produced a radical shift in the agenda for race relations in the United Kingdom. What was particularly noticeable in the anniversary debate was its exclusive concern with issues of race and discrimination with almost no reference to the exposed inefficiencies in police investigation. It is the impact of the Macpherson's definition of 'institutional racism' that is the key issue in the Report's legacy.

Writing in *The Guardian* of 21/2/2000, Younge concluded that Macpherson had provided 'a new conceptual framework for Britain's race debate'. For Tara Mack, a black American writer, in an *Observer* article, it represented 'Britain's racial coming of age'. In the same article, she included a quote from Trevor Phillips, the journalist, broadcaster and leader of the new Greater London Assembly:

> The UK has absolutely no sense at all for the reality of racism…it has no sense at all for the way its schools, its police produce a biased outcome.
>
> (Mack, *Observer Review*, 20/2/2000: p 2)

The Macpherson Report should change that lack of awareness. It shifted the definition of racism from one born of wilful personal malevolence to one which is, to borrow Mack's phrase, 'ingrained in intuition'. 'Institutional racism' applies to all organisations, but it is the police service that will be subject to the sharpest scrutiny, for its failings have been mercilessly exposed and the consequences of discrimination in policing are particularly pernicious.

'Institutional racism', or rather the lack of it, will provide the criteria by which organisations will be judged in terms of equity of service. It may be a broad term complicated by other social forces, (see Singh in this volume), but it is one that refers to corporate outputs rather than individual failings. If the police service is to emerge from the stain of institutional racism, powerful leadership will be required. It will no longer be sufficient for chief officers to lament the negativity of the 'canteen culture' and subscribe to the thesis that, whilst they are personally impeccably anti-racist, it is inevitable that the service contains a few racists because it represents the population as a whole. It is no longer simply a case of educating or eliminating explicitly racist individuals, for institutional racism is the product of an organisation's unexamined practices and discourses.

The response to Scarman, (1981), was the production of enlightened policy documents that we now know had little demonstrable effect on the interaction between the police and minorities. Such cosmetic tactics are no longer options, for it is by outcomes that the organisation will be judged, not the expenditure of energy on good intentions.

Some are already lamenting that little progress has been made. Michael Mansfield, QC, (*The Guardian*, 17/2/2000), alleges that the report is being ignored and, by the use of anecdotal evidence, suggests that 'daily policing remains largely untouched'. However, to expect 'quick fixes' is to deny the fundamental achievement of a new definition that requires deep and significant cultural change—unlikely to be made manifest in one year.

Lea, (1999), argues that the elimination of institutional racism requires a system of accountability to elected representatives to determine goals and priorities. Such an arrangement assumes that local democratic control is necessarily benign and ignores the fairly ineffectual history of local democratic police accountability. Jones and Newburn, (1997), contend that democracy is as much about values as constitutional arrangements. Those values may be defined and measured in terms of 'performance indicators'. That process is not without its problems, (see Hallam in this volume), but it does allow judgements to be made to inform a public debate. The 'managerial revolution' that followed the Police and Magistrates' Courts Act 1994 has shortcomings but it has introduced new mechanics of accountability through the ability of the Home Secretary to set priorities for the police service.

This has already been commenced in terms of recommendations 1 and 2 of the Macpherson Report, (Macpherson, 1999).

In assessing the capacity of police leadership to engineer such a transformation, police history is not particularly encouraging, (Waddington, 1999). Nevertheless, times have changed, and chief officers, now appointed on limited contracts and performance-related pay, have significant incentives to drive through effective reforms.

Her Majesty's Inspectorate of Constabulary (HMIC) have already produced critical reports on forces' community relations strategies which can hardly be regarded as 'pulled punches', (see Loveday in this volume). They have indicated that further scrutinies will be undertaken in 2000, which will, according to *The Times*, (28/2/2000), 'name and shame' where progress has not been made. Reforms in police disciplinary procedures will give new powers to deal with recalcitrant officers. The levers are in place. It is now up to chief officers to use them. Macpherson followed Scarman after eighteen years. The prospect of a similar condemnation in a couple of decades is too appalling to contemplate.

The structure of the book

After Macpherson: Policing after the Stephen Lawrence Inquiry is divided into three sections. Section 1 provides an analysis of reactions to the report.

In Chapter 1, **Alan Marlow** traces the responses to the Macpherson Report of members of the police service including officers accused of the identified failings. There have been comments that the process was unfair and there is no doubt that the criticisms within it were unrelenting. Nevertheless, it is perhaps best viewed as a moment of public catharsis as the messages relating to the unfair treatment of minorities had been ignored for far too long. The chapter also assesses the prospects for real change in the ethics of policing.

In Chapter 2, **Barry Loveday** analyses recent reports produced by Her Majesty's Inspectorate of Constabulary which demonstrate how ineffective policies and strategies on community and race relations have proved to be. Police leadership has made little impact on the negativity of police culture, or put in place training and support systems that encourage the recruitment and retention of minorities. Police supervisory ranks lack the incentive or moral courage to challenge discriminatory attitudes and behaviour. The Macpherson Report, he concludes, must stimulate better leadership to promote improved community relations; otherwise the civil courts and the Commission for Racial Equality may take on the task.

Section Two comprises a series of chapters that analyse some of the issues raised in the Report.

In Chapter 3, **Gurchand Singh** provides a complete and detailed analysis of the term institutional racism. He traces its history and the controversies that surround its use. He argues that it has become 'inflated' with no real power to identify causal relationships and needs to be 'deflated' to prevent it becoming vague and imprecise. The concept is useful as a challenge to the idea that racism emanates from individual prejudice but there is a danger that such an explanation is being substituted for something equally vague. In particular, the compounding effects of class and gender should be understood and delineated. Singh concludes that whilst it is helpful in directing attention to how racist discourses become embodied in social structures, a much more precise definition is required for it to be other than a signifier.

In Chapter 4, **Anita Kalunta-Crumpton** seeks to disentangle what she terms the academic battleground on the effect of racial discrimination in criminal justice. She takes issue with the left realists as to the extent that class and age produce a disproportionate involvement of black people in the criminal justice system. For her, the evidence is clear that the issue of race is the crucial determinant of disadvantage.

Lana Burroughs teaches Social Work at the University of Luton. Lana was requested to write on any possible lessons from anti-discriminatory practice in social work and also to reflect on her experience as a black woman growing up in London. Chapter 5 is the result. It is powerful, disturbing and moving. Its sets the experience of the Lawrence family into a distressing pattern of normality. It provides a chastening prelude to the chapters on disadvantage in criminal justice and the inequities of stop and search.

In Chapter 6, **Peter Kennison** examines the contentious practice of stop and search which he describes as the 'litmus test' of equality in policing. He sets out the origins and difficulties with the power and draws on his research to show that the disproportionate targeting of minorities for the exercise of the power produces high levels of resentment which tends not to be expressed through the police complaints procedure. The two factors have compounding influences.

Jock Young and Jayne Mooney analyse the findings from a research project involving the use of stop and search in North London. In Chapter 7, they assess the individual and organisational factors that motivate the exercise of the power. They conclude with some recommendations to ameliorate the pernicious effects of what they describe as a 'massive and blunt instrument'.

In Chapter 8, Stephen Hallam provides a critical analysis of the requirement for police forces to produce pleasing statistics to meet the performance standards set by government. In a number of the contributions, authors have pointed to the distorting effects of the 'performance culture' in policing. Hallam demonstrates how these imperatives may adversely affect the policing of those matters which are not priorities for measurement.

Eli Silverman has studied and written on the policing revolution in New York City. In his book *NYPD Battles Crime* he identified the elements that contributed to the dramatic improvement in the effectiveness of the force. However, in Chapter 9, he shows that the pressure to perform has resulted in some dramatic incidents of police victimisation of minorities. There are common themes—in New York, 'stop and frisk' is just as contentious as 'stop and search' in the United Kingdom. Silverman argues that the dilution of some of the principles that re-shaped the NYPD have contributed to the emergence of old racial tensions. In particular, the local accountability of precinct commanders has been compromised by a shift to centrally directed specialist units and poor personnel selection for pro-active policing.

Section Three is concerned with the delivery of policing after the Macpherson Report.

In Chapter 10, Michael O'Byrne, a Chief Constable, asks the question 'Can Macpherson Succeed Where Scarman Failed?' His answer is a conditional 'yes'. Advances in performance management allow a greater visibility, provided that they operate in an ethical and corruption intolerant culture. Additionally, the political climate is much more favourable to positive change than that which prevailed at the time of Scarman. Also critical is the political will at government level to drive reform and to provide the support and resources necessary for success.

Robin Fletcher has been concerned with policy development within the Metropolitan Police Service. In Chapter 11, he develops a model to facilitate an effective information exchange to satisfy recommendations in the Macpherson Report. What is required, he argues, is a 'neutral information unit', supported by all the local social agencies, but in which no single agency has supremacy. It is only with such an arrangement, he contends, that there can be a complete capture and shared use of the sort of information that may have allowed intervention in the sequence of circumstances that resulted in the Stephen Lawrence murder.

In Chapter 12, John Alderson thoughtfully examines the philosophical basis for ethical policing. For him, enterprising professional leadership is a pre-condition for principled policing and that leadership must be informed by fundamental tenets. By weighing the ideas of key writers on social justice, he develops guidance for enlightened police command.

References

Jones, and Newburn. (1997). *Policing After The Act*. London: Policy Studies Institute.

Lea, J. (1999). *The Macpherson Report and the Question of Institutional Racism*. Middlesex University, Centre for Criminology.

Mack, T. (2000). The US Isn't Great on Race. Are You Brits Any Better? *The Observer Review*, 20/2/2000.

Macpherson, Sir W. (1999). *Report on the Inquiry into the Stephen Lawrence Murder*. London: Home Office.

Mansfield, M. (2000). White On Black. *The Guardian*, 17/2/2000.

Scarman, Lord J. (1981). *Report on the Brixton Disorders*. London: HMSO.

Waddington, P. (1999). *Policing Citizens*. London: UCL Press.

Younge, G. (2000). A Year of Reckoning. *The Guardian*, 21/2/2000.

Chapter 1

Policing in the Pillory: Macpherson and its Aftermath

Alan Marlow

The Lawrence Inquiry Report is the most searing indictment of policing ever published. It is a catalogue of professional incompetence. It shows, with the help of hindsight, how mistake was piled on mistake, leading inexorably to the miscarriage of justice that has seen the murderers go free. It has also put the stamp of 'institutional racism' on the Metropolitan police and the rest of the service.

(**Police**, *The Voice of the Service*. **March, 1999: p 5**)

That was the verdict of the monthly magazine that reflects the views of the Police Federation—the staff organisation that represents police officers up to, and including, the rank of Chief Inspector. The ferocity of the criticism laid waste the defences of the Metropolitan Police, (McLaughlin, 1999), and left its management the single option of acceptance of the findings. For the participants, it had been a trial by ordeal—a modern version of the public pillory in which missiles of rotten vegetables were replaced by the equally bruising findings of racism and professional incompetence. At one point in the proceedings, the Commissioner Sir Paul Condon used the expression 'pilloried' when he complained of the heavy-handed cross-examination to which his subordinates were being subjected. However, he too was to become a target, was forced into contrition and finally offered an unreserved apology to the Lawrence family. Reiner, (1992), describes the long process of 'fall of police legitimacy' from its zenith in the late 1950s. If it had not already have been reached, the Macpherson Inquiry may be seen as the culmination of that process. The Metropolitan Police, so often portrayed as the elite of British policing, were shown to be at best incompetent and at worst both incompetent and racist in the business for which they were famed, in myth and legend—that of the investigation of murder.

The police service, by now accustomed to high profile criticism resulting from official enquiries, was particularly bruised by the Macpherson Report with its blanket attribution of 'institutional racism'. Reactions were muted and there seemed to be general if resigned acceptance of its findings.

This chapter reviews the responses of members of the police service to the Inquiry that have been published in its professional journals and periodicals. It also attempts to assess whether or not real change is a possibility or whether, like the aftermath of the Scarman Inquiry, (Scarman, 1981), it will result in documented good intentions that ultimately have little effect on interactions between the police and members of minority ethnic groups.

Voices from the stocks

The Macpherson proceedings seemed to embody the theatre of English class relations. The natural ability of the middle class lawyers to patronise was coupled with the unerring tendency of the police to present images of themselves as rather dim, working class 'plods'. In his report, Macpherson himself adds to the impression by precisely quoting, perhaps with relish or disdain, Superintendent Crampton's use of the expression 'strategical' in two places in the report, (Macpherson, 1999: p 93 and p 318). As Upton, (1999), puts it:

At the Inquiry they [the police] performed their usual trick of catching themselves out and stonewalling in the face of questioning by their social superiors.

(**Upton, 1999: p 8**)

He illustrates the process by the exchange between Michael Mansfield QC and Chief Superintendent Ilsley:

Mansfield   *Have you been aware of the more difficult kind of racism that sometimes appears within the police force?*

Ilsley   *No, I haven't.*

Mansfield   *Never?*

Ilsley   *Never, sir.*

(**Upton, 1999: p 8**)

The question, was, of course, a two-edged weapon with denial implying an ignorance of the obvious and acceptance taken as proof of institutional racism. Cross-examination in an adversarial and hostile atmosphere is never comfortable but a more considered response may have helped the officer's credibility.

Chief Superintendent Bill Ilsley was criticised by Macpherson for his 'failure to manage effectively and imaginatively in this highly sensitive murder investigation', (Macpherson, 1999: p 194). The officer himself considered himself to be very unfairly treated. As he later explained:

> We were treated worse than criminals. From the time we walked in we were abused, jeered at, laughed at and the chairman allowed it to happen.
>
> (Jenkins, *Police Review*, 26/2/99: p 16)

As he told the Inquiry, his difficulties were a lack of resources to conduct properly the investigation and despite his representations, an optimum level was not achieved. There were ten other high profile investigations in the area at the same time. He felt that the criticism was unfair:

> How can I be possibly criticised for an organisational problem that was accepted throughout the MPD? I put more resources into the enquiry than any other while I was on the AMIP (Area Major Investigation Pool). Most murders were understaffed through lack of resources and availability of staff and inadequate premises.
>
> (Ibid.: p 17)

In a celebrated incident reproduced in a television programme, Chief Superintendent Ilsley was accused in the public Inquiry by Mrs Lawrence of disregarding a piece of paper she gave him with a list of names of possible suspects. He commented:

> I folded the piece of paper up, put it my pocket, took it back to the station and it went straight into the system—and that has been proved.
>
> (Ibid.: p 17)

Superintendent Crampton, who initially led the investigation, conceded that mistakes had been made and 'these gave power to their elbow' by which he means police critics in general. It was Superintendent Crampton who took the decision, on the first weekend, not to arrest the suspects, a group of young men later to gain national notoriety. He defended this on the basis that, in his view, he possessed no evidence that provided reasonable grounds to arrest and the forensic transference of blood or other tissue was unlikely in the circumstances. Arrest was most likely to result in a decision to bail, thus releasing the suspects into a community from which they were trying to obtain evidence. Asked if he would, with hindsight, have arrested earlier, he agreed that he would:

> The strategy I adopted was unsuccessful and there was no successful prosecution. Therefore, with hindsight, I would be some sort of clown to say that by not arresting I would do exactly the same thing, knowing that that would be the outcome. Hindsight must tell me that the other option should have been tried.
>
> (Ibid.: p 18)

He concluded that every decision he took was fully considered and in his view he dealt with the matter in a professional way.

Detective Superintendent Brian Weedon became the Senior Investigating Officer on the Monday after the murder due to that attendance of Superintendent Crampton at court in another matter. He spent 14 months on the investigation and deferred his retirement to continue with it. He was accused of a lack of judgement when he took over from Superintendent Crampton in respect of the decisions not to arrest and, famously, that he failed to recite to the Inquiry the legal principles upon which such arrests may be justified. He explained the apparent lapse:

> I emphasised the need for evidence. Although I corrected myself, the media didn't cover my explanation. I did know my powers of arrest.
>
> (Ibid.: p 19)

Commenting that it was a difficult case, a 'stranger attack' in the street with little forensic evidence, he decided to continue with Superintendent Crampton's strategy of evidence gathering before arrest. He added that the racist character of the murder made it a high profile investigation, the inference being that these factors necessitated a cautious approach. Macpherson concluded that Superintendent Weedon gave an unsatisfactory explanation for the decision to arrest the suspects on May 6, 1993; the probability being that such a decision was influenced by outside pressures which included a meeting the Lawrence family had with Nelson Mandela, (Macpherson, 1999: p 114). The officer refutes this conclusion. Two circumstantial grounds for arrest had emerged and although he was still concerned about the lack of direct evidence, he was not prepared to delay arrests until after the weekend:

> I wanted the witnesses to attend identification parades. I've been criticised for not arresting without evidence and further criticised for arresting when I did get some evidence.
>
> (Ibid.: p 23)

Superintendent Weedon also conceded that, with hindsight, mistakes were made but their causes did not lie in racism or other ulterior motives. He also pointed to the lack of resources available to the investigation. He was particularly resentful of the implication that retirement resulted in him evading disciplinary proceedings:

> *Far from retiring early, I twice postponed my retirement*
> *to see the investigation through two important stages.*
>
> (Ibid.: p 24)

The three officers' careers were ended in the enduring bleakness of the Inquiry's criticisms. Superintendent Crampton commented:

> *If you'd have said to me you are going to spend 72 hours*
> *doing your job the way you normally do—and always*
> *had throughout your 30 odd year career; and for that*
> *you are going to have years of being pilloried, stalked by*
> *the press, you are going to be made to be one of the most*
> *hated people and it is going to be a ploy by a certain*
> *group of people, I would have said don't be silly; we are*
> *talking about the British justice system.*
>
> (Ibid.: p 24)

Chief Superintendent Ilsley concluded his explanation with the following:

> *At the end of the day, I can live with myself. And I have*
> *to go to sleep at night and think to myself: 'Was I wrong*
> *or not?'. I believe there was nothing that I could have*
> *done that would make the slightest bit of difference to the*
> *outcome.*
>
> (Ibid.: p 24)

The reviewing officer

Detective Chief Superintendent John Barker rues the day that he volunteered to review the murder investigation. Others had been asked to take on the task but he agreed as, he says, 'a willing volunteer'. He was given a two month deadline and was only able to devote three days a week to it. He secured the assistance of a detective inspector and the part-time services of a trained computer operator. Macpherson condemned his conclusions, adding:

> *We do not find evidence that its inadequacies were the*
> *result of corruption or collusion. Mr Barker's*
> *unquestioning acceptance and repetition of the*
> *criticisms of the Lawrence family and their solicitor are*
> *to be deplored. Others took the review 'as it was set out',*
> *in the Commissioner's words, and allowed themselves to*
> *be misled.*
>
> (Macpherson, 1999: p 207)

New rules on the disclosure of evidence to the defence were a key concern at the time and Chief Superintendent Barker considered it would have been clumsy, to say the least, to pass on information in a public document that might well jeopardise a future prosecution. He felt his role had been misinterpreted:

> *I went in with the well-intentioned aim of assisting the*
> *inquiry team and the family and to hopefully try to make*
> *sure we didn't have a repeat of this in the future.*
>
> (Ibid.: p 24)

He was criticised for not being more questioning of the fact that arrests had been delayed. He was to contend that he did point out that early arrests may have produced evidence and may have found weapons. Nevertheless, such a tactic was a gamble, as he pointed out to the Inquiry. He made twelve recommendations in his report which centred around the need for better family liaison, improved staffing levels and a clear press strategy. He also concluded that there was no new evidence that could be put before the Crown Prosecution Service to regenerate the charges that had already been dropped against the suspects.

The Inquiry concluded that the Barker Review lacked rigour. Where critical comments were made, they tended to be muted and unsupported by detailed analysis. In particular, the review had 'perpetuated the insulting and patronising way in which the family and their solicitor had been regarded by junior officers, and in turn by Mr Weeden', (Macpherson, 1999: p 200). Chief Superintendent Barker commented that he had, in fact, recommended that the family liaison arrangements were deficient and that better staff selection and training was necessary. He added:

> *I have great, great sorrow that the killers of Stephen*
> *Lawrence are still free. I felt I did all I could to assist the*
> *process [of investigation] and I am desperately disap-*
> *pointed that I have been accused of not doing that.*
>
> (Ibid.: p 25)

The Kent investigation

In February, 1997, Kent Police were asked by the Metropolitan Police to enquire into a complaint made by Mr and Mrs Lawrence alleging neglect of duty and racist behaviour. The investigation was led by Deputy Chief Constable Robert Ayling who was supported by a detective chief superintendent, two inspectors, one sergeant, eight detective constables and one civilian analyst. It was supervised by a member of the Police Complaints Authority who was himself advised by a Superintendent who had been a chairman of the Black Police Association.

In an article published in the *Police Review* of 12 March, 1999 and in *Policing Today* of 1 March, 1999, Robert Ayling commented on his findings and upon the Macpherson Inquiry. The main conclusions were that the original investigation suffered from incompetence and a failure of supervision and management. No evidence was found to support a discipline charge of racial discrimination against any of the Metropolitan police officers who were the subject of complaint. The Inquiry supported all of those findings.

The Inquiry's definition of 'institutional racism' was developed in the course of the proceedings and was not available to the Kent team. According to Mr Ayling, the basis upon which Sir William declared several officers to be 'institutionally racist' did not provide evidence for a discipline charge under police regulations. He was surprised at Sir William Macpherson's comment that if racism was not in the original terms of reference, it would have been better not to address the issue:

> I believe that Sir William has confused himself in this regard. My terms of reference included the phrase 'and any related matters' and quite clearly, the complaint made by Mr and Mrs Lawrence included an allegation against several Metropolitan Police Officers.
>
> (Ayling, *Police Review*, 12/3/99: p 16)

Mr Ayling welcomed the new definition of institutional racism but considered the evidence used to support the concept very limited. Each example was capable of much less sinister explanations. In his view, on no single occasion was the benefit of doubt given to any police officer and he questions the objectivity and fairness of such an approach. The Kent enquiry identified 28 major failings and tested them against a range of criteria to attribute incompetence, corruption or racism. In each case, the most plausible explanation was incompetence. The number and frequency of such failings were sufficient to allege neglect of duty against some senior officers.

The Deputy Chief Constable is critical of the public inquiry. Neither he nor members of his team were called to give evidence. This was unfortunate as wrong assumptions were made about the conclusions they had reached. He added:

> I have never been spoken to before, during or after the public inquiry by Sir William Macpherson or any of his team, which I regard as discourteous...I was horrified to discover that Sir William had included within his appendices my chronological list of the informants who gave details of their suspicions about the prime suspects

> ...I am confident that had Sir William made his final report available to Kent prior to general release, we would have spotted the now infamous Appendix 11 and insisted upon its removal or reduction.
>
> (Ibid.: p 18)

Deputy Chief Constable Ayling also points to the failings of the Barker Review, commenting that it did more harm than good. It promoted a false sense of security, deprived the later investigation of potential witnesses and prevented knowledge of the same to the private prosecution instituted by Mr and Mrs Lawrence. He also points out that the Inquiry used the Kent investigation as its framework upon which its final report was constructed and adds:

> As far as I am aware the public inquiry found nothing, not a single thing, that the Kent investigation had not found first. I doubt whether the public inquiry could have exposed many of these issues without the benefit of the Kent investigation having exposed the failures first.
>
> (Ibid.: p 18)

Macpherson recommended that, taking into account the strong expression of public perception in this regard, the Home Secretary should consider what steps can be taken to ensure that serious complaints against police officers are independently investigated, (Macpherson, 1999: p 333). In view of the foregoing, Deputy Chief Constable Ayling points to the implicit irony of the recommendation:

> While I would personally support such a move, the Stephen Lawrence case is not a good example of why such an investigation should be taken out of the hands of the police.
>
> (Ibid.: p 18)

Forensic detachment or crusading zeal?

There are some grounds for the officers' complaints that the Inquiry was the modern equivalent of the pillory. The criticism was unrelenting and whilst noble sentiments are easily inferred from success it is not easy to refute allegations of sinister motivations in the face of blunders. The following extract from the report itself shows a curious piece of reasoning by Sir William Macpherson:

> Judges do not like police officers who go on and on at a person who is advised to remain silent and shows rigidly that he will not speak. Indeed such interviews were not put before juries, since the risk is that the content of the questions posed may be taken as having some evidential quality when it has none at all. The six minute interview of

Jamie Acourt is plainly a 'let off' in one sense, and the interview showed very little if any evidence of preparation or technique. On the other hand Mr Acourt had spent an hour in consultation with his solicitor prior to the interview and the solicitor had informed DC Canavan that Mr Acourt would make no comment, and this proved to be the case. The officer would appear to have made the pragmatic judgement that he was wasting his time, and he brought the interview to a quick conclusion. In theory we accept that he has given up too quickly and that there were things that could have usefully been put to Mr Acourt. In practical terms, his judgement was probably right and that it would have no effect in any event. All in all the 'no comment' interviewing therefore carries little criticism compared with the other matters that are raised in this case.

(Macpherson, 1999: p 171)

The passage seems to imply censure that is only reluctantly suppressed as the officer was actually following guidance from Sir William's fellow judges and that a firmer line may have extracted information even though the legal representative had indicated the right to silence would be exercised.

Indeed, the whole affair was punctuated by a pathology of adversarialism that tends to stimulate bureaucratic and defensive responses. The Lawrence family solicitor, Imran Khan, took the view that confrontational awkwardness was the best way to represent the family's interests, even though the interests of the police and the family were, in theory, the same. As he explained to the *Law Society Gazette* after the Inquiry:

You shouldn't balk at taking action against the police if you have to…you've got to maintain a vigorous defence of your client…our attitude is that they prosecute, we defend, that is part of pluralism. I'd want their attitude to be the same.

(Upton, 1999: p 3)

He was true to this principle and made many demands for information, (*'bombardment' in the case of the police, 'sniper fire' in Khan's*) (Upton: p 3), against the threat of a report to the Commissioner. It is perhaps understandable that the investigating team were bemused by having to deal with two sets of defence lawyers. However, it was not for them to complain:

Again, however, it does seem to us that it is the duty of the police to be tolerant and understanding in cases of this kind, and to conduct of this kind by a solicitor. It is not unusual that requests should be made in somewhat peremptory fashion and in legal language so early in the investigation of a murder. But it is not for the police to tell a family and their lawyer how to behave.

(Macpherson, 1999: p 302)

The pernicious tentacles of the spectre of racism infected many of the assumptions, concerns and exchanges in the aftermath of the particularly vicious murder. Those who in other matters would see themselves as liberals and defenders of civil rights seemed to behave in ways in which in other circumstances would have been derided as naive or incompetent. As argued by Upton:

Again, if Michael Mansfield's conduct and decisions over the course of the many proceedings were to be taken as typical of his behaviour as a lawyer, his manipulation of the rules of evidence in order to secure admissions of the surveillance tapes at committal, his approval of a private prosecution that had no realistic chance of success and his criticism of defendants exercising their rights would mark him out as either an over-eager ally of Michael Howard or a novice advocate pushed in at the deep end.

(Upton, 1999: p 9)

Nevertheless, Mr Mansfield's performance at the Inquiry was much more professional. He had, after all, the results of the Kent investigation around which to structure his cross-examination.

Macpherson himself challenges long held fundamental protections in English law by recommending that there should be the prospect, albeit restricted, of retrial after acquittal and that it should be an offence to use racist language in private. It's almost as though the horror and viciousness of the murder justify exceptional amendments to the precepts that are the bedrock of criminal justice due process and notwithstanding that such changes may contravene the European Declaration of Human Rights—no doubt long championed by the lawyers involved in the case. Racially motivated crimes usually have a more pernicious quality than those of average circumstance. It is laudatory for the state to indicate its revulsion on such matters by the creation of special categories of aggravated offences and an insistence on exemplary sentences, (see Crime and Disorder Act 1998). It is quite another matter, however, to suggest that principles universally recognised in civilised liberal democratic states should be modified or abandoned.

The Black Police Officer's Association

Of all the police responses to the Inquiry and its themes of incompetence and 'institutional racism', perhaps the most pertinent are those from black police officers and the Black Police Officers' Association of the Metropolitan Police.

Leroy Logan, its chairman, was not entirely happy with the way that the Inquiry had progressed and that its nature involved a lot of emotion. However:

> *The BPA did not see the inquiry process as a witch hunt, it showed that it was a time for action rather than to paper over the cracks.*
>
> (Logan, 1999: p 27)

The Association welcomed the recommendation for an increase in the number of black officers as a step towards dismantling barriers. In particular, there was a need for greater representation in specialist departments such as the CID:

> *Many black officers won't even apply for these roles because they feel that their faces won't fit. There isn't overt racist behaviour against black officers any more. Behaviour has certainly changed but changing attitudes is more difficult. We want to make sure personal prejudices don't have any play when black officers are seeking advancement.*
>
> (Ibid.: p 27)

The BPA also wanted a review of current practices such as stop and search. An illustration of the operation of stop and search was given by Chief Inspector Ali Dizaei of Thames Valley Police. He had been stopped in his vehicle on three occasions in Southall, West London. He concluded that the only reasons for the stops were the facts that his appearance is similar to the South Asians who live in the area, (he is, in fact, of Iranian origin), and that he was driving a BMW. Apologies were offered when he produced his warrant card. In Britain, according to research he conducted, 24 per cent of white officers are above the rank of constable, whereas officers of minority origin constitute only 8 per cent above the bottom rank. He concluded:

> *We are still not overcoming the chill factor and it is still not an attractive career for the upwardly mobile members of the community. In the last 15 years the police service has been obsessed with recruiting from the minorities but it is not the recruiting which has to be addressed, it is the chill factor, it is advancement and progress of ethnic officers.*
>
> (Weeks, 1999: p 17)

Inspector Paul Wilson of the Black Police Association, (Police, March, 1999: p 23), refers to the police 'occupational' culture, a term he prefers to the more traditional 'canteen culture', as it extends beyond that preserve of the lower ranks, the canteen. He recounts how a Superintendent asked, when informed that the inspector had two children, 'are they both by the same woman?'. Inspector Wilson had visited Holland and Canada and found the same forms of discrimination. Waddington, (1999), also points to the international symmetry of police culture, (see also Silverman in this volume). The phenomenon is not confined to the police. Inspector Wilson recounts an experience of giving evidence to a Parliamentary Select Committee:

> *The thinly veiled racism behind some of the questions was quite hurtful. On the one hand I was pleased to be there, pleased to be given the opportunity to give my views, but I was astounded at some of the questions.*
>
> (Goodwin, 1999: p 23).

During his service he had seen many watersheds, the PSI Report, (Policy Studies Institute, 1983), and The Scarman Report, (Scarman, 1981), for example. Change implied organisational change, which training alone could not bring about. As he points out, the demographic profile of many parts of London means that black people may account for the majority of the population and there may be severe consequences for policing for not taking urgent and radical action.

Chief Superintendent Michael Fuller is the Metropolitan Police's most senior black officer. For him, to deny the Macpherson definition of institutionalised racism would be foolhardy, (*Police Review*, 30/4/99: pp 18–20). It is no longer acceptable for chief officers to maintain the status quo by claiming that racist attitudes within the police simply reflect the attitudes of society at large. A national diversity strategy is required— implemented by the Association of Police Officers and overseen by a government minister. Challenges to inappropriate behaviour must become the norm within the service:

> *Every police officer should regard him or herself as a role model on the premise that no amount of glossy advertising will improve the police image or relations with minority communities if people are not treated properly in their direct contact with police officers.*
>
> (Fuller, 1999: p 20)

Management cops versus worker cops

As Waddington, (1999), demonstrates clearly, tensions commonly exist between those who manage the police organisation and those who carry out the tasks of policing:

Since the inception of professional policing senior officers have struggled to control the organisation for which they are responsible.

(Waddington, 1999: p 227)

It is a problem for democratic societies all over the world, for the police service is not a classic bureaucracy in the Weberian sense. As James Q. Wilson observed many years ago, the defining characteristic of the police organisation is that discretion increases the nearer to the base of the bureaucracy one moves, (Wilson, 1968). Policing policy may appear enlightened but that is no guarantee that it will be reproduced in practice. The power of the lower ranks to subvert policies regarded as vacuous or unrealistic has been well documented, (see Waddington, 1999, Chapter 8). The assumptions that the attitudes and practices of the lower ranks tend to be impervious to change but they themselves are not part of this milieu often pervades the pronouncements of chief officers. As the issue of racism was being debated in the Inquiry, a number of chief constables issued statements to confirm that in their view, racism was a cancer in the service. In a letter to *The Times*, 14 October, 1998), Richard Wells, the former chief constable of South Yorkshire contended that racism was 'widespread' and even 'endemic'. Ian Blair, then Chief Constable of Surrey, John Newing of Derbyshire and David Wilmott of Greater Manchester all made similar statements. (Despite the fact that the latter has refused to allow the establishment of a branch of the Black Police Officers Association—see *Police Review*, 26/2/99). These public comments met with applause as honest statements of a disturbing reality, but one might be forgiven for asking difficult questions as to what these leaders were doing about the issue. How much had they challenged the systems and practices that produced racism during their already well established careers? It is to be hoped that they meant that 'we are all guilty' whether by intention or default rather than a posture of 'we are not to blame, it is the fault of those in the lower orders'.

Indeed, the point is conceded by Mr Newing:

The fault does not lie in race relations strategies and policies within the service—although these need to be more wide ranging and comprehensive. In my view, the fault lies in senior officers' failure to ensure that the intentions of their policies are being carried out.

(Newing, 1999: p 5)

The Police Federation was also clear that the fault lay with leadership. Whilst they have reservations over the clamour that followed the Macpherson Report:

There are disturbing similarities between the strident demands that have been made on the police service to acknowledge that it is riven with racism and the show trials in Eastern Europe fifty years ago, and the treatment of the victims of Mao's cultural revolution.

(Ibid.: p 5)

Nevertheless, for them it is clear where the blame lies. The Met is:

A force falling down on performance, and is perceived by its operational officers to be hampered by bad management and poor leadership, is in deep trouble.

(Ibid.: p 5)

One reason for these failings was that the CID had been 'emasculated' by decisions that had little to do with detective work, in particular the replacement of experienced senior officers with others who do not have investigative backgrounds as the result of *'an insensitive tenure regime'*. This argument is less than persuasive as the tenure policies were not in place at the time of the Stephen Lawrence murder and the officers at the forefront of the investigation were all career detectives.

The editorial is concluded as follows:

Society gets the police officers it deserves, and those officers are at least entitled to the leadership **they** *deserve.*

(Ibid.: p 5)

The Chairman of the Police Federation accepted the findings of the Report, commenting that it made 'painful but persuasive reading'. It was a 'watershed' (that word again) of opportunity for the police service to make 'a real and lasting change and put its house in order'. He concluded:

In accepting that racism exists in the police service, I believe the majority of officers honestly endeavour to police without prejudice. But systems have to be put in place to identify racism where it exists and ensure it does not flourish, either openly or unwittingly.

(Ibid.: p 9)

Reflections

There are some grounds for the sense of unfairness that the unfortunate officers felt after the ordeal of the Inquiry. It did, at times, resemble a ritual denunciation embellished with the public displays of the suspects and angry demonstrations. As a process of detached forensic scrutiny, it should not be regarded as a model. Exasperation pervades its pages rather than detached judicial enquiry. In a strange way, the force of the unremitting criticism allows the participants some sympathy for the mistakes they made and, over time, the bubbling up of a current of denial. Recent press releases now link low morale, a decline in the use of stop and search powers following the Macpherson Report, with increasing crime levels. Nevertheless, to pick at the imperfections is to profoundly miss the point. As McLaughlin puts it, the Inquiry was being forced to act as a 'de facto Truth Commission in which the concerns of the black communities could be publicly articulated and acknowledged', (McLaughlin, 1999: p 14).

In that sense, it represents a moment of public catharsis. The Lawrence family generated immense public sympathy as a result of their 'dignity' and 'typicality', (sentiments which may themselves have racial undertones). For all its imperfections, the outcome has forced a profound shift in public policy in this country, not only for the police service. It has drawn dramatic public attention to what Pitts describes as:

> *...the Eurocentric evaluations of the proclivities and capacities of black people by relatively powerful white ones. Such evaluations have come, over the period, to structure individual attitudes, social practices and social institutions.*
>
> **(Pitts, 1993: p 104)**

Or, to use the term preferred by Macpherson, 'institutional racism'. As McLaughlin concluded, it became clear that the officers involved:

> *...had a woefully inadequate understanding of how racial discourses were embedded in and constitutive of police work.*
>
> **(McLaughlin, 1999: p 14)**

This may be demonstrated by remarks made by Chief Superintendent Ilsley and Superintendent Crampton. 'Could you imagine what would have happened on the streets if the police had been given a clean bill of health in terms of racism, which we were cleared of by the Kent investigation' says Mr Crampton. 'There would have been a lot of unrest'. 'There could have been race riots', added Mr Ilsley, (Jenkins, 1999: p 16).

The Scarman Report of 1981 was also described as a watershed in policing. Its recommendations became, as Reiner points out, the orthodoxy of policing policy, (Reiner, 1992),

but whilst the rhetoric of police management changed, there was little impact on practice. Scarman provided an avoidance strategy by pointing to the importance of social disadvantage to which the police, and the Metropolitan Police in particular, could caste a knowing glance when addressing the difficult issues of racism in policing. Macpherson is profoundly different. It's central concern was the scrutiny of the core business of the police i.e. the investigation of serious crime. The incompetence and the contributing discriminatory discourses allow no side-steps. The 'few bad apples' thesis, so often rehearsed on such occasions, was substituted for a more universal one of 'unwitting racists'.

Most alarming has been the unresponsiveness of the organisation to the messages that have been emerging for the past thirty years. The central themes of Scarman, the Policy Studies Institute Report of 1983 and the many voices of protest have all tended to be rationalised with a 'we know best' attitude to what tends to be presented as the complex world of policing which only the professionals can understand. Earlier protests could often be dismissed as they became entangled with radical left politics in the 1980s. A feature of the success of the Lawrence campaign is that it avoided such entanglement.

The comments of the members of the Black Police Officers Association demonstrate clumsy discriminatory evaluations and are not unique to the lower ranks of the police service, but the difference is, however, that their effect is sharpened and often made concrete in the unequal power relationship of street policing, (Marlow, 1999). The emergence of the Black Police Officers' Association may be seen as a symptom of a failure to address these difficult issues. Any organisation that fails to heed its members, and a critical group of them at that, is indeed in crisis.

The potential for reform

The managerial revolution that was imposed on the police service in the wake of the Police and Magistrates' Courts Act 1994 is not without its critics, (see Hallam in this volume), but the mechanics of audit and scrutiny that have evolved do offer opportunities for increased transparency and the measurement of progress against the criticisms of Macpherson. The new, rigorous, publicly documented thematic inspections of Her Majesty's Inspectorate of Constabulary, (see Chapter 2 by Loveday), the probing of the Audit Commission and the power of the Home Secretary to impose key performance indicators, all offer yardsticks against which performance can be judged.

In his response to the Report's recommendations, the Home Secretary has accepted that a ministerial priority be established for all police services 'to increase trust and confidence in policing amongst minority ethnic communities', (Home Office, 1999: p 3).

It will be added to the existing objectives for 1999/2000 with the development of more comprehensive indicators from 2000 onwards, following consultation. In the immediate term, performance indicators will be limited but can be expected to embrace eventually most of the range set out in Macpherson:

- The existence and application of strategies for the prevention, recording, investigation and prosecution of racist incidents.

- Measures to encourage the reporting of racist incidents.

- The number of recorded racist incidents and related detection levels.

- The degree of multi-agency co-operation and information exchange.

- Achieving equal satisfaction levels across all ethnic groups in public satisfaction surveys.

- The adequacy of provision and training of family and witness/victim liaison officers.

- The nature, extent and achievement of racism awareness training.

- The policy directives governing stop and search procedures and their outcomes.

- Levels of recruitment, retention and progression of minority ethnic recruits.

- Levels of complaint of racist behaviour or attitude and their outcomes.

(Macpherson, 1999: p 327)

According to Fitzgerald and Sibbitt, (1997), monitoring against such criteria may be able to track developments and priorities to ensure that they do not further damage police relations with ethnic minorities by making the police aware of patterns of decision-making and 'by providing a peg for a dialogue between the police and ethnic minorities locally about issues of mutual concern', (Fitzgerald and Sibbitt, 1997: p 13). The authors are also clear that statistical data are not sufficient and that patterns need to explored qualitatively to elicit the reasons and redress for apparent discriminatory practice.

Developments in information technology now offer the potential for the performance of individual officers to be monitored under the regime of actuarial accountability. However, as Fitzgerald and Sibbitt, (1997), conclude, the best that these audit systems can do is to raise questions and to provide indicators of apparent discriminatory practice that the police will have to tackle or justify. These routines will necessitate much more sophisticated monitoring by individual police forces themselves to balance demographic factors and the complex interlinking of disadvantage, social exclusion and offending, (see Smith, 1997). Most difficult and politically sensitive will be accounting for those areas where minorities are over-represented in certain areas in certain types of crime.

The uncontested finding of the Inquiry was the 'wretched state of management and supervisory systems that pervaded the Metropolitan Police', (McLaughlin, 1999). During the investigation, managers at all levels seemed to be wringing their hands at the lack of material resources and allowing that consideration to justify and excuse inefficiency. In fairness to them, the managerial revolution that followed the Police and Magistrates' Courts Act 1994 had yet to occur and notions such as value for money and performance indicators had not entered the vocabulary of policing. Nevertheless, effective leadership in the Lawrence investigation was a rare and precious commodity. (The report of the Inspectorate *Policing London*, HM Inspectorate of Constabulary, 2000, also concludes that murder investigations in the Metropolitan Police District still tend to be under-resourced).

The Scarman Report is often cited for comparative purposes in this volume. Policies changed as a result of it but the ability to direct and address performance was demonstrably lacking. There has been significant learning within the police organisation since 1994. The twin disciplines of performance measurement and audit have improved effectiveness. Provided these are coupled with leadership and ethical monitoring, there is some ground for optimism. The real test for the service will be to confront the more insidious aspects of police culture that tend to categorise social groups by the attributes of the worst of their members or at the very least, to prevent those assumptions being made manifest in behaviour. Police leadership will have to demonstrate an effectiveness that the history of police management shows to be a rare phenomenon. There are models available. Silverman, (1999), has shown that the policing of

New York City has been transformed by a management that learned to insist on operational accountability through the gathering and use of information. Although, as he argues in this volume, some of those measures have been diluted with serious consequences. Nevertheless, the techniques may also be applied to the pursuit of fairness in policing.

Waddington, writing for a police readership, neatly summed up the principle task of the post-Macpherson era:

> *The oft-used defence that the police merely reflect the racism of the society from which they are drawn is not only morally bankrupt, it is ridiculous. Do first-class police drivers aspire only to achieve the same levels of driving skill as ordinary motorists? Do specialist firearms officers seek only the marksmanship expected of anyone? Of course not. Professionalism means achieving levels of exemplary performance.*
>
> **(Waddington, 1999: p 13)**

Nothing else will suffice.

References

Ayling, R. (1999). Fair Hearing. In *Policing Today*, 5:1. London: Police Review Publishing.

Ayling, R. (1999). Challenging Macpherson. In *Police Review*, 12/3/99. London: Police Review Publishing.

Bratby, L. (1999). NBPA Calls for Federation Recognition. In *Police Review*, 12/3/99. London: Police Review Publishing.

Fitzgerald, M., and Sibbitt, R. (1997). *Ethnic Monitoring in Police Forces: A Beginning*, Research Study 173. London: Home Office.

Fuller, M. (1999). The Legacy of Lawrence. In *Police Review*, 30/4/99. London: Police Review Publishing.

Goodwin, (1999). Black in Blue. In *Police*, March. Surbiton: Police Federation.

Her Majesty's Inspectorate of Constabulary (2000). *Policing London*. London: Home Office.

Home Office (1999). *The Stephen Lawrence Inquiry: The Home Secretary's Action Plan*. London: Home Office.

Jenkins, C. (1999). The Murder Detectives. In *Police Review*, 26/2/99. London: Police Review Publishing.

Logan, L. (1999). In *Police Review*, 26/2/99. London: Police Review Publishing.

Macpherson, Sir W. (1999). *The Stephen Lawrence Inquiry*, Cm 4262-1. London: HMSO.

Marlow, A. (1999). Young People, Drugs and Stop and Search. In Marlow, A., and Pearson, G. (1999). *Young People, Drugs and Community Safety*. Lyme Regis: Russell House Publishing.

Mason, G. (1999). Black Officers Call for More Say in Policing of Black Communities. *Police Review*, 26/2/99. London: Police Review Publishing.

McLaughlin, E. (1999). The Search for Truth and Justice. In *Criminal Justice Matters*, No. 35: Spring. London: ISTD.

Newing, J. (1999). Editorial. In *Policing Today*, 5:1; March. London: Police Review Publishing.

Pitts, J. (1993). Stereotyping: Anti-Racism, Criminology and Black Young People. In Cook, D., and Hudson, B. (1993). *Racism and Criminology*. London: Sage.

Police (1999). Editorial. *The Buck Stops Here*, 5/3/99. Surbiton: Police Federation Publishing.

Policy Studies Institute (1983). *Police and People in London*. London: PSI.

Reiner, R. (1992). *The Politics of the Police*. Hemel Hempstead: Harvester Wheatsheaf.

Scarman, Lord J. (1981). *Report on the Brixton Disorders*, Cm 8427. London: HMSO.

Silverman, E. (1999). *NYPD Battles Crime*. Boston: Northeastern University Press.

Smith, D. (1997). Ethnic Origins, Crime and Criminal Justice. In Maguire, M. Morgan, R., and Reiner, R. (1997). *The Oxford Handbook of Criminal Justice*. Oxford: OUP.

Upton, J. (1999). The Smallest Details Speak the Loudest. In *The London Review Of Books*, 21:13. London: LRB Publications.

Waddington, P. (1999). *Policing Citizens*. London: UCL Press.

Waddington, P. (1999). Think Tank. In *Police Review*, 26/2/99. London: Police Review Publishing.

Weeks, J. (1999). What Do You Call a Black Man in a BMW? 'Sir'; He's a Police Inspector. *Police*, 3:3. Surbiton: Police Federation Publishing.

Wilson, J.Q. (1968). *Varieties of Police Behaviour*. Cambridge, MA: Harvard University Press.

Chapter 2
Must Do Better: The State of Police Race Relations

Barry Loveday

Introduction

In his 1981 Report of an Inquiry twenty years ago, Lord Scarman was to comment that in terms of its composition, a police force ought to reflect the make-up of the society it served. As he observed, in the police, as in other important areas of society, this was not the case as the ethnic minorities were 'very significantly under-represented', (Scarman, 1981: para 5.6). Given the importance of ethnic minority recruitment attached by Scarman to the improvement of police/community relations it is interesting to note the continuing failure of the police service to respond to this perceived weakness. In 1981 the total number of black officers serving within the police represented just 0.3 per cent of the total police establishment. By 1999 the national average of black police officers had reached just 2 per cent of total police establishment. It is not a matter of any consolation, given it's centrality to events, that at the time of the death of Stephen Lawrence the 613 officers from ethnic minority backgrounds represented 2.2 per cent of the Metropolitan Police Services' police establishment.

Moreover, if recruitment of ethnic minority officers has proved to be a major obstacle to all police forces, that is more than matched by the problem of their retention, as they are clearly over-represented among those officers 'voluntarily resigning', (HMIC, 1996–97, *Winning the Race, Revisited*, para 6.2). All police forces, it would appear, have even more difficulty keeping ethnic minority officers in the service than they do in recruiting them. This might be thought a matter of surprise, given the very large expenditure on police training in ethnic awareness and the public commitment of all senior police officers to improved race relations. Moreover, while in the past, police forces may have identified pressure from other members of the ethnic community as an explanation for so many early resignations among ethnic officers this no longer enjoys much credibility. Thus the Lawrence murder and Macpherson Report may, inter alia, have finally forced the police service to look at its own organisational and management

structure in the search for an explanation for the poor record it has in both the recruitment and retention of officers from ethnic minorities.

Police Organisational Challenges

At this time, the long term impact of the Macpherson Report of the Stephen Lawrence Inquiry on police-community relations can only be guessed at. It is, however, clear that the Report can be expected to galvanise a commitment to address failings which exist within the police organisation. This would include both the management of personnel and the degree of control exercised by senior officers over the operation of the service. Interestingly, a leading critic of police internal organisational failures has proved to be Her Majesty's Inspectorate of Constabulary, (HMIC), which in a series of published reports has identified in some detail the problems that currently confront all police forces in England and Wales. These reports, it is argued here, have only reinforced the importance of internal police organisational failings. These may be closely linked to the apparent inability of senior officers to effectively manage a service for which they have ostensible responsibility. This is most likely to provide an explanation for the evident failure, in terms of police-ethnic relations, of the police service outside in the community. In many respects the apparent absence of managerial control over operational officers by senior officers could provide some explanation for the clear differences exhibited between police rhetoric about the need for good police/community relations and police action on the ground. This problem was to be particularly highlighted in relation to the attitudes exhibited by both junior officers and middle managers to ethnic minority officers in the course of their everyday duties.

In its 1997 Thematic Report on Policing Plural Communities, (*Winning the Race, 1996/7*), the Inspectorate was to note that meetings held with officers from ethnic minorities had only confirmed the existence of prejudice within the police service, (HMIC, 1997: para 2.73). As significant, they had also demonstrated that ethnic minority officers felt unsupported by line management and fellow officers in dealing with 'racist conduct' by police officers. Line management 'failure to intervene' is, within the police organisation, of crucial importance. This is because these officers, primarily sergeants, are first line supervisors to operational officers. Any failure here can as a result be expected to have a significant influence over the professional policing perceptions of officers for whom they are immediately responsible. This must ultimately impact on local police-community relations. Yet, as the same report was to note:

> *Sergeants were found to constitute the weakest link in the management of community and race relations. They were least likely to understand their responsibilities in this area and the least well prepared for meeting them. H.M. Inspector found clear examples of their failure to intervene following inappropriate behaviour or the use of racist or discriminatory language [by other officers].*
>
> (HMIC, 1997: para 2.75)

Elsewhere, the report was to comment on the disturbing evidence of what was described as 'indirect racial discrimination' within those police forces observed:

> *It must be recognised that racial discrimination, both direct and indirect, and harassment are endemic within our society and the police service is no exception There was continuing evidence during the Inspection of inappropriate language and behaviour by police officers, but what was even more worrying was the lack of intervention by sergeants and inspectors. This was reinforced during the observation of assessment panels for promotion to sergeant and inspector where potential supervisors demonstrated a reluctance to challenge colleagues who indulged in racist 'banter' and racist behaviour.*
>
> (HMIC, 1997: p 9)

The evident problems experienced by police forces in dealing equitably with ethnic minority officers was also highlighted in the Inspectorate Report. Police forces appeared unable to appreciate both the impact of such treatment of fellow officers on the public's perception of the police service or on the claims made by police as to their own impartiality. As was argued by HMIC:

> *Police officers, (and other personnel), cannot be expected to behave in ways which will enhance relations with minority populations in the public at large if they fail to treat colleagues from the same groups equitably.*
>
> (HMIC, 1997: para 3.63)

And that:

> *Community perceptions of inequitable treatment of minority officers (whether these perceptions derive from publicity about cases of discrimination or through the grapevine) will profoundly undermine not only the chances of increasing ethnic minority recruitment but the forces' investment in community and race relations more generally.*
>
> (Ibid.)

As a number of industrial tribunal cases and newspaper reports have made abundantly clear in recent years, behind the rhetoric of senior police as to the commitment of the service to equity and fairness, there remained a deep antipathy to the black community as a whole and to black police officers in particular. Most recently, as the Metropolitan Police Service's only black police officer to serve through to pensionable age, Norwell Roberts has identified the treatment received by colleague officers in that force. Experiencing, inter alia, verbal abuse from other officers, criminal damage to his car and the failure to respond to calls for 'back up' when on patrol, this officer was to state that had he known then what to expect 'he would never have joined' the police. As the same officer was to comment concerning the Lawrence case:

> *I joined the police force in 1967 but the first time I spoke up about racism was in 1985. Unfortunately, I have been vindicated but at the time people never took any notice of what I was saying…The problem of racism in the police could have been seen much earlier if I had said something. I used to tell people everything was fine, and I was lying, stomaching everything that happened because that was the only way I knew how to deal with it. Anyway, there was no one to help me.*
>
> (Fresco, 1999: p 6)

Elsewhere, evidence that many police officers continued to experience difficulties in dealing with black officers was to be demonstrated in the case of WPC Hendricks in 1999. This officer was to be acquitted of assaulting a senior colleague after the court heard that she had suffered 'prolonged racist abuse' from her fellow officers where, as a member of the Metropolitan Police Territorial Support Group, she was seen as little more than 'the token woman and token black' within that group. Following her acquittal it was to be WPC Hendricks hope that the Metropolitan police service would investigate all the previous allegations she had made 'that were ignored', (Gentleman, 1999).

HMIC fears as to what consequences these cases might have on the public's perception of the police have been more than warranted. As a 1999 MORI opinion poll was to discover, one in four of the public believe that 'most police officers are racist', (Travis, 1999a). As the same report was to argue in relation to public perceptions of police racism:

> *A particularly worrying finding is that an even higher proportion of younger people, 31 per cent, of the key 18 to 24 age group believe the blanket charge that most police officers tend to be racist or very racist.*
>
> (Travis, 1999a)

The internal failure of police forces to deal with the problem of racial harassment within their own organisation may have a heavy cost. The public may conclude that a service that cannot deal effectively with such an issue internally will not be able to deliver an equitable service to the public. On this issue the Police Inspectorate is however proving to be much more interventionist and ready to identify and condemn police racist behaviour. In its 1997 Thematic Inspection, HMIC was to report that it had been given evidence of racist behaviour among officers which, even allowing for exaggeration, clearly suggested that a problem existed which was not being addressed within police forces. As it was to note of the 1996/7 inspection:

> *The Inspection Team received a number of accounts from members of the public of racist behaviour by police officers. Even if these accounts are dismissed as either the product of third party articulation or even exaggeration, a picture still emerges of pockets of wholly unacceptable policing.*
>
> (HMIC, 1997: para 2.9)

The discovery by the Inspectorate of overt racism within police forces led it to ascertain the degree of commitment among police forces to community and race relations, (CRR). This, it suggested, would be apparent in each police forces' overall priorities and 'strategies to meet those priorities'. HMIC was to conclude however that very few police forces had shown any such commitment, other than in written form, at all, (HMIC, 1997: para 2.12). Indeed, where good practice was found this was almost entirely dependent on committed individuals rather than the service as a whole and 'was not guaranteed to continue if they moved on'.

Police and Community

A further element to the investigation of HMIC was the exploration of community views on current policing provision. Here the inspection confirmed that both black and white communities could suffer as victims of crime; as repeat victims; victims of 'anti social behaviour'

and also from threats and harassment on housing estates. More significant perhaps was a recognition that 'such conduct, targeted against individuals or families in their own locality, was usually racist in nature', (HMIC, 1997: 2.19). The recognition of the problem of black victimisation was important because, traditionally, police have been more ready to identify members of the black community as offenders than they were to view them as victims of crime. Yet successive British Crime Surveys have clearly demonstrated that for a range of offences, black households were more than twice as likely to be victimised than white households and that the incidence of victimisation may have reflected very clearly their own socio-economic position, (Home Office, 1992). Moreover, the frequent claim from this community of being 'overpoliced but underprotected' appeared to be justified by the apparent inability of police forces to respond to the problem of racial incidents or attacks. Reporting in 1997, HMIC were to note that while there had been an encouraging increase in the number of recorded racial incidents:

> *The figures have been volatile and recent evidence has confirmed long standing concerns that these incidents are significantly under-reported either because of officers' confusion over what is expected of them or because of a lack of sympathy with the issue or both.*
>
> (HMIC, 1997: 2.62)

While in terms of recording racial incidents the Inspectorate were to find evidence of good practice within some police forces it also became clear that very few operational (or other) officers were aware of the definition as developed by ACPO of what constituted a 'racial incident'. This definition offers a very wide discretion to the operational officer to so record an incident. It states that a racial incident is 'any incident in which it appears to the reporting or investigating officer that the complaint involves an element of racial motivation or any incident which includes an allegation of racial motivation made by any person', (HMIC, 1997: 3.10). Unfortunately this widely embracing definition appeared to have 'passed by' most operational officers who, as the Report makes clear, had not been provided with the definition for operational purposes or indeed, informed as to its content.

The evident failure to operationalise the ACPO definition of a 'racial incident' was unfortunate. This was because police refusal in the past to identify incidents as such generated high levels of animosity within the black community towards them. The most pressing example of this was probably to be the now infamous Deptford fire case where, in 1981, thirteen children were to burn to death. Police refusal to identify the fire as a potential racial attack was, at least in part, to fan the resentment that precipitated the Brixton riots which occurred later that year. It was noted, however, that there still appeared to be little commitment to recording such incidents. These, like other figures collected by the police, were 'still seen as a Home Office return' that had to be submitted, (HMIC, 1997: 2.56).

While those forces inspected appeared reluctant to implement the ACPO racial incident guidance, operational officers often did not exhibit a similar reluctance in the use of 'stop and search' powers, when directed at members of the ethnic community. In what might be viewed as a diplomatic approach to an extremely emotive issue, the Inspectorate were to comment that when levels of suspiciousness towards certain groups rose among police officers, there was some evident danger of police 'over-reaction'. This could generate a feeling among those who were the object of police attention that they were subject to police interest in a way that was both unfair and discriminatory. As the Inspectorate were to note in relation to 'overpolicing':

> *A much more general cause of concern is heightened levels of suspiciousness among police officers. This may combine with other factors to influence officers use of discretion with the effect that some groups may be treated less leniently than others. The cumulative result may be that they are treated considerably more punitively overall.*
>
> **(HMIC, 1997: 3.42)**

Official recognition of a stop and search policy that all too frequently is directed towards members of the ethnic community remains a major source of distrust of the police within these communities. It generates more than distrust when searches are also conducted in a rude and aggressive manner. This policing style, recorded very clearly by Roger Graef provides an good explanation as to why, among ethnic communities, they feel unprotected but are always 'over-policed', (Graef, 1989: p 128).

Police Training

Police commitment to training was to be given a substantial impetus by the Scarman Report which was to recommend, inter alia, an expanded training provision in community relations. As was stated within the Report:

> *Training courses designed to develop the understanding that good community relations are not merely necessary but are essential to good policing should, I recommend, be compulsory from time to time in a police officer's career up to and including the rank of Superintendent. The theme of these courses should be the role of the police as part of the community, the operational importance of good community relations, the techniques of consultation and the moral as well as legal accountability of the police to the public.*
>
> **(Scarman, 1981: 5.28)**

Given the importance attached to the training of police officers in community relations within the Scarman Report it is of interest that HMIC's 1997 Inspection was to also discover that many forces were not providing either sufficient or appropriate training. Of equal interest the Inspection was to target, more precisely, in fact, than the Scarman Report, those officers who might benefit most from this training. Those so identified were officers who were beyond their probationary period and were in daily contact with members of the public and also those 'with line management responsibilities', (HMIC, 1997: 2.90). The explanation for this particular concern within the Inspectorate is of immediate interest. It appeared to be what could be construed as an 'official' and public admission that something was very wrong within the police organisation. Furthermore, it also suggested a problem which all the 'community relations training' based on the earlier Scarman proposals had failed either to address or resolve. The Inspection was to stress that such training would mean that officers would be better equipped to deal with some of the complex and sensitive situations they would expect to face. It was also felt that such training would better equip them to:

> *Avoid the behavioural traits and norms of their more cynical peers. Without some counterweight to the 'canteen culture' they may fail to develop their ability to handle such incidents with confidence and sensitivity.*
>
> **(HMIC, 1997: 2.90)**

The same Inspection argued that, rather than being central to police training, 'community and race relations', (CRR), tended to be viewed as a 'bolt-on', optional extra, which was 'de-coupled from questions of service delivery'. As a result there was some doubt as to the general efficacy of such training, particularly as an antidote to police 'cynicism and the canteen culture'. Some insight into just how limited an impact any such training appears to have had on general police attitudes to the issue of race, has been provided by ethnic minority officers themselves. As one officer related, his experience raised serious questions as to the value of training in improving police behaviour. Leslie Bowie, one of the Met's longest serving black officers, in evidence to an industrial tribunal dealing with a case of racial discrimination, claimed that:

> As a probationer at Wimbledon police station in March 1993, he was driven around in a police vehicle with a golliwog tied to the blue light on the roof while words like nigger, coon, wog and spick were constantly bandied about in general conversation.

(Rufford, 1999: p 19)

Despite its apparent limitations, the Inspectorate remains committed to further training. Here, the reason for encouraging additional training throws some light on the real issues. For, as is argued by the Inspection:

> With regard to some line managers, their indifference (at worst) and lack of confidence (at best) in tackling inappropriate racist behaviour by officers is particularly worrying. Training to equip first line managers to deal appropriately with such behaviour would seem to be a priority. These supervisors are 'key' to combating racist attitudes and behaviour within the service, yet the unfortunate reality is that some actively perpetuate this type of conduct.

(HMIC, 1997: 2.91)

Some explanation for the apparent failure of current police training was to be identified within the Inspection. A 'lack of enthusiasm' was found among officers who attended Community and Race Relations training. Those who did attend were often not 'overly attentive' either. Nor was this Inspection to discover one example of good practice in either the 'proper monitoring' or 'evaluation' of community and race relations training. It appeared that neither senior police trainers nor police managers were very concerned about the lack of success that attended the provision of such training which in resource terms, was both expensive and futile. Elsewhere, it was discovered that many forces which sent officers for specialist training outside the service, rarely used them for in-force training thereafter. Officers who had undergone outside training were to comment on the 'very ad hoc' selection process and the failure to 'de-brief' on return to the force, (HMIC, 1997: 2.94).

The apparently ritualistic and empty approach adopted towards such training as was provided, was, however, more than matched by the ready acceptance of recruits who might be expected to exacerbate community relations problems. While it appeared to the Inspection that ethnic minority applicants were 'screened out' by police forces, white applicants, 'sometimes demonstrating racist views', appeared to be equally carefully 'screened in'. As the Inspection was to comment concerning this unfortunate pattern of recruitment:

> The other side of the recruitment and promotion coin concerns white officers. Although the Inspection was unable to examine these issues in detail, it was not apparent that systematic and effective steps were being taken to screen out recruits whose available skills in dealing with plural communities were in doubt, nor did the proven abilities of serving officers in this field count in their favour in career terms.

(HMIC, 1997: 2.74)

As the selection and promotion procedures explored by the inspection appeared to indicate, the system rewarded officers who exhibited racist characteristics while penalising those who sought to improve police-ethnic community relations. The discovery of these recruitment and promotion problems by the Inspection was to lead to a specific recommendation that in future all recruitment selection and promotion procedures 'should test individuals attitudes towards race and diversity', (HMIC, 1997: 4.13).

Revisiting the Scene

As is readily identifiable from the 1997 Inspection, HMIC was to demonstrate a refreshing honesty in confronting and publicising what they found in their inspection of the approach adopted within police forces to police community and race relations. With some notable exceptions the Inspection only appeared to provide official confirmation of the apparent failure of the police to pursue policies which might serve to improve often very difficult police community relations. The casual indifference exhibited within forces to matters of race in relation to recruitment, promotion and training may have only served to reaffirm that within the police 'organisational culture', these issues were of little account and could be ignored. Moreover, the absence of any effective management or leadership within the organisation which might have counteracted this, only confirmed existing prejudices. It was within this context that a number of recommendations were to be made by HMIC requesting police forces to respond. The recommendations were closely argued and, within the context of the police service, radical. They were, however, made during the enquiry into the death of Stephen Lawrence of which both HMIC and police forces were very much aware.

These required that forces should 'state that the behaviour of officers who showed racial or other prejudice' in their behaviour and language to colleagues or members of the public was 'completely unacceptable'. They also recommended that a community and race relations audit be made, along with the re-issuing of the ACPO definition of a racial incident. These recommendations are of interest because of the decision to return to the same forces in 1999. This visit was made to assess the impact of the first Inspection, but it also provides a remarkable insight into police organisational characteristics at the time the Macpherson Report was made public. It also offers a very useful insight into current policing priorities in relation to community and race relations.

As the 1999 report of the 'revisit' was to make clear, very few police forces were found to have implemented the earlier recommendations of the Inspectorate. Despite the salience of race and racial attacks it became readily apparent that little of this had permeated through to many police forces. As the 1999 report was to note:

> The conclusion of the findings indicates that progress has been less than satisfactory with many of the recom-mendations largely 'sidelined' and few forces placing the issue high on their agendas.
>
> (HMIC, 1999: 7)

Concern was expressed as to the apparent failure of most forces to establish a 'focused corporate approach' to the problem which might drive community and race relations, (CRR issues), as a 'mainstream and core element of policing'. This had not materialised at all. To HMIC it appeared to be the case that CRR issues, 'remain peripheral rather than at the core of policing for many forces'. While, for example, there had been some significant progress within some forces in terms of higher reporting and recording rates of racial incidents, it was also evident that the ACPO definition of a racial attack was still not understood. Alarmingly, it was also discovered that where such an understanding existed there were 'pockets' of personal resistance to it's acceptance 'as it is seen as giving special treatment perhaps to the undeserving', (HMIC, 1999: 4.2.2). Moreover, where operational officers had, using the ACPO definition of racial incident, correctly recorded an incident as racially motivated, this judgement

was to be often rescinded by front line supervisors. As was stated within the 1999 report:

> This is an intolerable situation that confuses constables, represents a gross gap in knowledge or serious errors of judgement on the part of some supervisors and poses pertinent questions of the role of management.
>
> (HMIC, 1999: 4.2.5)

Yet despite the clear evidence of continuing officer resistance to the recording of 'racial incidents' the Inspection was able to point to improved rates of recording. Over a ten year period, (1989–1999), recorded incidents had risen from 4,383 to 13,878, representing a rise of 217 per cent over this period. As important was a common acknowledgement that there was significant under-reporting of racial incidents in each force visited for the Inspection. This in itself presented a remarkable reversal of police assumptions which usually rejected any interpretation of an incident as being 'racially motivated'.

Police Organisational Culture

Recognition that the culture of an organisation must be addressed if change is to be effected within it, is clearly noticeable within the Inspectorate's report. This is probably why great emphasis is attached to the need for clear leadership from chief officers to a commitment to community and race relations, (CRR), issues as a marker of intent. Given the salience of the matter, it was surprising that many chief officers had not demonstrated that leadership which was expected of them. As HMIC was to note, along with front line supervision and effective sanctions that were both visible and unequivocal there was a need for leadership. While only one force had been found not to have published a policy statement that 'inappropriate behaviour among officers was not acceptable', this proved to be little more than formalistic and had not been reinforced by chief officers giving clear leadership on CRR. As the report noted, there could be life in the policy only 'if the message was consistently reinforced at chief officer' and other levels. Thus despite the evident importance attached to CRR by HMIC the report was to find that:

> It was disappointing to discover that there was so much uncertainty amongst officers as to who owned CRR in forces and who was driving the specifics forward. Many believed that CRR had a low priority in their forces.
>
> (HMIC, 1999: 5.1.8)

The lack of leadership on CRR was also to be identified by ethnic minority officers in each force with whom focus group meetings were held. In these, longer serving officers were to state they had noticed beneficial change. Yet clear evidence of profound problems experienced by minority officers within police forces was also identified. As the report noted:

> There were still too many accounts of distressing behaviour, or at best, managerial indifference towards ethnic minority staff. HMIC is used to exaggeration as a product of frustration but the accounts were so frequent and with so many common threads that elaborate over-exaggeration is not an acceptable explanation.
>
> **(HMIC, 1999: 5.1.10)**

Ethnic minority officers were to raise issues of 'inappropriate language' and behaviour of colleague officers in addition to that of supervisors and managers towards them. The most common characteristic of these incidents appeared to be the continuing indifference to this treatment among police managers. These consistently failed to treat their concerns seriously. Moreover, there was evidence of complaints being 'turned' against them by those to whom they reported them. Where a complaint against another officer made on the basis of racist language or behaviour was taken up by senior officers the complainants were left unsupported and 'often felt ostracised by the organisation'. This evidence of the lack of effective management was until recently compounded by the legal protections provided to officers which made it difficult to remove an officer from the service other than for the most serious misdemeanours. As new disciplinary procedures are introduced this may change. This might be thought appropriate for, as HMIC was to note regarding the attitudes and actions of some officers: 'there were a small number of officers whose behaviour was not only unprofessional but "morally wrong" '.

Yet for police forces a central problem has proved to be the difficulty experienced in getting rid of those officers who bring the service into disrepute. The case of DC Coles provides an illuminating example. During the Lawrence Inquiry, the fact that he was known to have had possible criminal dealings with the father of one of those suspected of the murder, was to result in the Metropolitan Deputy Commissioner commenting that he 'was appalled that this individual is still working for the Metropolitan police'. As was to be argued by one commentator in looking at the close similarities between the Lawrence case and earlier events involving police officers in the Los Angeles Police Department which had also been identified in numerous public complaints, they were seemingly immovable, given the considerable protections afforded to them by police 'disciplinary' arrangements. As the same commentator was to argue:

> There perhaps is the key. In Los Angeles the biggest obstacle to improving police performance and relations was the failure to implement an adequate, independent disciplinary process in the police force. Rogue officers could not be ejected.
>
> **(Rufford, 1999: p 19)**

Whilst there has of course been significant movement in the discipline field following the report of the Home Affairs Committee on police complaints and discipline, (Home Affairs Committee, 1997), how frequently the organisational culture will encourage the use of the new procedures, particularly in the apparent absence of any effective management within the police service, must remain a matter of conjecture. Just one year after the publication of the Macpherson Report, for example, DC Coles, on sick leave since 1998, was to be allowed to retire 'on medical grounds' in February 2000 receiving a police pension of around £20,000 a year, (Dodd, 2000).

Recruitment and Retention Problems

The 1999 HMIC report was to identify the recruitment and retention of minority group officers as a 'live' issue for the police service. There was at this time some concern that the impact of the Lawrence case might make the recruitment from minority groups more difficult. As a result, HMIC interest was directed to what measures police forces were adopting to retain existing ethnic minority group officers. HMIC was, in fact, to identify 'some good efforts' in attracting such applicants. But these efforts were largely undermined by the inability of many forces, thereafter, to retain these officers. As was to be discovered, while ethnic minorities accounted for three per cent of all appointments, they made up five per cent of all voluntary resignations and eight per cent of all dismissals. Given the very precarious position of all police forces in terms of retention of ethnic minority officers, HMIC found that:

> There was little evidence of any significant response to these issues and much to suggest that the rich seam of

experience and enthusiasm of ethnic minority officers is not being utilised to inform recruitment and retention strategies.

(HMIC, 1999: 7.11.2/3)

Police force indifference to what might appear to be a crucial issue within current debate about equity of provision of service also extended to a failure to confront clear differences in the use of stop and search powers by the police. As HMIC noted:

There remains a reluctance in forces to recognise the disproportionality of stop and search data. It would seem that a basic audit by forces of the grounds for stop and search and efforts to reinforce the strict criteria for exercising the power, would go a considerable way towards clarifying the picture.

(HMIC, 1999: 7.14.1/3)

Most recently a study of the use of stop and search powers within the Metropolitan Police district was to argue that in directing their attention towards young members of ethnic communities, the police were in danger of alienating them, particularly Asian youths. The study, based on research of over 700 police stop and search incidents in London was to conclude that:

Numerous findings throughout the study highlight the risk that searches may begin to criminalise young Asian men suffering high levels of unemployment and living in very overcrowded conditions. There is an obvious danger that an aggressive police approach to these searches increasingly risks alienating young people from this first British-born generation along with their peers and the cohorts following on behind them.

(Fitzgerald, reported in Bennetto, 1999)

The same study found that those Asians stopped by the police were likely to be younger than other suspects, less likely to have a criminal record and more likely to be picked up in groups. These conclusions only reinforced the case put forward by HMIC for police forces to be more aware of the impact of the use of stop and search on young ethnic minorities. As was to be argued by the Inspectorate:

The disparity in the ratio of stop and searches of black youth to their white counterparts is significant. The police must address disproportionality in their professional approach. The seeming endemic disproportionality in unemployment or employment non-commensurate with academic achievement, school exclusion and disproportion on almost any other social or economic scale is not of police manufacture. The frustration that feeds on restricted opportunity can place ethnic minority young people in real or potential conflict with police.

(HMIC, 1999: 3.4.2)

Policing London: The Metropolitan Police Experience

The issue of police ethnic minority relations is not and cannot be confined to the London Metropolitan Police area. It is the case, however, that the Metropolitan Police Service, (MPS), polices a geographic area that includes almost half of all the 'visible' ethnic minorities in England and Wales, (48.5 per cent), including the majority of those of African-Caribbean origin, (64 per cent). Over the last decade the diversity of the capital's population has grown more significantly than in the past, to the extent that around a quarter of London's population is made up of people from minority ethnic backgrounds. In terms of police recruitment however, the lack of success in the recruitment of ethnic minority officers remains very stark. In 2000 just 3.4 per cent of MPS police officers were from ethnic minorities, despite the far bigger recruitment pool from which they could draw, (HMIC, 2000: 5.1).

Most recently the problem of police ethnic relations, police recruitment and attendant matters has been addressed by HMIC in response to both the Macpherson Report and earlier HMIC reports, (HMIC 1996, 1999). It was indeed a specific recommendation within the Macpherson Report that HMIC, 'in order to restore public confidence', should conduct an inspection of the Metropolitan Police (Macpherson, 1999: p 328). The inspection was to find a number of positive developments within the MPS since the Macpherson Report, not least the establishment of the 'Racial and Violent Crime Task Force' and an increase in the report rate of racial attacks to the police. It was however, the analysis of earlier policy in relation to policing ethnic minorities, stop and search and police training within the MPS which proved to be enlightening, while providing some explanation for the police failure in the murder of Stephen Lawrence.

Police Use of Stop and Search in London

In relation to the use of stop and search, HMIC's inspection was to discover that whilst it was a 'live' issue, the supervision of its use by police managers continued to be conducted by way of 'paper supervision' through the analysis of paper records of completed stop and searches. As has been commonly recognised outside of the police organisation, such paper analysis provides no real guide to the actual exercise of this power by officers on the street. It was for this reason presumably that HMIC was to express concern that the same 'vigilance' by supervisors was not evident when stop and search powers were used on the streets. While data supervision was important, it was felt that 'effective frontline supervision to ensure the power was used lawfully and fairly was crucial', (HMIC, 2000: 3.54). More worrying than the complete absence of effective oversight of operational policing in the use of stop and search powers, was the discovery by HMIC of the use of stop and search as an individual and team 'performance indicator'. The impact of 'performance culture' has been the subject of earlier comment by the Inspectorate, particularly in relation to 'corrupting' police activity, (HMIC, *Police Integrity*, 1999). The HMIC were to express deep concern about its continued use within MPS as a measure of 'performance'. As was noted:

> HMI was very concerned to find that there is a residual belief by some operational officers that some frontline supervisors still make use of such quantitative data.
> (HMIC, 2000: 3.55)

While it was found that MPS had 'made clear in it's own policies' (sic), that stop and search was no longer subject to performance measurement, it became clear that this 'important message' appeared not to have permeated throughout the entire organisation. Indeed, the Inspection was to refer to a police constable's statement that:

> The team results of stop and search used to be posted in the canteen. This gave the impression that it was a competition. That doesn't happen any more but it is still a personal performance indicator.
> (HMIC, 2000: 3.55)

The extraordinary application of 'performance measurement' to an area of policing as sensitive as the use of stop and search, may perhaps have explained the frequent use of this power if not the bias in targeting members of ethnic minorities. While HMIC was to 'strongly recommend' that operational officers and every supervisor was made personally aware that stop and search activity was no longer either a 'personal or team performance indicator', it was silent as to how such a measure could, in the circumstances surrounding it's use, have been originally encouraged. This may have explained why, at a time when the number of stop and searches was apparently falling, officers from the Metropolitan Police still managed to 'stop and question', inter alia, two members of the House

of Lords, the Bishop of Stepney and the father of Stephen Lawrence. Given that in each case there did not appear to be 'sufficient grounds' to warrant the use of this power by the police, the explanation had to be that they were stopped primarily because they were black, (Phillips, 2000).

Police Training in the MPS

The acknowledged problems surrounding the use of the power of stop and search may have reflected a further failure within the MPS. This related to the evident difficulty MPS appeared to experience in the delivery of race relations training to its own officers. As HMIC was to note, the Scarman Report of 1981 was to lead to the publication of the report on 'Community and Race Relations Training for the Police' by the Home Office in 1983, (HMIC, 2000: 4.7). Following a decision to establish a community and race relations 'specialist support training unit' for the police service, a contract was to be awarded to 'Equality Associates', a consultancy company based in Turvey, Bedfordshire. This, in effect, became the primary race relations specialist training unit for the Metropolitan Police between 1989 and 1998. As a part of the Inspection, HMI was to assess the use made of the unit during this period by the MPS. Using the 'National Strategy for Community and Race Relations Training', (CRR Training), as a yardstick, it concluded that for this strategy to be effectively delivered within a police service the size of the MPS it would mean that only staff with sufficient potential to become effective CRR trainers were selected to attend courses at Turvey and that those returning from Turvey were fully utilised. It was also felt that CRR training would be given a high priority and that an evaluation strategy to measure the effectiveness of the training would be put in place.

As was to be discovered by HMIC, in each case MPS community and race relations training fell far short of meeting any of the criteria identified within the official national training strategy. HMIC was to find that the selection process for those attending training at Turvey was haphazard and was neither monitored or centrally co-ordinated. In many cases staff who attended were not chosen because they were the most suitable but because they either asked to go 'or were already in a training role'. Subsequently, many staff who attended the unit were never to be used in a police training or training management role, (HMIC, 2000: 4.19). The absence of any clear central CRR strategy and it's token nature within the MPS was to be again highlighted as it became evident in the course of the Inspection that senior management did not know 'with any degree of accuracy' how many staff had attended courses at Turvey. HMIC was to conclude that 'It therefore follows that the MPS is not in a position to make use of these staff because they do not know who they are or where they are located within the organisation', (HMIC, 2000: 4.20).

Following independent enquiries made by HMIC from Equality Associates at Turvey, it was to be learned that in the period 1989–1998 the MPS had sent 'at least' 149 staff to be trained there. The figure was to represent 'by far the biggest commitment any force' in the country had made to the training of CRR trainers and managers, (HMIC, 2000: 4.21). The estimated cost of this training between 1989 and 1998 was put at £780,000. Yet much had been wasted as there was no commitment on the part of senior (or other) management to ensure that those so trained were effectively used in any planned or co-ordinated way thereafter. In a survey of Turvey 'graduates' within the MPS, 67 per cent felt that the service had not made use of the skills they had attained. 89 per cent of respondents highlighted 'poor leadership, lack of co-ordination, lack of support, lack of commitment and the failure to use their skills' within the MPS. It was also discovered that 27 per cent of Turvey graduates had in fact 'never been used in the specialist role they were trained for', (HMIC, 2000: 4.26).

Given the evident lack of information held by senior management within the MPS as to how many trainers had attended the Turvey course, the cost to the MPS of so doing and thereafter how those trained officers were used, it is perhaps of no surprise to learn from HMIC that the inspection process had been 'unable to identify a policy, strategy or plan which outlined the MPS's commitment to CRR training covering the period 1989–1998'. As was noted, 'there was no substantive evidence of a cohesive and co-ordinated training plan, nor evidence of training packages or modules designed for delivery to the entire workforce of the MPS', (HMIC, 2000: 4.30).

Nor could HMIC discover whether there had been any attempt within the MPS to evaluate the overall effectiveness of what training in CRR was provided. It was to conclude that 'no evidence' was to be found that MPS evaluated any of its training to establish the effectiveness of the CRR element or the impact, if any, it had on service

delivery, (HMIC, 2000: 4.35). This may have only accurately reflected the priority accorded to CRR training within the MPS. As was to be noted by HMIC, it was significant that the 'equal opportunities/managing diversity training' that had been planned for delivery was allocated the lowest training priority level (Level 3) within the MPS. Indeed, of the 293 separate centrally provided courses and the number of student days allocated to these courses from April, 1998 to March, 1999, 'amounting to nearly 351,000 days', none of these student days, it was subsequently discovered, were allocated to centrally delivered CRR training courses, (HMIC, 2000: 4.39).

Following a request from HMIC to supply figures for the total number of staff trained in CRR over the previous three years, MPS was to identify a figure of 1,700. This, it was claimed, represented those staff trained as part of the initiative arising from the MPS response to the Macpherson Inquiry. Yet, as was argued by HMIC:

> *Given that the total number of staff in the MPS is approximately 36,000, the figure of 1,700 (4.6 per cent) suggests that at this time only a very small minority of MPS staff have received any CRR training to an agreed common minimum standard.*

(HMIC, 2000: 4.46)

It became increasingly apparent that in an area where the concentration of minority ethnic groups was highest the training in CRR relative to other police forces appeared to be lowest and that this was an accurate reflection of the importance attached to such training among MPS senior management.

Retention of Ethnic Minority Officers in the MPS

While MPS commitment to increase ethnic minority numbers was to be applauded by HMIC it became quickly evident that the real test would in fact be the level of retention of such officers who were already working in the MPS. It became clear the matter of recruitment had to be viewed 'within the context of minority officers leaving the force'. If this was seen as an indicator of commitment there appeared to be a major problem. If the MPS were able to substantially increase recruitment numbers from ethnic minority groups the evidence suggested they could also expect to very quickly loose them through early resignation. As was to be noted:

In 1998/99, 56 visible minority ethnic officers left the MPS compared with the 92 who joined. The MPS acknowledges that if they cannot retain ethnic minority staff in sufficient numbers then at best progress towards increased representation will be exceptionally slow or at worst suffer a decline.

(HMIC, 2000: 5.23)

Whilst the internal culture of the MPS had improved 'significantly' in recent years, it was still recognised that if an organisation was unable to retain minority ethnic staff, it raised a question as to the degree of trust that could be given to it to provide a 'fair and equitable service to members of minority ethnic communities', (HMIC, 2000: 5.24). Moreover, while it was found that at the senior level a commitment to support minority ethnic staff was clearly evident, 'the same was not apparent further down the chain of command'. In what might be seen as a clear failure of police leadership it was noted that:

A significant number of minority ethnic police officers and support staff felt that their line managers did not appreciate their particular circumstances. Indeed many Borough commanders who were interviewed believed that it was inappropriate to single out minority ethnic staff and engage in consultation regarding particular problems or issues that affected them.

(HMIC, 2000: 5.27)

The evident failure within the MPS of middle managers or line management to provide support to personnel for whom they had an immediate responsibility was an obvious source of concern. It was, however, to be matched by the serious reservations held among MPS staff as to the efficacy of established 'grievance procedures'. In what might be thought an interesting reflection of police organisational culture, it was to be discovered that staff generally had little confidence in the system 'and feared victimisation should they initiate a grievance'. Potential areas of grievance that might otherwise have been expected to arise included allocation (or non-allocation) of ethnic minority officers to specialist departments. While it seemed that some 'specialist departments' had experienced difficulty in attracting sufficient ethnic minority officers 'with appropriate skills', this may not have been entirely unrelated to the fact that:

Some minority ethnic officers felt they may not be made welcome in some of these specialist units. While HMI found no direct evidence of this, there was undoubtedly a need for a proactive approach by specialist depart-ments to encourage female and minority ethnic officers to apply for posts.

(HMIC, 2000: 5.49)

Some evidence of the need for substantial training in both CRR and equal opportunities was indeed to be provided in the case of WPC Hendricks, who as identified earlier was to be cleared in August, 1999, of assaulting a fellow police officer while on duty. As she was to state in court in relation to the MPS Territorial Support Unit which she joined in 1989:

*There were only two women allowed on the unit—one in each of two teams—and I had to wait for one to leave before I could join. On the TSG, I was treated like furniture, a token woman. They had to have a black—so they got two for the price of one. If they saw a white and a black together it would be 'there goes a salt and pepper team'. They would use comments like BIF which meant 'black, ignorant f***er' and 'groid' which was short for negroid. It was always going on.*

(Flynn and Sullivan, 1999)

The Hendricks case was to provide an interesting example of 'triple jeopardy' experienced by black and Asian women police officers and identified recently by researchers, (Holder *et al.*, 2000). But HMIC was to note, in relation to the recruitment of officers to specialist positions, that if officers, regardless of ethnicity, felt they could not equally apply on objective grounds for a specialist post 'this will have a direct impact upon job retention and job satisfaction'. Where specialist high profile, high status roles are seen to be predominantly for white male officers, 'this could have a negative impact on the recruitment of minority ethnic and female officers in forthcoming years', (HMIC, 2000: 5.49). If recruitment to specialist units is seen as important it is also the case that the most critical issue for ethnic minority officers remains the degree of support given to them by line managers. As the Hendricks case was also to demonstrate, the likelihood of such support could prove to be slight. This issue was to be identified within the Inspectorate's report where it was found that:

Consistently throughout the Inspection, staff at Borough level and within specialist departments felt that managers were too 'performance focused' and did not have sufficient human resource skills within their management tool kit [sic].

(HMIC, 2000: 5.27)

HMIC was to conclude that the makeup of staff within the MPS did not currently reflect the diverse population of London and that despite the commitment of senior management was unlikely to reach the target recruitment figures for ethnic minority officers of 5,662 by 2010. This was made even more unlikely given the attitudes identified among both uniform operational officers and those within specialist departments towards ethnic minority police officers.

Conclusion

At the most senior police rank the need to improve police-ethnic minority relations is recognised and understood. Nevertheless, successive reports from HMIC have identified clear weaknesses within forces. Irrespective of the good intentions of senior officers, the failure of operational line managers on the ground to abandon established prejudices runs like a fault line through the police service. Evidence from HMIC has also brought to public attention the clear managerial weaknesses which characterise the police service. This appears to allow some officers to both abuse their authority and to harass fellow officers on the basis of their race. The problem of police management, or it's absence, has been recognised by other observers. In 1997, for example, the Chairman of the Police Complaints Authority was to express concern about both sexual and racial harassment within forces and that:

> There was an apparent inability to manage some gross disharmony between officers [where] it had been claimed that chief officers had either failed to intervene or had connived in the harassment.
>
> (Campbell, 1997)

Unwillingness to intervene in internal situations identified as being clearly discriminatory to minority group officers must be a matter of concern. Reluctance among senior officers to exercise their authority could be explained by the absence of sufficient disciplinary powers. There must be a suspicion, however, that even with the introduction of new disciplinary powers, where there is no shared commitment to stop such abuses, they will continue. This may not mean necessarily that the police service is inherently 'racist'. Rather, the evidence may suggest organisational inertia which characterises the hierarchic and administrative structure.

This failing on the part of police forces was to be identified forcefully by HMIC. It was to note, for example, that following the review in 1996/7 the expectation was that police forces would at least have initiated a focused 'corporate approach' to implement recommendations made earlier. Yet it was noted:

> Disappointingly this has not been the case with too many forces failing to address adequately the key recommendations. Such a lack of progress has been all the more surprising [when] coupled with the current media attention and public concern regarding police interaction with ethnic communities [which] should have spurred forces into action.
>
> (HMIC, 1999: 8.1)

Concern expressed by HMIC was only reinforced by a further observation concerning 'front line' officers:

> The role of front line supervisors and managers is still the subject of concern. They are the individuals who are immediately responsible for service delivery and must fulfil the trust placed in them and respond, vigorously, whenever inappropriate behaviour is directed towards colleagues.
>
> (HMIC, 1999: 8.3)

The evident failure of the successive reviews conducted by HMIC on race and race relations to dent the organisational priorities of police bureaucracies was also made clear. In what might be seen as an open acknowledgement of failure, HMIC was to conclude that 'community and race relations do not currently receive the level of attention and priority they warrant in a significant number of forces in England and Wales', (HMIC, 1999: 8.5). Thus despite the huge publicity surrounding the cases of Stephen Lawrence, the Macpherson Inquiry and latterly the case of Michael Menson, police organisational culture has proved to be highly resilient to change. Notwithstanding the apparent decline in the use of police stop and search powers in London, there appears to be little evidence of underlying change in police organisational culture. In the absence of effective supervision, and of direct and close management of operational officers, the police organisation may not, as currently structured, respond positively to new demands placed upon it by Britain's multi-cultural society.

In the absence of effective management or clear leadership from senior police managers there may yet be a means of pushing a reluctant public service towards both the better policing of racially diverse communities and improving the internal relationships between officers of diverse racial backgrounds. The instrument which may achieve the goals identified by HMIC comes from the extension of the 1976 Race Relations Act to include the police service. The interesting feature here could prove to be not the 'symbolism' that may accompany the arrival of the Act but the financial implications which could quickly confront police forces that failed to respond to 'enforcement deficiencies'. This might prove to be particularly significant as no ceiling is placed on payments in discrimination cases involving employment, (Travis, 1999b).

As has been found in America, the discovery by the courts of the 'deep pocket' of public services has encouraged them to award exemplary damages in cases where any police abuse of their authority has been demonstrated, (Loveday, 1989). The very high awards are seen as the best and most effective way of punishing police departments that fail, while also encouraging them to improve performance. Should this approach be adopted within England and Wales, it would mean that on top of already very high police 'out of court' civil settlements, police forces will be paying for 'poor performance'. How much expenditure would be tolerated before managerial action on the ground was made manifest can only be a matter of conjecture. Chief Officer control of local police budgets may, however, encourage more decisive action on their part than has been the case in the past.

Additionally, the extension of the 1976 Race Relations Act to the police service could generate the prospect of the Commission for Racial Equality, (CRE), being able to carry out general and formal investigations into the police. This might be deemed appropriate if the efficient and effective enforcement against discriminatory action was not being seriously addressed within the police service, (Ouseley, 1999). This could in practice mean that the CRE would work alongside the Police Complaints Authority where there was a 'strong suspicion of racist practice' within the police. The financial penalties and investigatory powers provided under the Race Relations Act might appear severe. Yet the application of these powers to the police may be welcome if they succeed in improving police service. They may also bring an additional benefit in establishing a degree of equity in the professional treatment of all officers who join the police to serve the public.

References

Bennetto, J. (1999). Police Alienating Asians by Aggressive Tactics. *The Independent*, December 16th.

Campbell, D. (1997). Police Sex and Race Bias Rife. *The Guardian*, July 4th.

Dodd, V. (2000). Criticised Lawrence Case Officer Retires. *The Guardian*, February 19th.

Flynn, B., and Sullivan, M. Victory for Black WPC Put Through Racist Hell. *The Sun*, August 13th.

Fresco, A. (1999). In a Way it's my Fault, Says Black Policeman. *The Times*, February 23rd.

Gentleman, A. (1999). Racist Ordeal of Cleared PC. *The Guardian*, August 13th.

Graef, R. (1989). *Talking Blues: The Police in Their Own Words*. London: Collins Harvill.

HMIC (1996/7). *Winning the Race. Policing Plural Communities*. HMIC Thematic Inspection Report on Police Community and Race Relations. London: Home Office.

HMIC (1998/99). *Winning the Race. Policing Plural Communities Revisited*. A Follow-up to the Thematic Inspection Report on Police community Relations. London: Home Office.

HMIC (2000). *Policing London. Winning Consent*. A Review of Murder Investigation and Community and Race Relations Issues in the Metropolitan Police Service. London: Home Office.

Holder, K.A., Nee, C., and Ellis, T. (2000). Triple Jeopardy? Black and Asian Women Police Officers Experiences of Discrimination. In *The Howard Journal of Criminal Justice*, (forthcoming).

Home Affairs Committee (1997). *First Report. Police Disciplinary and Complaints Procedures*, Vol. 1: p 248–251. House of Commons.

Home Office (1992). *British Crime Survey*. London: HMSO.

Loveday, B. (1989). Recent Developments in Police Complaints Procedure: Britain and North America. *Local Government Studies*, May/June.

Macpherson, Sir W. (1999). *The Stephen Lawrence Inquiry. Report of an Inquiry*, CM4262-1 The Stationary Office.

Ouseley, Sir H. (1999). Enforce the Law. *The Guardian*, February 25th.

Phillips, M. (2000). Even the Bishop Had to be Stopped and Searched. *The Sunday Times*, February 6th.

Rufford, N. (1999). Dark Side of the Force. *The Sunday Times*, February 21st.

Scarman, Lord J. (1981). *The Brixton Disorders 10–12 April 1981. Report of an Inquiry*, Cmnd 8427. HMSO.

Travis, A. (1999a). One in Four Say Police Racist. *The Guardian*, February 9th.

Travis, A. (1999b) Police to Lose Immunity from Race Law. CRE to Get More Power. *The Guardian*, February 23rd.

Chapter 3

The Concept and Context of Institutional Racism

Gurchand Singh

Introduction

The concept of institutional racism is relatively new. It was developed in the late 1960s by radical 'black' American political writers and was then later taken up by academics on both sides of the Atlantic. 'Black' here refers to people of African and South Asian descent. The addition of the inverted commas indicates that there are problems with the term 'black', (see Modood, 1988; Cole, 1993). Despite these problems, the term will be used for the purposes of this chapter, although some of its shortcomings will be recognised.

In the process of its reproduction the term institutional racism has taken on a multiplicity of meanings and has often been inappropriately used. While the term has become stretched and conflated, it remains remarkably hollow. For many writers, if 'black' inequality exists, so does institutional racism. However, the causal relationships and processes that lead to the generation and reproduction of 'black' inequality are rarely identified and empirically demonstrated.

This chapter does not pretend to offer any final resolution to the debates surrounding the term institutional racism. Rather, it seeks to briefly chart the origins and context of the term and demonstrate some of the confusion surrounding the concept. It also seeks to highlight some of the key problems with the concept and suggests alternatives. The first section briefly charts the origins and reproduction of the concept of institutional racism as well as identifying its salient characteristics. The second section demonstrates some of the confusion over the term institutional racism. In particular, I want to highlight two instances in which there has been a considerable amount of disagreement over the nature of institutional racism—in the Scarman Report, (1981), and during the Macpherson Inquiry. The third section goes on to demonstrates several problems with the way in which the term has been used. Drawing on the work of Mason, (1982), Williams, (1985), Philips, (1987) and Miles, (1989), I want to argue that the term institutional racism suffers from several

problems. It has been conceptually stretched and inappropriately used over different levels of analysis, covering structural processes, groups of social actors, and individual prejudices. It sidesteps questions concerning causality; it conflates racism as the sole or primary cause of 'black' disadvantage, ignoring the impact of other processes relating to class and gender, and finally, it works on an erroneous theory of social stratification. In the last section, I want to argue that we can maintain the term institutional racism, although in a more precise and rigorous form. We would have to first 'shrink' the concept to refer only to institutional processes, 'deflate' it to refer only to divisions through the embodiment of racist discourses, as opposed to other process, and finally, make it empirically and theoretically more rigorous.

The Concept of Institutional Racism

The concept of institutional racism was developed in the continuing political struggles of 'black' Americans in the post-war period. During the 1950s and 1960s, the Civil Rights Movement had gained several victories, such as the 1965 Civil Rights Act and the 1965 Voting Act, which effectively ended the legal basis of discrimination against 'black' Americans. The Civil Rights Movement triumphed over de jure segregation. However, de facto discrimination remained. Despite the courtroom battles to secure equal rights, the lives of many 'black' people changed little: poor housing, high unemployment, crime, high infant mortality rates, and poor education all marked the experiences of 'black' Americans, (Farley and Allen, 1987; US Bureau of Census, 1992). The persistence of socio-economic inequalities in the midst of social and legal reforms led to the development of alternative forms of analysis and political action, evident in the rise of the Black Power Movement. Black radical leaders began to argue that the lack of any significant change reflected the fact that racism was entrenched within the structures, organisation, and power relations of American society. Change could only come when these power structures were challenged, (Williams, 1985; Marable, 1991; Hawkins, 1991; Fendrich 1993).

It was within this political context that Carmichael and Hamilton, (1967), coined the term institutional racism. Their use of the term indicated a shift in the analysis of racism, moving away from individual acts of prejudice, towards the role of racist power structures in the generation and reproduction of racialised division. This is evident in their 'typology' of racism. For Carmichael and Hamilton, racism exists at two closely related levels. Firstly, there is overt, explicit racism that is articulated by individuals. Secondly, at the level of the social formation, there is institutional racism—anti-black attitudes and practices, which are woven throughout all of the major institutions of society, that have the effect of maintaining 'black' disadvantage. In their work, Carmichael and Hamilton, (1967: pp 5–6), used the term institutional racism in parallel with internal colonialism, arguing that 'black' people stood as 'colonial subjects in relation to white society'. Hence, assimilation, integration, or legal reforms could not alleviate 'black' social disadvantage. Rather, militant political action against the white power structures of American society was required.

The term of institutional racism was soon taken up and reproduced by both American and British academics from the early 1970s onwards. Conceptually, it provided an important tool for challenging existing theories on racism. During the 1950s and 1960s, the dominant paradigms used to explain racism focused on individual prejudices, authoritarian personalities, and cultural pathology, (Adorno *et al.*, 1950; Allport, 1955; Moynihan, 1965). The use of the term institutional racism demonstrated a break with these paradigms. The emphasis was now on the organisation of society and power relations as opposed to individual prejudices and quirky personalities. This is more than evident in the way that writers began to highlight structural processes in their own definitions of institutional racism. For example, Jones, (1972: pp 121), defined institutional racism as 'those established laws, customs, and practices which systematically reflect and produce racial inequalities in American society. If racist consequences accrue to institutional laws, customs or practices the institution is racist whether or not the individuals maintaining those practices have racist intentions'. Blauner, (1972: pp 9–10), defined institutional racism as the

'interactions of various spheres of social life to maintain an overall pattern of oppression'. Other writers also began to emphasise the covert nature of institutional racism. Downs, (1970: p 79), argued that 'institutional racism is a process of placing or keeping persons in a position or status of inferiority by means of attitudes, actions, or institutional structures which do not use colour itself as the subordinating mechanism, but instead uses other mechanisms indirectly related to colour'.

In Britain, the term was taken up in order to explain the persistently poor social and economic position of 'black' migrants from the Commonwealth and Pakistan. It was also used to indicate a break with those studies that focused on prejudice, (e.g. Rose *et al.*, 1969). For example, Dummett, (1973: p 131), argued that a racist society 'has institutions which effectively maintain inequality between members of different groups in such a way that open doctrine is unnecessary, or even if operated partly by individuals who are not themselves racist in their beliefs, still has the effect of making and perpetrating inequalities'. By the 1980s, the concept of institutional racism began to be used extensively to identify how particular institutions, such as housing agencies, schools, the health service, and social services, generated and reproduced racialised divisions within their particular areas of concern. Although identifying a diverse range of processes the term institutional racism was used in two main ways in order to explain 'black' disadvantage. Firstly, to identify 'black' disadvantage as the outcome of normal bureaucratic and professional administrative processes and practices. Secondly, to argue that discrimination against 'black' people often occurred without intent. No matter how well meaning the personnel of any particular institution are, 'black' disadvantage could occur from the conscious and unconscious attitudes and practices of individual officers and professionals involved.

The concept of institutional racism also exists beyond academia. It is echoed in the 1976 Race Relations legislation in the notion of indirect discrimination. The predecessor of the 1976 Act, the 1968 Race Relations Act, was based on the notion of direct discrimination—when one person discriminates knowingly against another on the basis of colour, 'race', or ethnic or national origin. However, the notion of direct discrimination was limited for several reasons. Firstly, it was difficult to establish that discrimination had taken place. Proof was required of discriminatory intent. Secondly, the Act did not address practices and procedures that had the effect of excluding a disproportionate number of 'ethnic minority' members, irrespective of intention. The reality of the Act was that it did little to challenge racism and 'black' disadvantage. This was exposed in a number of studies that highlighted the continuing existence inequalities in the labour market between 'black' and 'white' workers, (Smith, 1977; Rex and Tomlinson, 1979). In the face of these problems, the 1976 Race Relations Act expanded the meaning of discrimination to include direct discrimination, prohibited by the 1968 Act, and indirect discrimination. The concept of indirect discrimination was based on the approach that the United States Courts had taken to the meaning of discrimination in Title VII of the 1964 Civil Rights Act. Both pieces of legislation attempted to circumvent the problems of proof, the intentionality of discrimination, and to go beyond an individualistic account of discrimination, (McCrudden, 1983). While the concept of institutional racism may have been echoed in the legislation, it was taken up more explicitly by the Commission for Racial Equality, (CRE), the body designated to implement and review the 1976 Act. The CRE, (1985: pp 2–3), in their definition of institutional racism stated:

> For too long racism has been thought of in individual psychological terms, reducible to the actions of prejudiced individuals. The concept of institutional racism draws attention to the structural workings of institutions, which exclude black people regardless of individual attitudes.
>
> (CRE, 1985: pp 2–3)

Hence, 'institutional racism can operate through the normal workings of the system' in rules, regulations, formal and informal procedures and practices, that discriminate against 'black' people.

In its various uses and associations, we can argue that the term institutional racism has several salient characteristics. Firstly, unlike other writers who sought to limit the use of racism to the realm of ideology, (e.g. Banton, 1970; Rex, 1970), the term institutional racism emphasised how racism could include ideas and actions. Secondly, the term institutional racism was used in such a way that it had a general rather than a specific referent. Racism was identified as all those beliefs, actions, and processes that led to the generation and reproduction of 'black' inequality. Thirdly, there was an emphasis on how racism permeated the organisation of

society and was not limited to the actions of a few individuals. However, this was often stretched, especially in the British social policy tradition, to focusing on individual attitudes and their roles in generating and reproducing 'black' inequality. Fourthly, the term has been used in such a way to emphasis that racism can be intentional and unintentional; evident in taken for granted assumptions by social actors as well as the bureaucratic processes of an institution. Finally, and following on from the last point, the term institutional racism has been used to argue that racism could be overt, evident in manifestations of individual racism, and covert, hidden in the organisation of society.

Although the term institutional racism was bounded by these salient characteristics, the extensive use and abuse of the term institutional racism, even within the characteristics above, has made it conceptually imprecise, vague, and obscure. Indeed, it has often been used with no formal definition, even in those works where it is highlighted within the title, (e.g. Anthony, 1980; Humphrey, 1980), or where it has occupied a central place in the work, (e.g. Knowles and Prewitt, 1969; John and Humphrey, 1971; Sivanandan, 1982; 1983). As Philips notes:

> The concept [of institutional racism] is often used in a loose, descriptive manner and has come to embrace a range of meanings, which are often imprecise, sometimes contradictory and frequently lacking theoretical rigour. Discussions of individual attitudes, stereotyping, implicit guidelines, explicit rules and procedures, organisational arrangements, power sharing and structural determinants of minority status have all been subsumed within the analysis of institutional racism.
>
> (Phillips, 1987: p 217)

This widespread use and disagreement was vividly exposed by Lord Scarman's Inquiry on the Brixton riots and the Macpherson Inquiry into the murder of Stephen Lawrence.

Developing Controversies

The Brixton riots, as well as later disturbances, were caused by an explosive mixture of elements: high unemployment, environmental decay, low levels of social provisions, political exclusion, and aggressive policing, all of which were exacerbated for black people because of the effects of racism. In most cases, it was aggressive policing that provided the spark that lit the inner city disturbances, (see Joshua et al., 1983; Small, 1983; Smith, 1983; Benyon, 1986; 1987; Benyon and Solomos, 1987; Keith, 1987; Solomos, 1993).

In the wake of the disturbances in Brixton, the Scarman Inquiry was set up in order to investigate the causes of the disturbances and to make recommendations.

The Scarman Inquiry identified some of the key elements behind the inner city disturbances. However, when it came to discussions on the nature of 'black' disadvantage and institutional racism it soon became evident how stretched the term had become. For example, Scarman implicitly rejected any definitions of institutional racism that stressed the organisations or institutions of society were racist. For him, the organisation of society was basically unproblematic: racism did not permeate or shape the organisation of British society. Similarly, Scarman explicitly rejected any definitions of racism that stressed discrimination could be covert and unintentional. For him, institutional racism was overt and based on intentional practices and policies designed to discriminate. It was on the basis of this definition that Scarman denied the existence of institutional racism in the police force as well as in British society:

> It was alleged by some of those who made repre-
> sentations to me that Britain was an institutionally
> racist society. If by that is meant that it is a society
> which knowingly, as a matter of policy, discriminates
> against black people, I reject the allegation.
>
> (Scarman, 1981: 2.22)

In the wake of the Scarman Inquiry there were serious attempts to give the concept of institutional racism more rigour (see below). However, while there were attempts to give greater clarity to the concept of institutional racism, it was still being defined and used in an eclectic manner throughout the 1980s and 1990s. This is more than evident in the Stephen Lawrence Inquiry. One of the key questions that arose was whether the handling of the murder investigation was marred by institutional racism. This question, however, was not easily resolved. This was because there was a plethora of meanings given to what constituted institutional racism. For example, there were those who defined institutional racism as practices and processes that either intentionally or unintentionally discriminated against 'black' people. In a letter to the inquiry, Herman Ousley, Chairman of the CRE, defined institutional racism as:

> Those established laws, customs and practices which
> systematically reflect and produce racial inequalities in
> society. If racist consequences accrue to institutional laws,
> customs or practices, the institution is racist whether or

not the individuals maintaining those practices have
racial intentions.

> (Ousley, 1998: p 2)

In their closing submission, the CRE, (1998), once more highlighted the irrelevance of intentions:

> The Commission accepts that there are a number of
> officers who gave evidence to the Inquiry who are not
> intentionally racist…That being said, the Commission
> does not accept that the absence of intentions removes
> the existence of racism or excluded the possibility of
> racial discrimination.
>
> (CRE, 1998)

A similar approach was also taken by SUA, (1998), an agency dedicated to the development of the 'black' voluntary sector, and the Runnymede Trust, (1998), in their submissions to the Inquiry.

At other times, institutional racism was used in an almost quasi-psychological manner, referring to attitudes, stereotypes, and 'internalised occupational cultures'. These usually contained little or no reference to the structures, organisation, or power relations. For example, Chief Constable John Newing, the then incoming President of the Association of Chief Police Officers, defined institutional racism as:

> the racism which is inherent in wider society which
> shapes our **attitudes** and behaviour. Those **attitudes**
> and behaviour are then reinforced or reshaped by the
> culture of the organisation a person works for. In the
> police service there is a tendency for officers to **stereotype**
> people. That creates problems in a number of areas, but
> particularly in the way that officers deal with black
> people. Discrimination and unfairness are the result.
>
> (Macpherson, 1999: 6.50)

Similarly, Inspector Paul Wilson, of the Black Police Association, argued that institutional racism has the effect of discriminating against people on the basis of their 'race' and emphasised how the source of this lies within the occupational culture. Wilson asserted that:

> The occupational culture within the police force, given
> the fact that the majority of the police force are white,
> tends to be the white experience, the white beliefs, the
> white values. Given the fact that these predominantly
> white officers only meet members of the black
> community in confrontational situations, they tend to
> stereotype black people in general. This can lead to all
> sorts of negative views and assumptions about black
> people, so we should not under-estimate the occupa-
> tional culture of the police service as being a primary
> source of institutional racism in the way that we
> differently treat black people.
>
> (Ibid.: 6.28)

However, the real controversy around institutional racism arose because many senior police officers accepted or rejected the existence of institutional racism in their police force on the basis of different definitions. For example, during the second part of the Inquiry, Sir Paul Condon, the Metropolitan Police Commissioner, accepted numerous accusations against the Metropolitan Police Service (MPS)—the existence of racism in the rank and file; discrimination and stereotyping of 'black' people; a lack of rigour in dealing with charges of racism against police officers and the abuse of discretionary powers such as stop and search, (*The Guardian*, 2/8/98; *The Times*, 2/8/98). However, Condon continually denied the existence of institutional racism in the MPS. Furthermore, he denied that the Stephen Lawrence murder investigation was marred by institutional racism. This Condon managed to do by clinging onto the definition of institutional racism that was provided by Scarman: racism that was consciously and deliberately a matter of policy and procedure. On the other hand, there were several senior police officers that were willing to accept that institutional racism did exist in their police force. The use of institutional racism in this context drew on the idea of unintentional racism as well as on quasi-psychological notions of attitudes and prejudice. For example, David Wilmott, the Chief Constable of Greater Manchester, accepted that institutional racism existed in his force: 'We have a society that has got institutional racism. Greater Manchester Police, therefore, has institutional racism. Some of it is not the overt type; it's that which has been internalised by individuals', (*The Guardian*, 14/8/98). Similarly, Lloyd Clarke, the Deputy Chief Constable of West Yorkshire, argued 'if institutional racism means unintentional prejudice, that such prejudice is subconscious, almost subliminal, than I totally accept the comment', (*The Independent*, 16/8/99).

The Macpherson Inquiry did not attempt to resolve the debate on the nature of institutional racism. Rather, it sought to develop a definition within the boundaries of the Inquiry. As Macpherson argued:

> We must do our best to express what we mean by those words [institutional racism], although we stress that we will not produce a definition cast in stone, or a final answer to the question. What we hope to do is to set out our standpoint, so that at least our application of the term to the present case can be understood by those who are criticised.

> (Macpherson, 1999: 6.6)

Macpherson defined institutional racism as the

> collective failure of an organisation to provide an appropriate and professional service to people because of their colour, culture, or ethnic origin. It can be seen or detected in processes, attitudes, and behaviour which amount to discrimination through unwitting prejudice, ignorance, thoughtlessness and racist stereotyping which disadvantage minority ethnic people.

> (Ibid.: 6.24)

This definition seems to have been developed in order to 'make sense' of the experiences of the Lawrence family and Duywane Brookes, Stephen's companion the night he was murdered, as well as the failures of the murder investigation and some of the wider problems of racism in the police force. Several areas were identified where institutional racism was seen to be manifest: the insensitive treatment of the Lawrence family and Duywane Brookes; the failure of many police officers to recognise that Stephen's murder was motivated by racism; the failure of racism awareness training in the police force; continuing disparities in stop and search figures, and the under-reporting of racist incidents, brought about by a lack of confidence in the police, (ibid.: 6.46).

In the wake of the Inquiry, many took on Macpherson's definition of institutional racism. The Home Secretary accepted the new definition of institutional racism, arguing that:

> any long-established, white dominated organisation is liable to have procedures, practices and a culture that tends to exclude or disadvantage non-white people. The police service, in that respect, is little different from other parts of the criminal justice system—or from Government Departments, including the Home Office —and many other institutions

> (Hansard, 24/2/99: col. 391).

Sir Paul Condon gave way and also accepted the new definition of institutional racism. Indeed, in the month after the Inquiry's publication there seemed to be an almost cathartic admittance of institutional racism in British society. Several local government organisations conceded that they suffered institutional racism under this new definition. The Chairman of the Association of Local Government, Lord Harris of Haringey, admitted that 'institutional racism is a reality in all large public organisations, in both private and public sectors', (*The Guardian*, 24/2/99). The British Medical Association admitted that there was institutional racism in the National Health Service, (*The Guardian*, 24/2/99). Similarly, the Royal College of Nursing accepted that it was guilty of institutional racism after its annual congress rejected moves to recruit more 'ethnic minority members'. Christine Hancock, the Royal College's secretary, told delegates: 'I do not believe the Royal College of Nursing is any freer of institutional racism than any other large organisation', (*The Guardian*, 12/3/99). At the Minority Lawyers Conference in March, delegates claimed (and admitted) that institutional racism existed in the legal profession, (*The Times*, 16/3/99). The Office for Standards in Education, (1999), report also warned that Britain's schools suffered from institutional racism. Although the term did not appear in the report, Cliff Gould, OFSTED's head of secondary education, echoed Macpherson's definition of institutional racism when he noted that 'the way some recent commentators have defined institutional racism certainly applied to many schools'. He went on to argue that teachers in schools were not 'intentionally racist' but that there were features and attitudes within some schools that put 'ethnic minority' pupils at a disadvantage, (*The Guardian*, 11/3/99).

However, there was also a backlash against Macpherson's use of institutional racism and indeed the concept as a whole, especially from the right wing press. For example, *The Telegraph* argued that the concept of institutional racism is insulting for several reasons: firstly, it taints all individuals who work within an institution as racist, and secondly, by arguing that it can be unintentional, it denies that we have conscious motivations, reducing us to 'worm like creatures incapable of self knowledge', (*The Daily Telegraph*, 15/3/99). Amongst some police officers there was also disquiet. Robert Ayling, the Deputy Chief Constable of Kent, argued that while he accepted Macpherson's definition of institutional racism, the claim that there is institutional racism in the police force was based on 'flimsy evidence'. Ayling also claimed that officers almost faced a form of McCarthyism during their submissions to the Inquiry:

> *Perhaps one should not be surprised that some gave a poor account of themselves and were led into making some controversial statements. They were in a no-win situation, often being asked questions like, have you ever heard a racist remark made by a colleague? If they said yes, it was taken as proof of institutional racism. If they said no it was taken as proof that they must be lying and covering up institutional racism.*
>
> (*The Daily Telegraph*, 9/3/99)

Indeed, before, during and after the Inquiry, the term institutional racism had a variety of meanings attached to it and was being used in a loose and imprecise way.

Key Problems

The widespread, imprecise and vague use of institutional racism led to a major re-evaluation of the concept in the 1980s, (see Mason, 1982; Williams, 1985; Philips, 1987; Miles, 1989). Several major problems were identified in the way in which institutional racism had been defined and applied. Firstly, the concept has been extended over different levels of analysis. In the early 1970s, institutional racism was pitched at the level of the social formation and was used to identify the inter-relationships between different institutions that generated and reproduced 'black' disadvantage. However, in later uses, institutional racism began to be used to identify practices and procedures within single institutional settings such as housing agencies, police forces, social welfare agencies, and educational institutions, that generated 'black' disadvantage within that particular area. To complicate matters more, institutional racism also began to be used to identify individual involvement, often in the form of staff attitudes, in the institutionalisation of racism through policy formulation and implementation. Hence, the term institutional racism covered three different 'levels': the organisation of the social formation, single institutions, and individuals. In turn, this generated a variety of different definitions that fitted the level of analysis. In effect, the concept of institutional racism became confused and muddled, (Philips, 1987).

A second key problem lies in the emphasis that discrimination can be intentional or unintentional. If 'black' disadvantage exists, then institutional racism is said to exist irrespective of the intentions or motivations of social actors. However, the relationship between intentions and outcomes is extremely complicated. Beliefs may or may not necessarily manifest themselves in logically appropriate actions. Similarly, actions can produce consequences which may or may not be logically consistent with beliefs, (see Williams, 1985; Philips, 1987; Miles, 1989). The concept of institutional racism ignores this debate. However, as Miles argues, there are a number of reasons why we should focus on this relationship:

> *If disadvantage is the consequence of intentionality and of a belief in the existence and inferiority of a certain 'race', rather than being the unintentional outcome of decisions or taken-for-granted processes by people who do not hold such beliefs, distinct interventionist strategies will need to be employed in each case. In other*

words, if the determinants are different, so should be the responses intended to prevent them from occurring in the future. Moreover, where there is no consistent or logical connection between ideas and actions, an analysis of the prevalence of racist beliefs may prove to be a very unreliable guide to the extent of discriminatory behaviour, and vice versa. By defining racism broadly by reference to consequences, use of this inflated concept absolves the analyst (and political activist) from the often difficult task of identifying the particularities of the processes that create and reproduce disadvantage. The simple distinction between, for example, overt and covert racism does not by itself resolve this problem: to designate racism as covert does not by itself reveal the complex, contradictory interplay of the determinant of disadvantage and exclusion.

(Miles, 1989: p 60)

In other words, the argument that racism can be covert unintentional racism has often meant, in practical terms, that social researchers do not even begin to identify causal relationships that structure 'black' inequality. Hence, the concept then is remarkably hollow, with little or no real power in identifying causal relationships.

A third key problem is that the concept has also become inflated—encompassing practises and processes that cannot be described as racist. As we noted above, writers have asserted that where 'black' inequality exists so does institutional racism. However, 'black' disadvantage can accrue from a number of areas. 'Black' workers are still overwhelmingly represented in the working classes. Hence, 'black' people's experiences will be shaped by disadvantages that accrue from their class position. Similarly, 'black' women face the 'triple oppression' of class, gender, and racism. Class and gender, then, are both influential in shaping 'black' disadvantage. However, can we say that practices and policies that discriminate along the lines of class and gender are racist? If we follow the logic of institutional racism the answer is yes because these are practices and policies that help generate and reproduce 'black' inequality. Thus, in effect we have an inflated concept of institutional racism that has no discriminatory powers between the effects of racism and other social processes. This, in turn, weakens the analysis and suggests inappropriate policies that are designed to alleviate 'black' disadvantage.

Finally, with the exception of a few Marxist writers, institutional racism is often couched in an erroneous theory of social stratification. Although there are variations, the description usually put forward identifies two main 'classes' in the social formation: 'blacks' and 'whites'.

These two classes are placed within a hierarchical relationship: 'black' people are identified as a subordinate class, or even underclass, while 'white' people are seen to be a dominant and exploitative class. Stress is laid on benefits which 'white' people accrue as a result of this relationship and the ways in which this dominance is sustained by institutional racism. However, there are several problems with this theory of stratification. Firstly, it ignores the fact, and cannot explain why, both 'black' and 'white' people occupy different class positions. On the one hand, as any first year sociology student can demonstrate, white people as a group occupy different class positions and have a differential access to social resources and power. On the other hand, 'black' people are not *all* located within some underclass. For example, various studies have identified the existence of a 'black bourgeoisie', whose social and economic circumstances differ from those of the black working class, (for America, see Franklin Frazier, 1957; Landry, 1987; 1991; Lewin, 1991; Dawson, 1994; Marks, 1995; for Britain, where much of the work has been on the development of an Asian bourgeoisie, see Waldinger, 1990; Cashmore, 1991; 1992; Daye, 1994; Srinivasan, 1995). Furthermore, feminist writers have also demonstrated how experiences of many 'black' women differ to those of 'black' men and 'white' people because of the intricate relationships between class, gender, sexuality, and racism, (Parmer, 1982; Carby, 1982; Feminist Review, 1984; Anthias and Yuval-Davis, 1992; Brah, 1996).

Secondly, this particular theory of social stratification assumes that 'black' people are the sole objects of racism. However, this ignores certain historical instances where 'white' people have become the objects of racism. For example, the Irish have been the objects of racist discourses and practices from at least the seventeenth century through to the early part of the twentieth century, (Handley, 1947; Curtis, 1971, 1984; Miles, 1982; Muirhead and Miles, 1986; Holmes, 1988; Rolston, 1993; Rai, 1993; Panayi, 1994). Similarly, Jews, gypsies, and travellers have also been the objects of racist discourses and violence, (Holmes, 1988; Kushner, 1996; Thurlow, 1996; MacLaughlin, 1995; 1998). More recently, a growing body of work is beginning to uncover how, under the auspices of the eugenics movement, many people of European origin were discriminated against in the name of 'racial' purity, (Brechin, 1996; Whitney, 1996; Klausen, 1997). The final problem with this theory of stratification is that it assumes that the struggles between the 'white' and 'black' classes are the sole or primary dynamic within the social formation. This ignores or obscures other axes of struggle such as class, gender, and sexuality, (Williams, 1985; Miles, 1989).

Alternatives

Despite these problems, we can still hold onto the concept of institutional racism, but only if it is 'shrunk', 'deflated', and analytically more rigorous. Firstly, we have to deflate the conceptual boundaries of institutional racism in order to avoid any inflation with class and gender divisions. Consequently, institutional racism must be seen as solely a product of racist discourses. As a side note, racism is defined as those discourses that signify phenotypical or genotypical characteristics, creating a system of categorisation, onto which negative/positive attributes are applied in a deterministic manner. This system of categorisation can be used to exclude groups in the process of allocating resources and services, (see Miles, 1989). The advantage of this definition is that it recognises how the objects of racist discourses can be 'white' and 'black' people. It also recognises that racism can exist at the level of an ideology *but can also be*, although not necessarily, embodied in practices and processes. As far as institutional racism is concerned, these changes may be best caught by a semantic shift, from 'black' disadvantage to racialised divisions. 'Black' disadvantage can be caused by the articulation between class and gender divisions. Racialised divisions, however, are the embodiment of racist discourses, therefore deflating the boundaries of institutional racism. Furthermore, racialised divisions can effect both 'white' and 'black' people. Following on from these points, Miles, (1989), argues that we can retain the concept of institutional racism to refer to two sets of circumstances. Firstly, there are circumstances where exclusionary practices arise from, and therefore embody, racist discourses but which may no longer be explicitly justified by such a discourse. Secondly, there are circumstances where an explicitly racist discourse is modified in such a way that the explicit racist content is eliminated but other words carry on the original meaning. However, as Miles argues:

> ...*the concept of institutional racism does not refer to exclusionary practices per se but to the fact that a once present discourse is absent and that it justified or set in*
> *motion exclusionary practices which therefore institutionalise that discourse. An ideology of racism is therefore embodied in a set of practices but this warrants classification as institutional racism only where the process of determinacy can be identified. Thus, in order to determine the presence, or otherwise of institutional racism one has to assess not only the consequences of actions but the history of a discourse in order to demonstrate that prior to the silences (or to the transformation) a racist discourse was present.*

> (Miles, 1989: p 85)

Secondly, the concept of institutional racism must also have explanatory power, it has to be able to point us towards particular structures and processes that lead to racialised divisions. Furthermore, we have to empirically investigate whether institutional racism exists. Too often academics and commentators have asserted that institutional racism is the cause of 'black' disadvantage without any substantial supporting evidence. However, if we are to sustain the claim that institutional racism exists, we have to empirically demonstrate the causal relationships that leads to racialised divisions. Coming back to our point above, if we simply assume that certain processes create disadvantage, or that racism is the sole cause of 'black' inequality, then there is a danger of ignoring the influences of other processes and divisions in structuring disadvantage. This opens the way to an erroneous analysis and equally erroneous policy solutions.

Thirdly, we have to 'shrink' the concept of institutional racism. As we noted above, the term institutional racism was originally used to refer to processes occurring at the level of the social formation. However, it was later extended to cover single institutions and individual attitudes. This, in turn, led to a plethora of definitions and meanings being attached to institutional racism. In order to sharpen the meaning of institutional racism, I would argue that it is necessary to limit the term to processes occurring at the level of the social formation. This is one of the real strengths of institutional racism—it shows how racist discourses can become embodied in the structures of a social formation. To move beyond this level, towards prejudice, attitudes, and culture, takes away from the strength of institutional racism. However, it may be necessary to highlight all three levels, (the social formation, institutions, and social action), if we are to have a holistic picture of how institutional racism generated and reproduced racialised divisions. For example, we cannot analyse single institutions in isolation. Rather, we have to recognise, as the early American writers did, how institutional racism is a process involving a mutually reinforcing structure that generates and reproduces racialised divisions. In practical terms, this means that a research project would have to take account of the inter-relationships between different institutions and the cumulative disadvantage arising from them.

Furthermore, if we are to have a fuller understanding of how an institution operates, we must highlight the role of social actors. In sociological parlance, we need to understand and demonstrate how structure and agency interact. Unless we recognise this interaction, there is a danger that we will slip into erroneous assumptions as well as a partial or skewed analysis. For example, there is a danger that we reify institutions. This is evident in the work of Rodriguez, when she argues that:

> *Institutions have great power to penalise. Institutions reward by providing career opportunities for some people and foreclosing them to others. They reward as well by the way social goods and services are distributed, by deciding who receives training and skill, medical care, formal education, fair treatment by the law, decent housing, self confidence, and the promise of a secure future for self and children.*
>
> (Rodriguez, 1987: p 130)

However, institutions do not decide on the distribution and allocation of social resources. These institutions, their organisation and processes, are the product of groups of active and creative social actors. In order to understand the shape and organisation of an institution, who receives rewards and who is disadvantaged, we must be aware of why certain groups of social actors established the institution, whose interest it operates in, under what conditions has it been reproduced, and again in whose interest.

The role of the social actors working within an organisation marked by institutional racism must also be recognised. How do social actors interpret and act upon rules, practices and procedures? To what extent do they draw on racialised discourses both from within and outside of the institution, in order to 'make sense' of and resolve situations? When asking these questions, we should also be aware of the different class or occupational positions occupied by different social actors. This is because the way that racialised discourses will be drawn upon and reproduced will vary according to class position or the position occupied within the institution. For example, Katz, (1978), argues that racism is equal to prejudice plus power. What of those

who occupy positions without power in institutions? Can we not say that if they articulate racialised discourses in their practice that its form and nature will be shaped because these social actors are powerless? Similarly, the role of social actors who become objects of racialised discourses and divisions needs to be recognised, especially in their challenges to institutional racism. Too often, the objects of racialised discourses have been seen as passive, somehow simply being the objects of racism. However, this ignores the active role that social actors play in challenging the shape of an organisation. This is more than evident in the Lawrence case, where the tenacious pursuit of justice by the Lawrence's led to a judicial review as well as subsequent changes in police practice. However, it has to be emphasised again that this 'level' of analysis stands outside the concept of institutional racism. Nonetheless, if we are to have a complete picture of the workings of any institution(s) we have to recognise the role of the social actor.

Conclusion

One almost feels loathe to criticise the concept of institutional racism. In Britain and America, the term has been used to attack existing theories that locate the origins of racialised divisions in individual prejudices or cultural pathology. It has also been influential in shaping policies designed to eliminate those practices and polices that generate and reproduce racialised divisions. However, the concept has been used in such a vague and imprecise manner that it actually presents a hamper to the formulation of effective anti-racist strategies. In its various uses and applications, the term institutional racism has become conceptually stretched over different levels, covering broad processes at the level of the social formation, individual institutions, and the attitudes of social actors. The term institutional has also become conceptually inflated. As we saw, 'black' disadvantage that has been shaped by the class and gender divisions can be defined as institutional racism. Hence, the term has lost any discriminatory powers or analytical rigour. While the term has been stretched and inflated, it is also remarkably hollow. Through asserting that racism can be unintentional and covert, it avoids the task of empirically identifying causal relations. Indeed, the term has often been used simply as a slogan. Finally, the term has also been used in association with a misleading caricature of social stratification and racism. On the one hand, with the exception of a few writers, most writers put forward a theory of social stratification in which there are only two 'classes', 'black' and 'white', which stand in a hierarchical relationship to each other. On the other hand, racism is presumed to be the prerogative of white people, and 'black' people are seen to be the sole objects.

This, however, does not mean that we should abandon the term. It is useful in directing our attention to how racist discourses can become embodied within the structures and organisations of society. However, if we are to retain the concept, it not only has to be 'shrunk', but also 'deflated', and made conceptually precise. Firstly, the term should have the power to discriminate between the effects of racist discourses and those divisions structured by class and gender. Hence, institutional racism should refer to only those instances where a racist discourse has become embodied in certain institutional practices. Secondly, rather than simply assuming that institutional racism exists, or stating that it is covert, we should seek to empirically demonstrate the causal relationships that structure racialised divisions. Thirdly, we should be clear about the levels at which institutional racism works. Our analysis should be pitched at the level of the social formation and institutions. However, we should be aware of how the different levels of analysis articulate together in order to structure racialised divisions.

References

Adorno, T., Frankel-Brunswick, E., Levanson, D., and Stratford, R. (1950). *The Authoritarian Personality*. New York: Harper.

Allport, G. (1955). *The Nature of Prejudice*. New York: Addison-Wesley.

Anthias, F., and Yuval-Davis, N. (1992). *Racialised Boundaries: Race, Nation, Gender, Colour and Class and the Anti-racist Struggle*. London: Routledge.

Anthony, B. (1980). Parallels, Particularities, Problems and Positive Possibilities Related to Institutional Sexism and Racism. In *Women's Studies International Quarterly*, 3:4; pp 339–346.

Banton, M. (1970). The Concept of Racism. In Zubaida, S. (Ed.). *Race and Racialism*. London: Tavistock.

Benyon, J. (1986). The Spiral of Decline: Race and Policing. In Layton-Henry, Z., and Rich, P. (Eds.). *Race, Government and Politics in Britain*. London: Macmillan.

Benyon, J. (1987). Interpreting the Civil Disorders. In Benyon, J., and Solomos, J. (Eds.). *The Roots of Urban Unrest*. Oxford: Pergamon Press.

Benyon, J., and Solomos, J. (1987). British Urban Unrest in the 1980s. In Benyon, J., and Solomos, J. (Eds.). *The Roots of Urban Unrest*. Oxford: Pergamon Press.

Blauner, R. (1972). *Racial Oppression in America*. New York: Harper and Row.

Brah, A. (1996). *Cartographies of Diaspora: Contesting Identities*. London: Routledge.

Brechin, G. (1996). Conserving the Race: Natural Aristocracies, Eugenics, and the U.S. Conservation Movement. In *Antipode*, 28:3; pp 229–245.

Carby, H. (1982). White Women Listen! Black Feminism and the Boundaries of Sisterhood. In Centre for Contemporary Cultural Studies. *The Empire Strikes Back*. London: Hutchinson.

Carmichael, S., and Hamilton, C. (1967). *Black Power: The Politics of Black Liberation in America*. New York: Vintage.

Cashmore, E. (1991). Flying Business Class: Britain's New Ethnic Elite. In *New Community*, 17:3; pp 347–358.

Cashmore, E. (1992). The New Black Bourgeoisie. In *Human Relations*, 45:12; pp 1241–1258.

Cole, M. (1993). 'Black and Ethnic Minority' or 'Asian, Black and Other Minority Ethnic': a further note on nomenclature. In *Sociology*, 27:4; pp 671–675.

Commission for Racial Equality (1985). *Birmingham Local Education Authority and Schools: Referrals and Suspensions*. London: Commission for Racial Equality.

Commission for Racial Equality (1998). CRE's oral evidence to the Lawrence inquiry. Commission for Racial Equality.

Curtis, L.P. (1971). *Apes and Angels: The Irish in Victorian Caricature*. Newton Abbot: David and Charles.

Curtis, L. (1984). *Nothing but the Same Old Story: The Roots of Anti-Irish Racism*. London: GLC.

Dawson, M. (1994). *Behind the Mule: Race and Class in African-American Politics*. Princeton University Press.

Daye, S. (1994). *Middle Class Blacks in Britain*. London: Macmillan.

Downs, A. (1970). *Urban Problems and Prospects*. Chicago: Rand McNally College Publishing Co.

Dummett, A. (1973). *A Portrait of English Racism*. Harmondsworth: Penguin.

Farley, R., and Allen, W. (1987). *The Colour Line and the Quality of Life in America*. New York: Russell Sage Foundation.

Feminist Review (1984). Many Voices, One Chant: Black Feminist Perspectives. In *Feminist Review*, 17.

Fendrich, J.M. (1993). *Ideal Citizens: The Legacy of the Civil Rights Movement*. Albany: State University of New York.

Franklin Frazier, E. (1957). *The Black Bourgeoisie: The Rise of the New Middle Class*. New York: The Free Press.

Ginsburgh, N. (1988). Institutional Racism and Local Authority Housing. In *Critical Social Policy*, 8:3.

Glasgow, D. (1980). *The Black Underclass*. New York: Jossey Bass.

Greaves, G. (1984). The Brixton Disorders. In Benyon, J. (Ed.). *Scarman and After: Essays Reflecting on Lord*

Scarman's Report, the Riots and their Aftermath. Oxford: Pergamon Press.

Handley, J. (1947). *The Irish in Modern Scotland*. Cork: Cork University Press.

Hawkins, D. (1991). The Discovery of Institutional Racism: An example of the Interaction Between Law and Social Science. In *Research in Race and Ethnic Relations*, 6: pp 167–182.

Henriques, J. (1998). Social Psychology and the Politics of Racism. In Henriques, J., Hallway, W., Urwin, C., Venn, C., and Walkerdine, V. (Eds.). *Changing the Subject: Psychology, Social Regulation and Subjectivity*. London: Routledge.

Hoggett, P., and Jeffers, S. (1995). Like Counting Deckchairs on the Titanic: A Study of Institutional Racism and Housing Allocations in Haringey and Lambeth. In *Housing Studies*, 10:3; pp 325–344.

Holmes, C. (1988). *John Holmes Island, Immigration and British Society 1871–1971*. London: Macmillan.

Humphrey, C. (1980). Salient Characteristics of Institutional Racism in Policing. In *Social Developmental Issues*, 4:1; pp 26–30.

John, G., and Humphrey, D. (1971). *Because They're Black*. Harmondsworth: Penguin.

Jones, J. (1972). *Prejudice and Racism*. MA: Addison-Wesley.

Jones, T. (1974). Institutional Racism in the United States. In *Social Work*, 19:2; pp 218–225.

Joshua, H., Wallace, T., and Booth, H. (1983). *To Ride the Storm: The 1980 Bristol 'Riot' and the State*. London: Heinemann.

Katz, J. (1978). *White Awareness: Handbook for Anti-racism Training*. Norman: University of Oklahoma Press.

Keith, M. (1987). Something Happened: The Problems of Explaining the 1980 and 1981 Riots in British Streets. In Jackson, P. (Ed.). *Race and Racism: Essays in Social Geography*. London: Allen and Unwin.

Keith, M. (1993). *Race, Riots and Policing*. London: UCL.

Klausen, S. (1997). 'For the Sake of the Race': Eugenic Discourses of Feeblemindedness and Motherhood in the South African Medical Record, 1903–1926. In *Journal of Southern African Studies*, 23:1; pp 27–50.

Knowles, L., and Prewitt, K. (1969). *Institutional Racism in America*. Englewood Cliffs: Prentice-Hall.

Kushner, T. (1996). Anti-Semitism and Austerity: The August 1947 Riots in Britain. In Panayi, P. (Ed.). *Racial Violence in Britain in the Nineteenth and Twentieth Centuries*. London: Leicester University Press.

Landry, B. (1987). *The Black Middle Class*. California: University of California Press.

Lewin, A. (1991). A Tale of Two Classes: The Black Poor and the Black Middle Classes. In *Black Scholar*, 21:3; pp 7–19.

MacLaughlin, J. (1995). *Travellers and Ireland: Whose Country, Whose History*. Cork: Cork University Press.

MacLaughlin, J. (1999). Nation-Building, Social Closure and Anti-Traveller Racism in Ireland. In *Sociology*, 33:1; pp 129–151.

Macpherson, W. (1999). *The Stephen Lawrence Inquiry: Report of an Inquest*. HMSO.

Marable, M. (1991). *Race, Reform, and Rebellion: The Second Reconstruction in Black America, 1945–1990*. London: University Press of Mississippi.

Marks, C. (1995). Separate Societies: Negotiating Race and Class in the 90s. In *Sociological Focus*, 28:1; pp 49–61.

Mason, D. (1982). After Scarman: a Note on the Concept of Institutional Racism. In *New Community*, 10:1; pp 38–45.

McCrudden, C. (1983). Anti-discrimination Goals and the Legal Process. In Glazer, N., and Yong, K. (Eds.). *Ethnic Pluralism and Public Policy: Achieving Equality in the United States and Britain*. Aldershot: Gower.

Miles, R. (1982). *Racism and Migrant Labour*. London: Routledge and Kegan Paul.

Miles, R. (1989). *Racism*. London: Routledge.

Modood, T. (1988). 'Black', racial equality and Asian identity. In *New Community*, 14:3; pp 143–160.

Moynihan, D. (1965). *The Negro Family: A Case for National Action*. Washington: Department of State.

Muirhead, L., and Miles, R. (1986). Racism in Scotland: A Matter for Further Investigation. In *The Scottish Government Year Book 1985*. Edinburgh: University of Edinburgh.

O'Day, A. (1996). Varieties of Anti-Irish Behaviour in Britain. In Panayi, P. (Ed.). *Racial Violence in Britain in the Nineteenth and Twentieth Centuries*. London: Leicester University Press.

OFSTED (1999). *Raising the Attainment of Minority Ethnic Pupils*. HMSO.

Ouseley, H. (1998). *Letter to the Lawrence Inquiry*. Commission for Racial Equality.

Panayi, P. (1994). *Immigration, Ethnicity and Racism in Britain 1815–1945*. Manchester: Manchester University Press.

Parmer, P. (1982). Gender, Race and Class: Asian Women in Resistance. In Centre for Contemporary Cultural Studies. *The Empire Strikes Back*. London: Hutchinson.

Philips, J. (1987). The Rhetoric of Anti-racism in Public Housing Allocation. In Jackson, P. (Ed.). *Race and Racism: Essays in Social Geography*. London: Allen and Unwin.

Rai, M. (1993). Columbus in Ireland. In *Race and Class*, 34:4; pp 25–34.

Rex, J. (1970). Race Relations. In *Sociological Theory*. London: Weidensfeld and Nicolson.

Rex, J., and Tomlinson, S. (1979). *Colonial Immigrants in a British City: A Class Analysis*. London: Routledge and Kegan Paul.

Rodriguez, A. (1987). Institutional Racism in the Organisational Setting: An Action Research Approach. In Shaw, J., Nardile, P., and Shapiro, R. (Eds.). *Strategies for Improving Race Relations: The Anglo-American Experience*. Manchester: Manchester University Press.

Rolston, B. (1993). The Training Ground: Ireland, Conquest and Decolonisation. In *Race and Class*, 34:4; pp 13–23.

Rose, E. *et al.* (1969). *Colour and Citizenship: A Report on British Race Relations*. London: Oxford University Press.

Runnymede Trust (1998). *The Inquiry into the Matters Arising from the Death of Stephen Lawrence, Part Two. Evidence Submitted by The Runnymede Trust*. London: The Runnymede Trust.

Scarman, Lord J. (1982). *The Scarman Report: The Brixton Disorders; 10–12 April, 1981.* Harmondsworth: Pelican.

Sivanandan, A. (1982). *A Different Hunger: Writings in Black Resistance.* London: Pluto Press.

Sivanandan, A. (1983). Challenging Racism: Strategies for the 80s. In *Race and Class*, 25:2; pp 1–11.

Smith, D. (1977). *Racial Disadvantage in Britain.* Harmondsworth: Penguin.

Smith, D. (1983). *Police and Black People in London: A Survey of Londoners.* London: PSI.

Small, S. (1983). *Police and Black People in London.* London: PSI.

Solomos, J. (1993). *Race and Racism in Britain.* London: Macmillan.

Srinivasan, S. (1995). *The Asian Petty Bourgeoisie in Britain.* Avesbury.

SUA (1998). *The Inquiry into the Matters Arising from the Death of Stephen Lawrence, Part Two. Evidence Submitted by the SUA: The National Development Agency for the Black Voluntary Sector in Partnership with the National Racial Harassment Network.* London: SUA.

The 1990 Trust (1998). *Submission to the Second Part of Sir William Macpherson's Inquiry.*

Thurlow, R. (1996). Blaming the Blackshirts: The Authorities and Anti-Jewish Disturbances in the 1930s. In Panayi, P. (Ed.). *Racial Violence in Britain in the Nineteenth and Twentieth Centuries.* London: Leicester University Press.

United States Bureau of Census (1992). Poverty in the United States: 1991. *Current Population Reports*, Series P-60: No. 181.

Waldinger, R. (1990). *Ethnic Entrepreneurs.* London: Sage.

Whiteny, G. (1996). Whatever Happened to Eugenics? In *Mankind Quarterly*, 37:2; pp 203–215.

Williams, J. (1985). Redefining Institutional Racism. In *Ethnic and Racial Studies*, 8:3; pp 324–348.

Chapter 4
Black People and Discrimination in Criminal Justice: The Messages from Research

Anita Kalunta-Crumpton

Why has research into the role of race in criminal justice response towards black people been shrouded in contradictions? Much of the complexity features in the area of black over-representation in crime figures, which has become an established academic battle ground as to whether or not racial discrimination affects the criminal justice process. At both the empirical and theoretical levels of studying race and criminal justice, there have arisen inconsistencies and conflicts ultimately amounting to controversies over conclusive evidence. The main problem is seen to lie with methodological difficulties: just as empiricists have often been critiqued for grounding their findings on limited sample data for instance, theorising in the absence of empirical research has also gained theorists the criticism of a methodological flaw. In the face of all these, I am forced to ask: 'what is so complicated about this subject that we cannot conclude one way or the other?' What sort of evidence do we need to this effect? To address such questions requires taking a look at the major points of disagreement in race-crime-criminal justice research with the view to unravelling some of the complexities. Whilst the intention here is not to exhaust the literature on the subject, the chapter will draw on a wide range of data sources concerning black-criminal justice encounters.

The Black Presence in Crime Statistics: Convergence and Divergence in Research Findings

At least as far as the position of black people in the crime statistics is concerned, there has been no disputing the fact that this racial group is disproportionately represented when compared to their number in the general population. Until recently with the regular compilation of national arrest statistics following the introduction of Section 95 of the 1991 Criminal Justice Act, (Home Office, 1998), information on arrest figures had been gleaned from London-based arrest statistics put together by the Metropolitan Police. Since the late 1970s, the Met have compiled data on the racial composition of arrestees and those statistics have contributed to a series of Home Office statistical information, (Home Office, 1983; 1984; 1989), other Home Office studies, (Stevens and Willis, 1979; Willis, 1983), and academic works, (Demuth, 1978; Roberts, 1982; Walker, 1988; 1989). Findings from these show the arrest rate for black people to be disproportionate in comparison to the London population. It is higher than that of other racial groups in every category of offence. Recent studies and statistics have replicated the same scenario, (Home Office, 1992, 1998). At the national level of recording crime statistics by ethnic background, data from the prison population compiled since 1985 have constituted a major source of information. The over-representation of black people in penal institutions including the remand prison population has been consistently pictured in the national prison statistics of England and Wales, (Home Office, 1986; 1993; 1994; 1998).

To account for this racial disparity in crime statistics has entailed studies into various stages of black contact with the criminal justice process. The outcomes of such studies provide differing findings, even at the front-end of the criminal justice system, particularly police stops and search where there is vast evidence of a disparity. The discretionary powers of stop and search accorded the police has called into question their impact on the high black arrest rate as shown during the period of the 'sus' law. Arrest figures for 'sus' showed black people to be more frequently arrested than their white counterparts; in 1975, black people made up 40.4 per cent of all 'suspected person' arrests in the Metropolitan Police District, and in 1977 and 1978, the figures of 'sus' arrests for blacks were 44 per cent and 43 per cent respectively, (Roberts, 1982; Demuth, 1978). That black arrest rate can be influenced by black stop rate is contradicted for instance by findings of the Policy Studies Institute's (PSI) survey of Londoners which having agreed a link between stop and arrest rates found no racially based difference in relation to Afro-Caribbeans and whites, (Smith, 1983a, b). However, the study reveals significant evidence of a disparity between the proportions of people stopped on the basis of ethnic origins: not only were higher proportions of Afro-Caribbeans stopped than whites, the rate of multiple stops was also higher for Afro-Caribbeans than white people, (Smith, 1983a).

The PSI findings bear similarities with other studies. For example, a Home Office study of recorded stops at four police stations shows stop rates for blacks to be disproportionately higher, (Willis, 1983); according to the Islington Crime Survey the stop rate for black males under the age of 25 was disproportionate in comparison to whites, (Jones *et al.*, 1986); and in the 1988 British Crime Survey, (BCS), more Afro-Caribbeans were shown to have reported being subjected to police stops than whites even after controlling for other relevant factors, (Skogan, 1990), a pattern similar to the findings of the 1992 BCS, (Skogan, 1994). But this pattern of findings has had some doubt cast upon it. Tuck and Southgate's, (1981), study conducted in Manchester uncovered no notable difference in the use of stop, search and arrest powers where blacks and whites were concerned, and this finding, according to Jefferson, (1988), emerged because of the homogenous nature of the studied area in terms of socio-economic characteristics. In a more recent analysis by Jefferson *et al.*, (1992; see also Jefferson, 1993), following a study carried out in Leeds, this point is made clearer in the connection made between black and white stop rates. In the Leeds study, blacks had a higher stop rate than whites or Asians in areas with a low concentration of black people and a high concentration of whites, whereas in areas with high black and low white concentration the stop rate was higher for whites than for blacks and Asians. Related to this 'area' influence is the similarity in the socio-economic makeup (that of deprivation) of those areas from which black and white arrestees were drawn

The Leeds study showed this pattern relating to stops to be more apparent in relation to arrest rates where, alongside the area influenced differences according to racial groups, blacks had a higher arrest rate than whites and Asians, (Jefferson *et al.*, 1992). This observation about arrest mirrors the findings of previous and more recent studies, exemplified above, which demonstrate the higher likelihood for black people to be arrested by the police than their white counterparts. There is evidence to show that following on from arrest, police charging decisions, prior to the introduction of the Crown Prosecution Service, (CPS), demonstrate that there is less likelihood of black people receiving a

police caution than white people. This is an observation mostly derived from studies conducted by Landau, (1981), and Landau and Nathan, (1983), into police use of cautioning for juveniles in London, which reveal that black juveniles are more likely to be charged even as first offenders whilst white juveniles with more previous convictions than blacks are several times more likely to receive a caution. A study by the Commission for Racial Equality, (1992), confirmed that black juveniles are more likely to be prosecuted than white juveniles, after controlling for some relevant variables such as offence type. The higher probability of a police caution for whites than for blacks is also shown in a recent Home Office publication, (1998), which however treats this disparity with caution, given that there may be legitimate reasons for the variation ranging from admission of guilt to offence type and seriousness.

Once charged, the position of black people when they come in contact with the court has attracted a huge debate, especially as it is the court's decisions that in the main lead to the high imprisonment rate for black people, including remand. Remand decisions have been known to work to the disadvantage of black defendants who are more likely to be refused bail and instead are remanded in custody pending trial, (Home Office, 1989; 1992; Shallice and Gordon, 1990; Hood, 1992). The proportion of black defendants remanded in custody by magistrates to stand trial at the crown court, and those on police remand, is higher than of white defendants, (Walker, 1989). This disparity in magistrates' remand practices occurs 'even when seriousness of offence and other relevant factors are taken into account', (Home Office, 1992: p 15). And even when fewer black defendants are granted bail by magistrates, they are more frequently placed on conditional bail, (Gordon, 1983; Shallice and Gordon, 1990).

Much of the in-depth research studies of the courts and the disproportionate numbers of black people in the crime figures has focused on the sentencing patterns of the court. Until the recent study of *Race and Drug Trials*, (Kalunta-Crumpton, 1999), which provides a detailed account of a link between conviction or acquittal processes and black over-representation in crime statistics, there was very little information on this subject. Previous findings have merely indicated that black people are more likely than other racial groups to be convicted, (Home Office, 1983) or have a higher acquittal rate, (Walker, 1988). In any case, research studies of court disposal of defendants according to race have produced mixed findings—some have disclosed that differential treatment permeates the courts' sentencing practice whilst others have portrayed the court as adopting similar sentencing patterns for different racial groups. Based on their survey of *The Influence of Race and Sentencing in England*, McConville and Baldwin, (1982), hold that the judicial system does not permit variables such as race to influence sentencing decisions. Findings from studies carried out by Crow and Cove, (1984), and Moxon, (1988), point in the above same direction. On the other hand are findings that have identified unequal treatment in the trend of sentencing which is argued to work to the disadvantage of black people who are more likely to receive a custodial sentence than white people. This observation applies to the juvenile court, (Tipler, 1985), and to the magistrates' and crown courts, (Hudson, 1989; Walker, 1988). Black defendants, unlike their white counterparts have less chances of receiving other sentencing options such as a probation order but more frequently receive a custodial sentence even when important sentencing criteria are accounted for. For example, Hudson, (1989), has claimed that white defendants on average have more previous convictions than black defendants, however, the latter with fewer past convictions are more likely to be imprisoned than the former with strings of worse criminal offences, (Voakes and Fowler, 1989; Day, 1989). Hudson also notes that more black defendants receive custodial sentences than whites for offences which can be considered as minor. Although she observes that factors such as age can determine the difference in imprisonment rates, she nevertheless argues that injustice surfaces especially in relation to the ordinary offences against the person and minor robbery offences.

Hudson's overall line of argument is given credence by Hood's detailed study, *Race and Sentencing*, (1992). Acclaimed for its large scale focus, the study identifies a race effect in sentencing in some circumstances independent of factors such as black defendants being more likely to enter a not guilty plea and opt for trial at the crown court, instances which have been claimed to account for the high possibility of a custodial sentence for blacks. In Hood's study, more blacks entered a not guilty plea than whites but regardless of that, blacks in this category, received longer prison sentences than whites in the same category and in similar circumstances. The high imprisonment rate for blacks has also been attributed, in past and more recent studies,

to a higher likelihood of being tried and sentenced at the crown court for offences triable on indictment, such as robbery, that is more likely to attract a custodial sentence upon conviction, (Walker, 1988; Jefferson and Walker, 1990; Brown and Hullin, 1992; Hood, 1992). However, within this category of serious offences, there is evidence that blacks are more likely to be imprisoned than whites, (Walker, 1988). Furthermore, even when cases are triable either way, the likelihood of a higher proportion of blacks being committed by magistrates or recommended by the CPS to stand trial at the crown court is higher than for whites, (Home Office, 1992; Brown and Hullin, 1992).

Race in Gender and Crime Figures: The Case of Black Women

Women's presence in the arrest, conviction and prison statistics is overall lower than that of men, (Morris, 1987; Heidensohn, 1996, 1994), and explanations for this sex difference in crime figures has been contentious as reflected broadly speaking in these varying views that:

- Women's offending levels are lower than men's.
- Unlike men, women receive lenient treatment.
- Women are favourably treated in the criminal justice system.
- Women are more harshly treated by law enforcers.

This conflicting nature of gender-criminal justice analyses is acknowledged by Heidensohn in her statement:

> *If the police were particularly ill-disposed and punitive towards women then, logically, there should be more, not fewer, women criminalised and processed as deviant. In short, evidence on this topic is patchy, and conclusions necessarily tentative.*

> (Heidensohn, 1994: p 1008)

When black women's position in the criminal justice process is incorporated into these discrepancies in gender studies of criminal justice, the whole issue becomes more complicated. So far, research which interacts gender with race and criminal justice is relatively limited. In considering the encounters of black people with the criminal justice system, the bulk of the research is related to black men. This is not surprising given that traditional theories of crime and deviance have focused on men—a situation which formed the starting-point of feminist critique of mainstream criminology for its neglect of women, (Smart, 1977). In both studies of race and gender as they influence criminal justice practices, black women occupy a relatively marginalised position. Yet, like their black male counterparts, their presence in the crime statistics is far from marginalised when compared to white females; like black males, they are disproportionately represented in the prison population.

On 30 June, 1985, when the prison population of England and Wales stood at 47,503, about 8 per cent of the male prisoners and 12 per cent of the female prisoners were black which compared unfavourably to their general population of between 1–2 per cent, (Home Office, 1986). For whites, their prison population was made up of 83.1 per cent males and 77.8 per cent females, whereas they accounted for 93–94 per cent of the population, (ibid.). By 30 June, 1989, the black female prison population had increased to 20.1 per cent out of the 1,756 female prison population in England and Wales; this figure catapulted to 22.9 per cent in 1990, (Home Office, 1993). This problem of black female over-representation in the prison population has subsequently remained constant: 20.4 per cent in 1994, (Smith, 1997), and 20 per cent in June, 1997, (Home Office, 1998). However, there is evidence to considerably attribute this overall disproportion to the significant numbers of black foreign nationals charged or convicted for importing illegal drugs, (Green, 1991; Richards *et al.*, 1995). In June, 1997, black foreign nationals made up 80 per cent of the female foreign nationals serving a prison sentence for a drug offence, (Home Office, 1998).

The disparity that unfavourably confronts black men in the criminal justice process is also witnessed, albeit doubly, by black women who are disadvantaged by their gender position as women and their racial background as black. The likelihood of being subjected to police suspicion, stopped, denied a police caution and arrested is higher for black women than for white women. Chigwada, (1991, 1997), provides us with examples of where such differential police behaviour towards black women is clearly evident. One is the abuse of immigration laws by the police to indiscriminately harass black women, and men, as possible illegal immigrants. Secondly and very worrying is the police use of Section 136 of the Mental Health Act 1983 to detain and refer black women, and men, to psychiatric hospitals. According to Chigwada, a

police officer is allowed under this provision to 'remove' a person 'who appears to him to be suffering from mental disorder and to be in immediate need of care or control' to 'a place of safety' if 'he thinks it necessary to do so in the interests of that person or for the protection of other persons', (1997: p 42). In this context, disproportionate numbers of black women, and men, have found themselves detained in police stations or referred to psychiatric hospitals for behaviours labelled by the police as an indication of mental abnormality, which in a considerable number of cases have turned out to be a wrong diagnosis. Some of the negative effects of being received into a mental hospital under Section 136 are outlined by Chigwada to range from indefinite detention in hospital to the adverse implications on one's future in the wider society.

Black women's contact with other aspects of the criminal justice process has unveiled evidence of differential treatment that has tended to discriminate against them. They face a higher possibility of being refused bail but instead remanded in custody; their chance of receiving a custodial sentence and a lengthier prison sentence, especially for foreign nationals sentenced for drug importation, is higher than that of their white counterparts in similar situations. Black women's chance of receiving a community sentence is relatively limited. According to Chigwada, (1997: p 52), whereas probation orders 'may be used as an alternative to imprisonment for white defendants…for black women they may equally be used as an alternative to a discharge, fine or some other lesser punishment, thereby limiting the scope for community sentences in the future'. The observation that black people in general are less likely than white people to receive a probation order has already been noted. In fact, Hudson, (1993: p 10), clearly states: 'one of the undisputed facts about race and criminal justice is that black offenders are less likely than their white counterparts to be made the subject of probation orders'. This claim had earlier been made in Whitehouse's study, (1983), of social inquiry reports, now pre-sentence reports, and again noted by Hood, (1992). Not only are black offenders less likely to have a social inquiry report prepared on them, partly because of their higher tendency to enter a 'not guilty' plea, they are also less likely to be recommended for probation, (ibid.). This finding contrasts with an earlier observation made by probation officers that the non-placement of black offenders on supervision, as an alternative to incarceration, does not emerge from social inquiry reports and recommendations made on their behalf, given that they are more likely to receive recommendations for supervision. Notwithstanding that, they are still more likely to receive a custodial sentence, (Inner London Probation Service, 1982; West Midlands Probation Service, 1987).

The Criminal Justice Response to Black Victims of Crime

Existing information about black people as perpetrators of crime far outweighs what there is about black people as victims of crime, which is not to say that this fact is a manifestation of black offending and victimisation rates. As far as the level of victimisation according to racial groups is concerned, research shows that the victimisation rate is higher for blacks than for whites. For instance, the 1988 British Crime Survey shows this to be the case for both personal and household crimes. Afro-Caribbeans made up 16 per cent of victims of personal crimes such as assaults, Asians 15 per cent and 10 per cent for whites; for household crimes, the figures were 33 per cent for Afro-Caribbeans, 36 per cent for Asians and 30 per cent for whites, (Mayhew *et al.*, 1989).

To a large extent, this disparity, showing greater victimisation for minority ethnic groups has been attributed to social factors such as belonging to the lower class, residing in inner city or high crime areas and belonging to a high risk age group, (Fitzgerald and Hale, 1996), rather than the race factor that has often accompanied complaints made by victims of personal and household crimes from minority ethnic groups. Despite the fact that racially motivated crimes in the form of violence and harassment are not new phenomena, it was only in the 1980s that they gained recognition as a notable issue in the political agenda, (Home Office, 1981; Home Affairs Committee, 1986). This was acknowledged by the police, resulting, according to Virdee, (1995), to an increase in the reportage of such incidents and consequently, a rise in police statistics of racially motivated crimes. However, amongst those who have experienced racial violence and harassment, those at risk of victimisation and organisations with an interest in this problem, the popular feeling, prior to the recent 1998 Crime and Disorder Act and its notable recognition of racial violence and harassment, is that legislative and

law enforcement responses have been inadequate in addressing this problem.

In 1919, black people in the dock areas of Britain such as London and Liverpool witnessed a series of racial attacks, (Gordon, 1983; Hiro, 1992). There were further incidents of such violent attacks in the 1940s and 1950s following black immigration into post-1945 Britain. The 1970s saw an escalation of racial violence, a situation which worsened in the 1980s and showed a dramatic increase in the 1990s, (Mayhew, *et al.*, 1989; Gordon, 1990; Hesse, *et al.*, 1992; Virdee, 1995). But as Solomos has argued, the 'nature of the response to racial attacks both by the government and the police for most of the past decade' remained 'low key'. This, he adds:

> *...contrasts sharply with the oft-expressed views of the police and government on the criminal activities of young blacks, and the amplification of images of black crime in the popular media on an almost daily basis. By contrast, the policy response to racial attacks and related phenomenon has been muted and at worst non-existent.*
>
> (Solomos, 1993: p 192)

While incidents of racial violence and harassment escalated, police reactions showed a failure to protect the victims, (Gordon, 1983). Law enforcement response has been that of disinterest and disdain whilst transferring blame on to the victim or re-defining the attack to exclude its racial connotation, (Institute of Race Relations, (IRR), 1987; Virdee, 1995). The IRR states:

> *The police's apparent indifference to racist activity and their playing down (often with the help of the media) of the significance of racist attacks is matched by an increasing tendency to blame the victim.*
> *Despite claims by senior officers that policing racist attacks is a major priority, the attitude ordinary police officers display is that racist attacks are not a policing problem. The police's noncommittal attitude to those who report attacks is too often derived from the view that the presence of black people invites racial harassment.*
>
> (IRR, 1987: p 156)

Such law enforcement response survived into the 1990s as is clearly demonstrated in the Stephen Lawrence case.

Very interestingly, the common trend in the mode of response to racial violence and harassment, since its emergence, has situated the victim as the focus of attention. In the early and mid 20th century the race riots that emanated from white on black attacks in parts of the country received the blame. The political discourse blamed the tension on the black presence, and law enforcement embarked on arrests, of which the vast majority involved black people, (Gordon, 1983; Miles and Phizacklea, 1984; Cashmore, 1989). Recent years have seen responses to victimisation through accounts of victims' experiences and the nature and extent of victimisation. But the perpetrator has featured as insignificant in both the discursive and practical attitude towards racial incidents. In a London-based study conducted by Victim Support, (1991), into 700 cases of racial incidents in Southwark, Camden and Newham, findings show that it was often the case that 'nothing appeared to be done to arrest or charge the perpetrator' despite the evidence that the police dealt with reported cases sympathetically. The insignificant position of the perpetrator is further highlighted in a recent Home Office study which observes:

> In the debate on racial harassment and violence, the perpetrators have long been conspicuous by their absence. Police crime reports, newspaper reports and local surveys describe examples of specific incidents in terms of the victims.
>
> (Sibbitt, 1997: p 2)

There are those who would argue, in contrast, that criminal justice response to black victims of crime is no different to response to white victims of crime. Thus the question that this raises is whether what is considered to be criminal justice indifference to black victims' experiences of victimisation is not merely a perception rather than a reality. In the 1981 PSI study of Londoners the police were claimed to be 'more likely to take some action, to make a full investigation, to move quickly and to catch the offender' where 'the victim was a West Indian' than 'where the victim was white or Asian', (Smith, 1983a: p 84). On the other hand the study also shows that black people were less satisfied with police response to their cases of victimisation.

Is There Racial Discrimination in the Criminal Justice System?

It only takes a reading of a number of works relating to race and criminal justice, for example, Smith and Gray's, (1997), contribution in the Oxford Handbook of Criminology entitled *Ethnic Origins, Crime, and Criminal Justice*, to realise that arriving at a straightforward 'Yes' or 'No' answer to the above question is more often than not presented as an impossibility. In the first place questions will be asked pertaining to the context within which an answer to the above question is

expected and, as illustrated in the above contextual situations, what will then follow would be a display of controversies. The complicated stance about race and criminal justice had never been made clearer to me than the reaction aroused in various spheres across the country to the Macpherson Report published on 24 February, 1999. That reaction—expressed by the media, politicians, the police, academics and so forth—was that of shock in the disbelief principally caused by the allegation of institutional racism levelled against the Metropolitan Police by Sir William Macpherson who went on to define institutional racism as:

> ...consisting of the collective failure of an organisation to provide an appropriate and professional service to people because of their colour, culture or ethnic origin. It can be seen or detected in processes, attitudes and behaviour which amount to discrimination through unwitting prejudice, ignorance, thoughtlessness and racist stereotyping which disadvantage minority ethnic people.
>
> (Macpherson, 1999: 6.34)

My own state of shock, also in disbelief, to the post-Macpherson Report period of widespread excitement was not at the accusation of racism but at the response it generated, which portrayed institutional racism in the police force as some kind of a new phenomenon. It is not clear whether that atmosphere was premised on the belief that institutional racism never existed, or does not exist, in the police force, or whether it was influenced by the fact that the Metropolitan Police were publicly accused of being institutionally racist on the basis of a public inquiry, a route not taken by Lord Scarman in his inquiry into the 1981 Brixton riots. Unlike Macpherson, Scarman had stated:

> It was alleged by some of those who made represen-tations to me that Britain is an institutionally racist society. If by that it is meant that it is a society which knowingly, as a matter of policy, discriminates against black people, I reject the allegation. If, however, the suggestion being made is that practices may be adopted by public bodies as well as private individuals which are unwittingly discriminatory against black people then this is an allegation which deserves serious consideration, and where proved, swift remedy.
>
> (Scarman, 1981: 2.22)

Instead, what Scarman emphasised to be the crucial cause of the riots was the deprived socio-economic position of black people, itself a product of racial disadvantage and 'its nasty associate racial discrimination'. He then very importantly observed that it is the social and economic circumstances of young black people that force them out in the street and into the 'seedy commercially run clubs of Brixton'; it is there that they meet 'criminals, who appear to have no difficulty in obtaining the benefits of a materialist society', (para 2.23).

In reasoning and analysing black-criminal justice relations, especially in the suspect/defendant/offender context, the class position of black people has been tied in as a vital explanatory feature, with its primary purpose having been to wholly or partly dismantle the race factor that has formed the subject of contention particularly around the issue of crime rates. Attempts to prioritise class in terms of black people's marginalised socio-economic position have, broadly speaking, revealed two schools of thought, although there are instances of an overlap: one which has discussed the black offending rate within a class framework, and the other which has looked at how class might directly or indirectly affect criminal justice policies and practices to the detriment of black people. Both views found much of their importance in the left realist thought of the 1980s, expressed as part of the race and crime debate principally pursued by the disparate approaches taken by left realism and critical criminology. The main line of argument advanced by left realists is that to understand black crime rates—and invariably the relatively high black victimisation rate of which a substantial proportion is linked to high black offending—would fundamentally require coming to terms with the realities of the political economy of crime. In a capitalist society where inequalities in material wealth and unequal legitimate opportunities to acquire material success are a part and parcel of capitalism, crime is inevitably bound to be more prevalent amongst those situated at the lower-end of the social strata—a theoretical justification stemming from the strain theories articulated by Merton, (1938), Cohen, (1955), and Cloward and Ohlin, (1960). Relatedly, given that the black community suffers an adverse and complex form of deprivation not experienced by other racial groups, a situation also compounded by their experience of racial discrimination, they are more likely to make the crime choice in response to their deplorable socio-economic condition, (Lea and Young, 1984, 1993).

Through the concept of relative deprivation, Lea and Young, (ibid.), made an assertion that a high black crime rate is consistent with black people's awareness and feelings of being relatively deprived in comparison to white people. Much as this link between relative deprivation and crime seems plausible, unfortunately it is merely a convenient assumption that only stands a chance of credibility if backed up by empirical research. How can we assume that a feeling of relative deprivation exists where it probably does not, given that there are people who, despite our perception of them as disadvantaged, do not in reality perceive themselves as such? Some of those who fall into this category may commit crime, not because of the circumstances of marginalisation, but as a response to the greed, associated with wanting more and more, created by capitalism. It is from this perspective that relative deprivation can logically account for middle/upper class crimes although it is a concept that is nevertheless adapted in left realist thought to explain lower class criminality and in particular black criminality. By illustrating the notion of relative marginalisation within the realm of race, left realists have simply reinforced the widespread racialised notion about deprivation, criminalised black deprivation and invariably solidified the racialisation of crime.

If it is the case that black people's experiences of relative deprivation inevitably creates a high black offending rate and thus constitutes a fundamental cause of their disproportionate presence in the crime figures, then the question of race as it affects their encounters with the criminal justice system begins to lose its validity. To left realists any form of racially based discriminatory practices by the police toward black people would proceed from a high black crime rate rather than precede it. This means that high crime rates in black communities, engendered by socio-economic deprivation, arouse coercive law enforcement, such as indiscriminate stop and search tactics, which in turn gives rise to black hostility toward the police—an interaction process that amounts to a vicious cycle of deviancy amplification. In this observation, no allowance is made for middle-class black people who happen to be or reside in the so-called high crime areas. Perhaps this absence of recognition of this class is down to that deep-rooted belief that deprivation is a permanent structural feature amongst black people. This probably explains why, for instance, a black person driving what is believed to be an expensive car, regardless of area, is as likely to be subjected to police suspicion, stop and search as a black person on foot, (Willis, 1983), for the simple reason outlined by the Indian Workers' Association, (1987: p 2), that 'the police assume that all blacks are on the dole, and if they are not they ought to be'. In other words black disadvantage—rather than black advantage—is conceivable and expected.

In a slightly different context, trivialising the race effect in criminal justice practices by capitalising on class has also meant tracing contemporary law enforcement back through history from where the present focus on the lower class originated. Traditionally, the perception of the unemployed, the deprived, the poor as the 'dangerous' class deserving of control has justified differential law enforcement in which the lower-class, and not their middle-class counterparts, are liable to criminalisation. With the arrival of black migrant workers to meet the unskilled labour shortage, came an emerging new addition to the already existing category of the 'dangerous' class. The high black unemployment and homelessness rates instance features of the 'underclass'. So if black people are stopped and searched by the police it is not simply because of their racial origin but, as Jefferson, (1993), argues it is instead because 'they are...'rough' working class and black'. Why middle-class blacks are similarly susceptible to indiscriminate police stops and search is removed from this analysis even though Jefferson, in an earlier study, (1988), gave recognition, albeit minimally, to such experiences faced by middle-class blacks.

The tendency within criminology to undermine the reality that there is an absence of a divide and rule strategy in criminal justice attitudes toward black people seems to be a major hindrance to any attempt to paint an accurate picture of black-criminal justice relations. Despite that black middle-class, 'older' blacks, who are over-represented in crime figures, and black females, also over-represented in crime figures, are not exonerated from the indiscriminate law enforcement practices, interpreting the disproportionate black presence in the crime figures has prominently attributed it to being male, young, working class and black, (Reiner, 1985; Lea and Young, 1984; Jefferson, 1993), a combination of characteristics which supposedly interact with high rates of black offending with criminal justice discrimination against black people. But how much of the problem is due to black offending on the one hand and discrimination on the other, is unknown.

Rather than thrive on this narrow-minded approach we ought to be asking if being 'deprived' or young for example is a crime? Because black unemployment rate is high and those who are employed are mostly found in unskilled or semi-skilled employment, or because black people are over-represented in the younger age profile, itself another criminogenic element and a pointer to the criminal justice system, does this make all lower class blacks or all black youths potential criminals? In practice, such factors have been known to be employed indiscriminately in the criminal justice response to black people, and not their white counterparts. Socio-economic variables such as unemployment and homelessness are legally relevant criteria that have been known to influence critically not only policing but other criminal justice decisions such as prosecution, bail and sentencing— pertaining to black people given that they are disproportionately represented in those areas, (Box and Hale, 1986; Carlen, 1988; Chigwada, 1989; National Association for the Care and Resettlement of Offenders, 1993; Crow and Simon, 1987). However, Hood's quantitative research showed how 'being unemployed was a factor significantly correlated with receiving a custodial sentence if the defendant was black but not if he was white or Asian', (1992: p 86). In my own qualitative study of drug trials at a London crown court, (Kalunta-Crumpton, 1998, 1999), being unemployed or even in irregular self-employment formed a very crucial predictor of guilt from the standpoint of the prosecution but only in drug cases concerning black defendants. For white defendants, being in similar socio-economic circumstances was not a criterion upon which their possible guilt was assessed.

Therefore it is not a question of how black people are unfortunately disadvantaged by those generic criteria applied by the criminal justice system but whether there is a consensus and uniformity in their relevance and application, when it comes to race. Another example: black people may statistically be shown to have a higher rate of not guilty pleas than whites, which is one of the reasons, according to studies, why they receive a heavier sentence as against the sentence discount that accompanies a guilty plea. But to take such statistical information as given is to ignore the highly influential role of subjective processes on those facts. In my observation of drug trials, black defendants pleaded not guilty no more than their white counterparts as was the case with guilty pleas, but that is only if we remove the effect of the negotiated plea settlements and prosecutorial discretion that favoured a significant number of white defendants who changed their plea from not guilty to guilty. In exchange, the more serious drug offence charges were dropped, thus further revealing that the gravity of an offence, which is a legally provided criterion for variations in charges, is not necessarily manifested in the charge instituted.

Such are instances of the subtle but powerful forms of indirect discrimination, which is often relegated to the bottom by the search for direct discrimination pursued in quantitative research. That focus on 'hard' data has involved placing substantial inventories of variables under statistical evaluation as if this process is mechanically controlled. Apparently the variations and opposition in findings attest to this, which is not to take for granted the importance of quantitative research to our understanding of the problem of black over-representation in the crime figures. However, it does point to the urgent need to ascribe a privileged position to qualitative research for the purpose of uncovering the subjective influences in the criminal justice system as a whole. There is ample evidence that the police hold racial stereotypes about black people as being crime prone, violent and so forth, (see, for instance, Holdaway, 1983, 1996). There is also evidence that racial stereotypes and imageries greatly inform how the police and other criminal justice agents discriminatorily perceive and respond to black people in terms of crime, (see Kalunta-Crumpton, 1999), and how the police respond to black victims of crime, particularly racial violence and harassment, (IRR, 1987; Macpherson, 1999).

To fully comprehend black-criminal justice relations is to have a clear grasp of the macro- and micro-level processes of criminalisation in which racial imageries that associate black people with crime—and not victimisation—are constructed, (Centre for Contemporary Cultural Studies, 1982; Keith, 1996). The 1970s moral panics about mugging, (Hall *et al.*, 1978; Solomos, 1993), the reactions toward the 1980s urban disorders, (Solomos and Rackett, 1991; Keith, 1993), and the 1990s description of the 'yardies' and drug trafficking are illustrative of popularised ideological constructs which manifested a convergence of race, inner-cities and crime, and further justified repressive and discriminatory law enforcement strategies.

Conclusion

The approach taken above is not to be viewed as an attempt to deny the possibility of a disproportionate black offending rate. Instead, the fundamental argument is that this possibility,

which is based on assumption and not on fact, should only be emphatically presented as such, in the same way as we can relate the possibility of a disproportionate white offending rate. Establishing the offending rate for any racial group has proved difficult; both the victims' reports survey which claim high black offending rate, (Fitzgerald and Hale, 1996), and the analyses of self-reported offending which show no difference in black and white offending rates, (Graham and Bowling, 1996), harbour their own limitations in terms of reliability and validity.

To assess the extent to which black offending accounts for the crime figures first of all requires that we establish that the criminal justice system has no racially-determined influence on those figures. As already illustrated, this issue has been controversial. However, aside from a number of findings with a clear cut indication of the absence of a race factor in criminal justice practices, (McConville and Baldwin, 1982), most have situated race in the criminal justice process, whether as a sole determinant of discrimination, (Gilroy, 1987a, b) or a part of it, (Reiner, 1985). With the latter view being predominant, one crucial question that has been pursued is the extent to which racial bias is evident in the criminal justice system. Providing an answer to this question has seemingly resulted in the trivialisation of the role of race. For instance, individualising police racism, that is, employing the 'bad apple' approach is quite a weighty strategy utilised in the interpretations surrounding the contribution of race in police practices, (Smith and Gray, 1983; Matthews and Young, 1986). Consequently, the police role is seen to have an insignificant effect. Despite Macpherson's description of police racism in institutional terms, it is understood as unwitting, thus raising the question as to whether the Metropolitan Police was really accused of racism? It is perhaps in a similar context that Hood's revelation of racial discrimination in the crown court is viewed given that 'its measured effects were rather small, especially when compared with the effects of other variables', (Smith, 1997: p 750). What we tend to downplay in this 'numbers game' is nicely summed up in Dholakia and Sumner's observations regarding Roger Hood's findings:

The degree of difference in the use of custody for black and white offenders attributable to the 'race effect' may not be large but it is important to bear in mind its impact. A greater probability of 5 per cent in the likeli- hood of a black person going to prison may not sound a large figure but it becomes much more alarming when translated into actual numbers of people. As Hood has pointed out, if no 'race effect' had been operating on his sample, then 479 blacks would have been sent to prison in 1989 rather than 503. If this is multiplied throughout the country, then many people's lives are being severely damaged and their future prospects impaired for no reason other than that they are black.

(Dholakia and Sumner, 1993: p 38)

Conversely, some may argue against this argument on the basis that because elements of racial bias surfaced in 'A' court does not mean 'B' court will display the same, in effect it is meaningless to assess such findings in generic terms. Even where findings have shown evidence of bias at various stages of the criminal justice process, that there is no evidence of a cumulative bias through the process has been indicated as a flaw in research in this area, (Smith, 1997).

To argue that there is evidence of a race influence in police stops and not in search, recording or use of cautioning for instance, or in the sentencing practices of one out of 20 courts in 'C' city, or that such evidence is down to a number of criminal justice officials, does not make the issue of discrimination any less problematic. As it stands we need to move beyond any form of denial to search for more promising ways of promoting racial justice in the criminal justice system.

References

Box, S., and Hale, C. (1986). Unemployment, Crime and Imprisonment and the Enduring Problem of Prison Overcrowding. In Matthews, R., and Young, J. (Eds.). *Confronting Crime*. London: Sage.

Brown, I., and Hullin, R. (1992). A Study of Sentencing in Leeds Magistrates' Courts: The Treatment of Ethnic Minority and White Offenders. *British Journal of Criminology*, 32; 1.

Carlen, P. (1988). *Women, Crime and Poverty*. Milton Keynes: Open University Press.

Cashmore, E. (1989). *United Kingdom?* London: Allen and Unwin.

Centre for Contemporary Cultural Studies (1982). *The Empire Strikes Back*. London: Hutchinson and Co.

Chigwada, R. (1989). The Criminalisation and Imprisonment of Black Women. *Probation Journal*, 36; 3.

Chigwada, R. (1991). The Policing of Black Women. In Cashmore E., and. McLaughlin, E. (Eds.). *Out of Order*. London: Routledge.

Chigwada, R. (1997). *Black Women's Experiences of Criminal Justice*. Winchester: Waterside Press.

Cloward, R., and Ohlin, L. (1960). *Delinquency and Opportunity*. New York: Free Press.

Cohen, A. (1955). *Delinquent Boys*. Chicago: Free Press.

Commission for Racial Equality (1992). *Cautions v. Prosecutions: Ethnic Monitoring of Juveniles by Seven Police Forces*. London: Commission for Racial Equality.

Crow, I., and Cove, J. (1984). Ethnic Minorities and the Courts. *Criminal Law Review*, pp 413–417.

Crow, I., and Simon, F. (1987). *Unemployment and Magistrates' Courts*. London: NACRO.

Day, M. (1989). Naught for Our Comfort. In Russell, E. (Ed.). *Black People and the Criminal Justice System*. London: The Howard League for Penal Reform.

Demuth, C. (1978). *'Sus': A Report on the Vagrancy Act 1824*. London: Runnymede Trust.

Dholakia, N., and Sumner, M. (1993). Research, Policy and Racial Justice. In Cook D., and Hudson, B. (Eds.). *Racism and Criminology*. London: Sage.

Fitzgerald, M., and Hale, C. (1996). *Ethnic Minorities: Victimisation and Racial Harassment, Findings from the 1988 and 1992 British Crime Surveys*. London: Home Office.

Gilroy, P. (1987a). *There Ain't No Black in the Union Jack*. London: Hutchinson.

Gilroy, P. (1987b). The Myth of Black Criminality. In Scraton, P. (Ed.). *Law, Order and the Authoritarian*. Milton Keynes: Open University Press.

Green, P. (1991). *Drug Couriers*. London: The Howard League for Penal Reform.

Gordon, P. (1983). *White Law*. London: Pluto.

Gordon, P. (1990). *Racial Violence and Harassment*. London: Runnymede Trust.

Graham, J., and Bowling, B. (1996). *Young People and Crime*. Home Office Research Study 145. London: Home Office.

Hall, S., Critcher, C., Clarke, J., Jefferson, T., and Roberts, B. (1978). *Policing the Crisis*. London: Macmillan.

Heidensohn, F. (1994). Gender and Crime. In Maguire, M., Morgan, R., and Reiner, R. (Eds.). *The Oxford Handbook of Criminology*. Oxford: Clarendon Press.

Heidensohn, F. (1996). *Women and Crime*. London: Macmillan.

Hesse, B., Rai, D., Bennet, C., and McGilhrist, P. (1992). *Beneath the Surface: Racial Harassment*. Aldershot: Avebury.

Hiro, D. (1992). *Black British White British*. London: Paladin.

Holdaway, S. (1983). *Inside the British Police*. Oxford: Blackwell.

Holdaway, S. (1996). *The Racialisation of British Policing*. London: Macmillan.

Home Office (1981). *Racial Attacks*. London: HMSO.

Home Office (1983). Crime Statistics for the Metropolitan Police District Analysed by Ethnic Group. *Home office Statistical Bulletin*, 22/83. London: Home Office.

Home Office (1984). Crime Statistics for the Metropolitan Police District Analysed by Ethnic Group, 1977–1983. *Home Office Statistical Bulletin*, 22/84. London: Home Office.

Home Office (1986). The Ethnic Origins of Prisoners: the Prison Population on 30 June, 1985 and Persons

Received, July, 1984–March, 1985. *Home Office Statistical Bulletin*, 17/86. London: Home Office.

Home Office (1989). The Ethnic Group of Those Proceeded Against or Sentenced by the Courts in the Metropolitan Police District in 1984 and 1985. *Home Office Statistical Bulletin*, 6/89. London: Home Office.

Home Office (1992). *Race and the Criminal Justice System*. London: Home Office.

Home Office (1993). The Prison Population in 1992. *Home Office Statistical Bulletin*, 7/92. London: Home Office.

Home Office (1994). The Ethnic Origins of Prisoners: Ethnic Composition of Prison Population 1985–1993; Study of Population on 30 June, 1990 and Person Received in 1990. *Home Office Statistical Bulletin*, 21/94. London: Home Office.

Home Office (1998). *Statistics on Race and the Criminal Justice System*. London: Home Office.

Home Affairs Committee (1986). *Racial Attacks and Harassment*. London: HMSO.

Hood, R. (1992). *Race and Sentencing*. Oxford: Clarendon Press.

Hudson, B. (1989). Discrimination and Disparity: The Influence of Race in Sentencing. *New Community*, 16: p 2.

Hudson, B. (1993). Racism and Criminology: Concepts and Controversies. In Cook, D., and Hudson, B. (Eds.). *Racism and Criminology*. London: Sage.

Indian Workers' Association (1987). *The Regeneration of Racism*. Southall: Indian Workers' Association.

Inner London Probation Service (1982). *Probation and Aftercare in a Multi-Racial Society: A Working Party Report*. London: Inner London Probation Service.

Institute of Race Relations (1987). *Policing against Black People*. London: IRR.

Jefferson, T. (1988). Race, Crime and Policing: Empirical, Theoretical and Methodological Issues. *International Journal of the Sociology Law*, 16: pp 521–539.

Jefferson, T. (1993). The Racism of Criminalization: Policing and the Reproduction of the Criminal Other. In Gelsthorpe, L. (Ed.) *Minority Ethnic Groups in the Criminal Justice System*. University of Cambridge Institute of Criminology.

Jefferson, T., and Walker, M. (1990). Ethnic Minorities in the Criminal Justice System. *Criminal Law Review*, pp 83–95.

Jefferson, T., Walker, M., and Senevirate, M. (1992). Ethnic Minorities, Crime and Criminal Justice: A Study in a Provincial City. In Downes, D. (Ed.). *Unravelling Criminal Justice*. London: Macmillan.

Jones, T., MacLean, B., and Young, J. (1986). *The Islington Crime Survey*. Aldershot: Gower.

Kalunta-Crumpton, A. (1998). The Prosecution and Defence of Black Defendants in Drug Trials. *British Journal of Criminology*, 38: p 4.

Kalunta-Crumpton, A. (1999). *Race and Drug Trials*. Aldershot: Ashgate.

Keith, M. (1993). *Race, Riots and Policing*. London: UCL Press.

Keith, M. (1996). Criminalization and Racialization. In Muncie, J., McClaughlin, E., and Langan, M. (Eds.). *Criminological Perspectives*. London: Sage.

Landau, S. (1981). Juveniles and the Police. *British Journal of Criminology*, 21: p 1.

Landau, S., and Nathan, G. (1983). Selecting Delinquents for Cautioning in the London Metropolitan Area. *British Journal of Criminology*, 28: p 2.

Lea, J., and Young, J. (1984). *What is to be Done about Law and Order?* Harmondsworth: Penguin.

Lea, J., and Young, J. (1993). *What is to be Done about Law and Order?* (2nd edn.). London: Pluto.

Macpherson, Sir W. (1999). *The Stephen Lawrence Inquiry: Report of an Inquiry by Sir William Macpherson of Cluny*, cm 4262-1. London: Home Office.

Matthews, R., and Young, J. (Eds.) (1986). *Confronting Crime*. London: Sage.

Mayhew, P., Elliott, D., and Dowds, L. (1989). *The British Crime Survey*. Home Office Research Study 111. London: HMSO.

McConville, M., and Baldwin, J. (1982). The Influence of Race on Sentencing in England. *Criminal Law Review*, pp 652–658.

Merton, R. (1938). Social Structure and Anomie. *American Sociological Review*, 3.

Miles, R., and Phizacklea, A. (1984). *White Man's Country*. London: Pluto.

Morris, A. (1987). *Women, Crime and Criminal Justice*. Oxford: Blackwell.

Moxon, D. (1988). *Sentencing Practice in the Crown Court*. Home Office Research Study 103. London: HMSO.

National Association for the Care and Resettlement of Offenders (1993). *Evidence of the Links Between Homelessness, Crime and the Criminal Justice System*, Occasional Paper. London: NACRO.

Reiner, R. (1985). *The Politics of the Police*. Brighton: Wheatsheaf Books.

Richards, M., McWilliams, B., Batten, N., Cameron, C., and Cutler, J. (1995). Foreign Nationals in English Prisons: II. Some Policy Issues. *Howard Journal of Criminal Justice*, 34: 3.

Roberts, B. (1982). The Debate on 'Sus'. In Cashmore, E., and Troyna, B. (Eds.). *Black Youth in Crisis*. London: George Allen and Unwin.

Scarman, Lord J. (1981). *The Brixton Disorders 10–12 April, 1981: Report of an Inquiry by the Rt Hon. The Lord Scarman*. London: HMSO.

Shallice, A., and Gordon, P. (1990). *Black People, White Justice?* London: Runnymede Trust.

Sibbitt, R. (1997). *The Perpetrators of Racial Harassment and Violence*. London: Home Office.

Skogan, W. (1994). *The Police and Public in England and Wales: A British Crime Survey Report*. London: HMSO.

Smart, C. (1977). *Women, Crime and Criminology*. London: Routledge and Kegan Paul.

Smith, D. (1983a). *Police and People in London: A Survey of Londoners*, Vol. 1. London: Policy Studies Institute.

Smith, D. (1983b). *Police and People in London: A Survey of Police Officers*, Vol. 2. London: Policy Studies Institute.

Smith, D., and Gray, J. (1983). *Police and People in London: The Police in Action*, Vol. 4. London: Policy Studies Institute.

Smith, D., and Gray, J. (1997). Ethnic Origins, Crime, and Criminal Justice. In Maguire, M., Morgan, R., and

Reiner, R. (Eds.). *The Oxford Handbook of Criminology.* Oxford: Clarendon Press.

Solomos, J. (1993). *Race and Racism in Britain.* London: Macmillan.

Solomos, J., and Rackett, T. (1993). Policing and Urban Unrest: Problem Constitution and Policy Response. In Cashmore, E., and McLaughlin, E. (Eds.). *Out of Order.* London: Routledge.

Stevens, P., and Willis, C. (1979). *Race, Crime and Arrests.* Home Office Research Study 58. London: HMSO.

Tipler, J. (1985). *Juvenile Justice in Hackney.* Hackney: Research, Development and Programming Section, Social Services Directorate.

Tuck, M., and Southgate, P. (1981). *Ethnic Minorities, Crime and Policing: A Survey of the Experiences of West Indians and Whites.* London: HMSO.

Victim Support (1991). *Racial Attacks in Camden, Southwark and Newham.* London: Victim Support.

Virdee, S. (1995). *Racial Violence and Harassment.* London: Policy Studies Institute.

Voakes, R., and Fowler, Q. (1989). *Sentencing, Race and Social Enquiry Reports.* Wakefield: West Yorkshire Probation Service.

Walker, M. (1988). The Court Disposal of Young Males by Race in London in 1983. *British Journal of Criminology,* 28: 4.

Walker, M. (1989). The Court Disposal and Remands of White, Afro-Caribbean and Asian Men, London 1983. *British Journal of Criminology,* 29: 4.

West Midlands Probation Service (1987). *Birmingham Social Enquiry Report Monitoring Exercise.* West Midlands Probation Service.

Whitehouse, P. (1983). Race, Bias and Social Enquiry Reports. *Probation Journal,* 30: pp 43–49.

Willis, C. (1983). *The Use, Effectiveness and Impact of Police Stop and Search Powers.* London: Home Office.

Chapter 5

'Dirty Babylon': Reflections on the Experience of Racism and Some Lessons from Social Work

Lana Burroughs

The Central Council for Training and Education in Social Work, (CCETSW), once said that 'Racism is endemic in British Society', (CCETSW, 1990). Very little notice was taken but then political pressures brought about the closure of CCETSW's Black Perspectives Section who were considered to be too radical and therefore too great a risk for the government funded body responsible for the training and regulation of the social work profession. The word 'endemic' carries many negative connotations and is usually associated with disease. Dictionary definitions refer one to synonyms such as infectious, contagious, transmissible, and spreading: scary stuff when one considers that this word was used to describe the extent of racism in our society in the late 20th century. CCETSW was, of course, right, and one only has to reflect on the events leading up to and after the tragic and unnecessary death of young Stephen Lawrence in 1993 to realise that the disease of racism permeated every step. In British society there is an unwillingness to consider the real impact of racism on black people and their lives. It is more palatable for white and some black people if racism is viewed more generally in that it affects all types of people regardless of colour. Of course this is true, but the black experience of racism in British society is unique in its destructiveness and its undermining of a people, their abilities and their contribution to society over several generations.

Even those black people who have seemingly 'made it' continue to struggle against its onslaught and it is harder at the top where black people are fewer in numbers with less support systems. Tony Sewell who writes for the *Voice* and used to write for the *Sunday Mirror* would have us believe that we have 'made it' since some of us can be referred to as members of a black middle class. I fear he forgets the struggle that has shaped our way, our personalities, our very survival skills. The survival skills that out of necessity we now pass on to our own children so that they will know how to fight against becoming victims of racism. He forgets that regardless of class, we still have black skins and therefore we are still subject to the dreaded disease of racism in our daily lives. Issues of class and gender are obviously pertinent to discussions about racism and other forms of oppression but there is no denying that for black people its our 'blackness' that gives us a shared experience and unites us in the fight against racism, regardless of the other 'isms' and oppressions we may also suffer.

In considering the death of Stephen Lawrence and how we as black people came to have such poor relations with the police, I reflected on my own experiences as a British born black teenager. I was born in North London in the early 60s. My mother instilled in me from a very young age the need to always do better in my endeavours than my white counterparts. She considered that this would be my passport to a good future career and life. Receiving a grade B at school, the same as my white friend, wasn't good enough in my mother's view because if we both competed for a job I had the additional hurdle of racism to overcome. I can hear her encouraging me to get an 'A' grade but reminding me that even then they might not give me the job due to racism. That's a lot of pressure for a little girl to take on but experience was to show me that my mother was right about the racism that was and is still out there.

Mother didn't have the words to describe how this evil permeates society at different levels as in Thompson's personal, cultural and societal analysis, (Thompson, 1998), and that I'd be affected at every level, but her own experience taught her that it was a destructive powerful force and she needed to protect her offspring from it. Yes, most parents want to protect their offspring from harm but how often does that harm include racism? The answer is, every day if you happen to have black skin.

My parents believed that the education system was our best ammunition and that it would offer some relief if we used it to our advantage. They didn't understand about its unfairness which resulted from its institutionalised racism manifested in policies, teachers attitudes, exam papers etc. There is overwhelming evidence to prove that the education system in British society failed and continues to fail black children,

(Rampton, 1981; The Swan Report, 1985; Kelly and Cohen, 1988). Even today research shows that teachers have negative attitudes towards African Caribbean boys, (Brodie and Berridge, 1997). So I listened to my parents and with their help overcame each of the many hurdles thrown in over the years to make me stumble. I remember clearly, however, how my teachers wanted me to do CSEs instead of 'O' levels and how they insisted that I was too young and inexperienced to take the social work option on my degree course, even though I had life experience that they in their middle class cosy world could only imagine. They had not bargained on my appeal, during which they could not justify my not taking the social work option. When they asked me, as part of the appeal process, what I would do if I knocked on a white client's door and they refused to see me because of my black skin, I mumbled some reply about explaining to the client that I was qualified and then seeking advice from my manager. My mother was livid with them and with me for what she viewed as a 'weak' response. She told me that in future I should turn such questions back on them and ask what they would do when a black client doesn't want them as their social worker because of their white skin. I wished so hard that I could have thought of that answer at the time and said it. It was hard being young and black, trying to obtain qualifications and assert my rights because of racism but eventually I achieved academic qualifications and a professional social work qualification.

Nothing my parents did could have prepared me for the never-ending racism from the police. I lost count of the amount of times as a teenager that I was pulled over in my car by the police. I passed my driving test at age 18, mother's idea, but I couldn't drive down the road without flashing lights behind me. I grew to hate 'producers', forms requiring the production of driving documents at a police station, but I'd just obediently produce my documents and shrug away the inconvenience. If I was in a boyfriend's car, my boyfriends were black, then it was worse. We often had to get out of the car whilst it was searched by the police. Sometimes they searched us too. We called them 'Dirty Babylon'. Those readers with biblical knowledge will know that Babylon was an ungodly city and the term was also a symbolic name for false religion in the bible book of Revelation. The emphasis here is on evil, an apt term used by black youth to describe oppressors who came in the form of the police.

My generation of black teenagers grew to hate Dirty Babylon. We didn't start off hating them,

they harassed us into it. Hate is such a negative and destructive emotion and certainly one which we could have done without. We stopped being polite when they pulled us over, we became more assertive and gave them 'lip', often using patois to curse them. We knew that even though they could tell we were not being friendly, they wouldn't understand the degrading depth of the insults that we threw their way. We always had to back down though because we couldn't match their power and we knew that the consequences would be a cell for the night, a hassle that our law-abiding parents could do without. Whilst the parental generation understood that we were often harassed by the police due to being black and were sympathetic, they didn't understand the expression of our anger through retaliative behaviour, this in their view only caused more trouble which would in turn lead to conflict and violent confrontations. Their generation feared for our safety and knew from their own struggles with racism, the race riots in Nottingham and Notting Hill, 1958, that to retaliate does not mean that you win the battle. We were different, however, we were born in Britain. We couldn't talk fondly about 'going back home', we were home and we didn't want racial harassment in our home. We were a generation, however, with great respect and concern for our parents so we retaliated only within reason. Dirty Babylon should be grateful for that because the riots of late 70s and 80s might have happened earlier otherwise.

It was not possible to trust the police to help you when you became victims of crime or racial injustice so you didn't bother to report incidents that should have been police business. If you were naïve enough to report criminal activity, you quickly saw how the tables were turned and you became the 'suspect'. The police became the number one enemy of black youths. Even now I can visualise them clearly in their uniforms with their cocky attitudes as they overdosed on power and made our lives hell. They started to raid our clubs and parties. They stopped us on the streets for no reason and used the so-called 'sus' law as a legitimisation of their racist behaviour. The bombardment of harassment was intense and relentless. For my brothers, boyfriends and male cousins it was even worse, sometimes as a girl you were left alone but the boys had no respite from police racism. What kind of young adulthood was this? The kind that only a black teenager would know.

Other things happened. The catalogue of black people who have died under suspicious circumstances during or following police involvement are far too numerous to mention but there are the names of a few that I distinctly remember, probably because they happened in or near the communities within which I grew up and spent my adolescent years. Michael Ferreira died in Stoke Newington Police Station in 1978. Winston Rose from East London died in a police van in 1981. Paul Worrell died in Brixton prison in 1982. Colin Roach died in Stoke Newington Police Station in 1983. Cynthia Jarrett from Tottenham, North London, died after a police raid on her home in 1985. John Mikkelson died in Hounslow police station in 1985. Stephen Bogle died in the cells of Thames Magistrates court in 1986. Martin Richmond died in Brixton prison in 1988.

They also refused to take action when other racists killed us. An awful dread came over me in January, 1981, when racists were suspected of killing thirteen of us in a house fire in Deptford New Cross. The murderers have never been brought to trial and the police insisted that the killing of these young black people was not racially motivated, but we knew differently. I was later to work alongside a colleague who lost two of her children in the Deptford fire. She had a quiet dignity about her and admirable strength but I remember the tremendous and overwhelming sadness in her eyes, evident even when she smiled. The same sadness that we now see in the eyes of Doreen and Neville Lawrence, parents of Stephen. These parents and many others have been robbed of justice and live with the belief that their children's racist killers are roaming around free to kill again because Britain's police are indifferent to the murders of black children.

Some of my black counterparts took to crime. Call this what you like, self-fulfilling prophecy, revenge on the so-called law keepers, lack of legitimate opportunities in a racist society. Some leaned towards music and used reggae to express our oppression. Some were influenced by Rastafarianism and grew dread locks to signify a new black youth identity. Some took to Rastafarianism in its full religious and life style sense. All of us continued to hate. That hatred spilled over into, and was simultaneously fuelled by, police behaviour in the Notting Hill riot of 1976 and subsequent riots all over England in 1981. One only has to read the literature to know that there were undeniable links between police racism and the 1981 riots, (Sivanadan, 1982; Scarman, 1981; Fryer, 1984; Gilroy, 1987). I have vivid and frightening memories of going to a fun fair with my sister, feeling excited about the rides and lights only to get caught up in a riot. There was chaos everywhere and the police had shields and batons presenting as a menacing force in their anger. They did not appear to be keeping order, they were hitting, kicking and beating anything black that moved. Young, old, female, male, as long as it was black it was caught, hit and thrown into the back of one of those vans that black teens had come to loath. My sister and I ran screaming through the streets. Shop windows were being broken and black youths were expressing their pent up anger. We didn't want to get caught up in the looting and violence and we didn't want to get caught by the police to be beaten and thrown into the van. We watched the police beat the innocent. We shouted at them to stop but then had to run because we'd drawn attention to ourselves. We tried not to get trapped by the police, we were terrified trying not to be separated from each other as the crowds surged and people fell. We stumbled, we fell, we got up, we ran and we screamed. We survived by lying flat on our bellies in someone's front garden just as the enemy van searching us out drove by. We triumphantly reported to our friends and families that we were in the riots— our glee at escaping unharmed and outwitting the police was indescribably huge but no joy could mask the reality of what we had witnessed—the viciousness of the police was inhuman. If you were there and you saw, then you knew for a fact that they came there to get as many of us as they could through any means.

Over the years I learnt to let go of both my hatred and my anger. Police racism is so widespread that a black person could not really live, could only exist if you allowed the negative emotions that it brought to permeate and decay your life. Just as you learn to deal with racism on a daily basis, you learn to dip into your survival kit and deal with the racist backlash from the police. I went into child protection as a social worker and learnt how to work with the police. I became less angry with black police whom I'd previously viewed as betrayers, traitors, Judas's, and above all I learnt not to generalise about all white police just as I now refuse to do so about white people in general. My anger would be rekindled however by various events over the years and more recently by Stephen's death at the hand of racists and the police racism that prevented justice.

It is clear and well evidenced that police relations with black youths and black people in general have not improved much since I was a teenager. To this day my husband and teenage son are still being harassed and large numbers of black men and women have current experiences of police harassment and unfair treatment that they could cite. My son at aged 13 was walking home from school minding his own business only to be called over by two police officers and asked if he had a problem. On replying that he did not, he was informed that this was good otherwise there would be trouble. My husband who is a young black social worker, on escorting a white child to a police station in capacity as an appropriate adult is asked if he has come to report for bail. On taking white children looked after by the local authority on outings he is approached by the police with enquiries about his activities/motives. These are a few minor examples of police activity based on racist stereotypes that criminalise the actions of black people. We shrug them off after initial feelings of fury and rage but we know that we have a right as human beings not to be subject to this racist treatment.

Sir Herman Ousley, chairman of the Commission for Race Equality states that the pace of reform has been slow and complaints of racism have doubled over the past 10 years, (Ousley, in Jones, 2000). Even Neville Lawrence, whose suffering after the callous racist murder of his son is unimaginable and compounded by the police mishandling of subsequent events, receives no respite from police racism. He was stopped by police in December, 1999, searched and questioned about a robbery of which he had no knowledge, (Brough, 2000). They had no reason to stop Mr Lawrence apart from their racist stereotypical beliefs that black men rob shops and even when it was obvious that he had not been involved in the robbery they questioned him about his car, again because of racist beliefs that black men steal cars. This is the reality for black people in their dealings with the police. As we have seen, many lose their lives. This was certainly the case for Christopher Alder, a young black father of two children who never again drew breath after the police got hold of him and dragged him out of their van in 1997. The verdict on the cause of his death was 'multi factorial''. His sister is still fighting for justice two years after his death, (Macey, 1999).

Mr Lawrence maintains that things are not improving and that there is a great deal of resistance to change. He is reported to have said:

They hope it will all wash over but its not going to wash over. They have to change…

(Lawrence, in Brough, 2000)

Like many other black people he will continue the struggle until he is content that society is safe for his children and other black people. Sir Herman Ousley is of the opinion that the present government is committed to change in the area of racism but that it fears a backlash. I am not convinced that anti racism is wholly and firmly on the political agenda and doubt if it ever will be because it doesn't serve the self centred interests of those with power who inevitably emerge as the political decision makers and promoters of public policy. The police dealings with black people are permeated with racism which is endemic to the police and the structures of British society that allow it. Racism is a political evil and it exists because those who sit in the decision making seats of our society want it to, otherwise they might have to vacate those seats which are synonymous with power, prestige and privilege. Racism will always exist, as Bob Marley said:

…until the philosophy which holds one race superior and another inferior is finally and permanently discredited and abandoned, until the basic human rights are equally guaranteed to all without regard to race, until the colour of a man's skin is of no more significance than the colour of his eyes, everywhere is war.

(Bob Marley, 1977)

Regardless of political support, black people will continue to struggle against oppression which manifests itself in the form of racism. We will do so step by step, day by day and each goal achieved, no matter how small, will be a victory in the ongoing war against racism. If non-black people are to join us in the war then they too will have to be prepared to take that step forward on some days along with the inevitable steps backward on other days whilst viewing each tiny achievement as worthwhile. The reality is, however, that non black people can choose whether or not to join this frustrating war, they can dip in and out of it if they want to. For the black person however there is no choice, the war against racism is part of survival in British society. To give up is to lie down and die.

I contemplated my own social work career and subsequent move into social work education and wondered if there was anything that the police could learn from the development of anti racist social work practice in our society. Social work is supposed to be at the forefront of anti-oppressive practice. The profession has not cracked it, racism is still institutionalised in the very fibre of social work practice but there are arguably some real attempts to address it and that, in my opinion, is what is lacking in policing. CCETSW's attempts to incorporate anti racist practice into social work education bore fruit in 1991 with the then new requirements for the Diploma in Social Work outlined in CCETSW's Paper 30 2nd edition, (CCETSW, 1991). Paper 30, however, received an onslaught of criticism from a wide range of sources reinforced by media exaggeration, (Philips, 1993; Pinker, 1993). This criticism was typical and should have been anticipated by CCETSW. They were naïve to think that the political climate would permit statements about the endemic nature of racism in British society. The backlash was ruthless and effective in its effort to mock and deride the attempts to train social workers within an anti racist framework. The term 'political correctness' was coined in order to add insult to injury, complete the mockery and place the final nail in the coffin of Paper 30.

By the mid 1990s, CCETSW had disbanded its black perspectives group as mentioned at the outset of this chapter and many in the social work profession were relieved at its back tracking on this crucial issue. After all, they did not want to belong to a profession whose members were considered to be 'loons' and ridiculed by the media and political right. CCETSW reviewed its Paper 30 and introduced a revised version entitled *Assuring Quality in the Diploma in Social Work* in 1995 which contained a diluted version of the anti racist requirements. In effect, CCETSW gave in to political pressure. It is unsurprising then that we have not moved much further forward in our pursuit of a non racist society since CCETSW's example, and precedence has shown us that the objectors will come out in powerful force in order to thwart any effort deemed likely to be influential. Those who make the effort subject themselves to ridicule at best and counter accusations of racism at worst. If CCETSW, the government, the police and other institutions had black people in higher decision making and influential positions then efforts to promote anti racism in society would likely be more successful. It is black people out of necessity for their own survival who have the staying power and can ride the waves of racist ridicule, racist scepticism and racist academic critique.

Despite the criticisms of CCETSW and social work education, social work still has a value base which incorporates a respect for diversity and difference. It is the only profession which has braced itself against political and public outcry by making attempts to redress racism in society even if the bracing ended up with some cowardly flexing and bending. We can undoubtedly learn from CCETSW's mistake in backtracking when considering suggestions for improving relations between the police and black people and in countering police racism by ensuring that we do not backtrack in the quest to see some changes in our police force. We can start by dismissing the unhelpful term of 'unwitting racism', (Macpherson, 1999), which is just a watering down of the seriousness of this disease and its effects. Whether racist behaviour is deliberate, aware, covert or overt, it is still racist and its effect devastating and sometimes fatal as we have seen. There was in any case nothing 'unwitting' about the catalogue of racist police blunders following Stephen's death. You cannot unknowingly not give a dying person first aid at the scene, unknowingly not take note of black eye-witness accounts, unknowingly not offer victim support to the family, unknowingly treat the dying victim and his friend as perpetrators of crime. The list of heartless action by the police after Stephen's death is endless and, as Doreen Lawrence sums it up, the police acted towards her family like '...white masters during slavery', (Lawrence, in Hirst, 1999). The police behaviour stemmed from racism at personal and institutional levels, and to say this was unwitting racism is to minimise it and nothing about the tragic murder of Stephen Lawrence should ever be minimised. There is no excuse in the 21st century for police officers to be unaware of their own racism or of any one else's. British history is saturated with racism and those who work in public services should not do so unless they are aware of this fact and the implications for their own practice. Racism is criminal, and just as our judicial system will not accept ignorance as a form of defence against law breaking, so it should be for racism. Ignorance is no excuse and is in fact a lethal weapon often used to minimise sanctions for racist behaviour and crimes.

Dominelli, (1997), highlights a series of strategies often utilised by white people to undermine black people and to perpetuate and contribute to racism in society. In my training of social work students I encourage them to consider these strategies and honestly reflect on which ones they employ in an attempt to raise their awareness of racism in general but also of their own racism. I have utilised CCETSW's value requirements in training social work students and have found that it is in the area of anti racist and anti oppressive practice that the students believe they have made the greatest shift in terms of self awareness and the implications for practice. I have used CCETSW's value base to emphasise that commitment to anti racist and anti oppressive practice are integral to the social work role and task. I teach the theory base, integrating this with the professions value base in order to illustrate how oppression exists at various levels and how this will impact on practice but also on the practitioners personal responsibility. There is a great deal that the police can learn from the social work value base. If police business is to maintain law and order and reduce crime then they must make a move towards being concerned about the crime of racism. They cannot do this until there is a commitment to anti racist practice in the police force. This commitment must manifest itself in practice at the personal, cultural and societal levels of police activity and needs to be informed by a value base. The Macpherson Report recommendations must be implemented and not dismissed as the barrage of racist criticism crashes in like flood waves in an attempt to sweep the recommendations out to sea— remember lessons can be learnt from CCETSW's back tracking!

The racism in Britain's police force is so deeply entrenched that it may not be penetrable, but in the optimistic hope that it can be combated, I offer the following suggestions in terms of how to commence improving the relationship between the police and black people. Mine is a common sense approach stemming from my own personal and professional experiences as well as from a heartfelt hatred of racism and all other forms of oppression experienced by human kind. I make the suggestions in the hope that things may improve for my sons and future generations of black children so that Stephen's death was not in vain.

- The development of a police value base which has at its core a deep respect, regard and value for difference.

- Police recruitment strategies should be tightened up so that selection of new police officers incorporates a testing/checking out of the individual's attitude towards anti racist practice. A commitment to promoting anti racist practice should be a requirement.

- Initial training for new recruits and ongoing training for all police officers and police personnel should include an exploration of values, attitudes and personal awareness in an attempt to promote self awareness by accepting ones own deep seated racism/prejudices in order to take action to address it.

- Trainers should be experienced in anti racist training and development and be able to utilise creative and up to date training materials. These might include role plays of real racist situations and an exploration and critique of the events. Old school police/home office trainers are out of their depth and should be replaced.

- The impact of racial stereotyping, labelling, myths and how these have developed historically and continue to perpetuate racism should also be a focus in training. Police officers must have knowledge about the black person's experience of racism and how this impacts on life chances. They must also learn how they add to this oppression.

- An awareness or racism and oppression at the personal and structural levels in society is necessary if effective steps are to be taken to bring about change at both levels in order to combat it. This will entail an overhaul of police practice, policies, legislation, and procedures that disadvantage people of colour.

- The selection of significant (not tokenistic) numbers of black personnel at higher management and decision making levels through recognition and promotion of those in the force who should be in these positions already and through the process of positive action in terms of future recruitment strategies.

- The development of effective procedures to handle complaints of racism from the public and to handle internal 'whistle blowing' to identify those who persist in discriminatory attitudes or practice.

- Zero tolerance of racism in the police force so that sanctions are enforced against those committing this heinous crime.

Note: the term 'black' used in the context of this chapter refers to people of African, African Caribbean and Asian origin

References

Brodie, I., and Berridge, D. (1997). *School Exclusion: Research Themes and Issues.* Luton: University of Luton Press.

Brough, G. (2000). Grieving Neville Lawrence on his New Agony. In *The Daily Mirror*, 5/2/00.

CCETSW (1991). *Paper 30 Rules for the DipSW*, 2nd edn. CCETSW.

CCETSW (1995). *Assuring Quality in the Diploma in Social Work Rules and Requirements for DipSW.*

Dominelli, L. (1997). *Anti-racist Social Work*, 2nd edn. BASW, Macmillan.

Fryer, P. (1984). *Staying Power: The History of Black People in Britain.* London: Pluto Press.

Gilroy, P. (1987). *There Ain't no Black in the Union Jack.* London: Hutchinson.

Hirst, J. (1999). The Stephen Lawrence Enquiry: What Now for Social Services. In *Community Care*, 4–10 March.

Jones, G. (2000). Race Relations Chief Hits Out at Tony Blair. In *The Daily Mirror*, 29/1/00.

Kelly, E., and Cohen, T. (1988). *Racism in Schools: New Research Evidence.* Trentham Books.

Macey, P. (1999). Inquest Ordered into Alders Death. In *The Voice*, 13th December.

Macpherson Sir W. (1999). *Stephen Lawrence Inquiry.* The Stationery Office.

Marley, R. (1977). Song entitled *War.*

Philips (1993). Oppressive Urge to end Oppression. In *The Observer*, 1st August.

Pinker, R. (1993). A Lethal Kind of Looniness. *The Times Higher Education Supplement*, 10 September.

Rampton (1981). *The Rampton Report of the Committee of Inquiry into the Education of Children from Ethnic Minority Groups: West Indian Children in our Schools.* HMSO.

Scarman, Lord J. (1981). *The Brixton Disorders.* London: HMSO.

Sivanadan, A. (1982). *A Different Hunger: Writings on Black Resistance.* London: Pluto Press.

Swan (1985). *The Swan Report, Education For All.* London: HMSO.

Thompson, N. (1998). *Promoting Equality: Challenging Discrimination and Oppression in the Human Services.* London: Macmillan.

Chapter 6

Being Realistic about Stop and Search

Peter Kennison

Introduction

This chapter looks at the impact of stops and search exercised under the Police and Criminal Evidence Act 1984, (PACE). It analyses evidence from research data taken from various national surveys and victim studies and against this backcloth considers the relationship between the public and the police. The study reviews issues of disproportionate victimisation, public dissatisfaction and complaints against police arising not only from indiscriminate use of stop and search but also police behaviour generally. It seeks to show how police discipline and complaints bring into focus the issue of control and accountability of the police. The key theme of the chapter shows that the 'litmus test' of equality in policing is the issue of stop and search. The dysfunctional effects, when compared to the proportion of minorities in the population, indicate to police managers the impact of stop and search powers. Additionally, the damaging effects of disproportionate use of stop and search which, when coupled with under use of the complaints process tends to put a 'stopper in the bottle' of fermenting discontent. The chapter concludes by stressing the need for change in stop and search and complaints policies by outlining constructive proposals which would help to increase public confidence, perceived legitimacy and respect for the police.

What is Stop and Search?

People are generally aware that the police have a legitimate right to stop and search them should the need arise, although these powers are considered personal, intrusive and potentially frightening. The police consider the use of stop and search as an essential element in the fight against crime, (Fitzgerald, 1999: iii) Against this, civil libertarians question the effectiveness of these powers, which authorise an officer at street level to confront, question and interrogate before deciding whether to detain, arrest or prosecute. Furthermore, the high level decisions on policing

strategies, like stop and search, arouse the greatest public anxiety especially when they concern control of the streets, demonstrations and other operations which have more to do with public order rather than fighting crime. Fitzgerald and Sibbet expressed the importance of stop and search by stating:

> *Of the three main aspects of policing covered by the ethnic monitoring requirement of 1996, the question of stops and search has attracted the greatest interest: from the police, politicians, the media and community groups alike.*
>
> **(Fitzgerald and Sibbet, 1996)**

The Lawrence Inquiry report specifically referred to the issue of stop and search in these words:

> *If there was one area of complaint which was universal it was the issue of stop and search. Nobody in ethnic minority communities believes that the complex arguments which are sometimes used to explain figures of stop and search are valid.*
>
> **(Macpherson, 1999: p 312)**

Prior to the introduction of PACE there was no general or universal police power which authorised police officers to stop people or vehicles for the purpose of searching and seizing property. There was, however, stop and search legislation relating specifically to drugs and firearms. Traditionally, stop and search was a local phenomenon, managed, regulated and controlled at station level where it was seen not only as a means to fight crime, but also as a method to gather intelligence, aid detection and clear up offences. These ad hoc powers lacked managerial influence and control, resulting in policing styles that targeted certain areas which for civil libertarians added to the general perception that the police were not accountable to the public. Neither was there accountability upwards regarding this matter. Before 1986, stop and search statistics were not collated by chief officers in their annual reports to the Home Secretary for example. Profound dissatisfaction with policing styles, not least regarding stop and search, like *Swamp 81* in Brixton, London in 1981, became the catalyst for rioting and disorder.

Until 1984, stop and search powers varied nationally according to geographical locale. In London, for example, these powers derived from the Metropolitan Police Act 1839. In the counties, some police forces relied on local council regulations or by-laws. These ad hoc powers were often unclear. If an offence had been suspected the police officer would often resort to arresting the suspect, which may have involved the use of 'sus' in order that a search could be carried out. 'sus' was the offence of being a suspected person or reputed thief being in or on any highway etc. with intent to commit a felony contrary to Sec. 4 Vagrancy Act 1824. The historical tradition of stop and search had more to do with control of the streets, often being used for order maintenance rather than fighting crime.

It was against this background that the Royal Commission, (1981), considered police powers and criminal procedure and this set the agenda for much of the Police and Criminal Evidence Act, (Leishman, 1996: p 48). PACE attempted to put right some of the civil libertarian concerns in respect of police accountability as these concerns gathered momentum between the mid 1950s and the early 1980s. Kinsey et al., (1986), identified two key transitional periods. The first, between 1955 and 1975 was a period in their eyes characterised by a crisis of effectiveness in the police fight against crime. The second, from 1975 onwards they referred to as the 'hyper-crisis': the result of ineffective policing methods, and the unrealistic expectations that the police alone could tackle the problems of a range of serious crimes, particularly in inner city areas. These problems appear rooted in police re-organisations in 1964, the unit beat policing strategy, technological advancement, stop and search tactics and the notion of fire brigade policing methods involving a fast response to incidents and 999 calls.

PACE defined the rights of citizens who were stopped and searched by the police, or detained at police stations. These rights included fixed procedures relating to interviewing, searching of premises and access to legal representation. The legislation contained the explicit intention of reducing levels of police discretion on the streets, by issuing a 'code of practice' (Sec 66) which tightly defined and interpreted meanings, assumptions and rules. These rules meant that any breach of PACE 'codes of practice' could be dealt with not only according to law but also, and for the first time, against police discipline, (Sec 67). This dual liability intentionally placed constraints on the police in an effort to win back public approval, promote satisfaction and enhance public legitimacy. The codes are amended at periodical intervals without recourse to further legislation.

On an operational level the police were unprepared for such a drastic change in legislation since training support for street level practitioners, certainly as far as the Metropolitan Police were concerned, was insufficient and inadequate, though it represented perhaps the most important change to policing since 1829. Even today there is concern within the senior levels of the police that many street level officers and detectives are unaware or have insufficient knowledge of large sections of PACE. During the Lawrence Inquiry one senior detective appeared not to recognise *'a basic tenet of criminal law'* relating to reasonable grounds for suspicion, (Macpherson, 1999: pp 107–108). This said, the legislation is not easy and appears complex, intricate, and difficult to understand. Add to this a lack of training and practical understanding, and it may in part answer the criticism in explaining the high numbers of civil actions being conducted annually by dissatisfied complainants.

The Test of Reason in Stop and Search Practice

When the legislation for PACE was put together, following extensive public consultation, care was taken to avoid such difficult matters as random searches, stereotyping and embarrassment of suspects in the wording of the Act. Civil libertarian concerns highlighted the need for reasonable explanations to be given by the police to those being stopped and searched. It was deemed reasonable for an officer to be in a position to provide six pieces of information. These are:

1. The officer's name.

2. The name of the station to which he is attached.

3. The object of the search.

4. The grounds of the search.

5. If not in uniform he must show his warrant card.

6. The entitlement, within one year, to a written record of the search.

Legislators ensured that the 'codes of practice' provided both sufficient guidance and warnings to practitioners thus:

It is important to ensure that powers of stop and search are used responsibly and sparingly and only when reasonable grounds for suspicion genuinely exist. Over use of the powers is likely to be as harmful to police effort in the long term as misuse; both can lead to mistrust of the police among sections of the community. It is also particularly important that any person searched is treated courteously and considerately if police action is not to be resented.

(Codes of Practice, 1985: p 13–14)

On the issue of stereotyping, the 'codes of practice' provides further warning:

A person's colour of itself can never be reasonable grounds for suspicion. The mere fact alone that a person is carrying a particular kind of property or is dressed in a certain way or has a certain hairstyle is likewise not in itself sufficient.

(Ibid.: p 20)

There is evidence to suggest that police have failed to heed this advice. Mistrust of the police is widespread amongst the young, unemployed and socially excluded. Furthermore the brunt of stop and search policy has led to the alienation and marginalisation of the minority ethnic community, (Young, 1994; Mooney and Young, in this volume).

The code of practice says that:

Where an officer has reasonable grounds for suspicion necessary to exercise the power of stop and search he may detain the person concerned for the purpose of and with a view to searching him. There is no power to stop or detain a person against his will in order to find grounds for a search.

(Codes of Practice, 1985: p 14)

The term 'reasonable suspicion' has attracted critical comment not only because of its abstract nature but because its application relies heavily on discretion.

Reasonable suspicion

The codes of practice define the term 'reasonable grounds for suspicion' as 'not requiring certainty nor satisfaction beyond doubt but that there must be some concrete basis for the suspicion'. Mere suspicion was no longer enough for stopping people; decisions needed to be grounded in terms of objective facts respecting whether his or her action appears reasonable, (Polyvios, 1983). Civil libertarians regarded the term 'reasonable suspicion/grounds' in its traditional formulation with English law as too imprecise, (Brogden, 1985), whilst orthodox liberals viewed the powers enshrined within PACE as unworkable,

too vague, unnecessary and as harmful to more important policing objectives. A review of stop and search practices in 1995 by Haringey Community and Police Consultative Group, in association with the National Association for the Care and Resettlement of Offenders, (NACRO), and the Metropolitan Police, entitled *The Tottenham Experiment*, recommended that the term 'reasonable suspicion' should be re-defined and clarified to make it more positive.

Young, (1994), identifies three methods the police may use when determining suspicion, as 'stereotypical', 'democratic' and 'information led' suspicion. He argues that stereotypical focusing leads to low yields of information for the police because it alienates the very people who possess information about crime. Democratic suspicion suspects every person, group, sub group equally. Young, (1994), and Fitzgerald and Sibbett, (1997), concur that both methods are unfeasible and illogical although the latter authors recognise the police could not do their job without being selective in their suspicions. Mooney and Young, (1999), argue instead for suspicion to be determined by hard evidence (information led), which in their view would reduce the chances of public alienation and increase the flow of crime information, (Young, 1994).

The use of discretion during a stop and search may be a pretext for some other reason, illegally gathering information or intelligence or preventing a crime. For example, a known serious offender may be stopped on several occasions by uniform officers as part of a strategy of surveillance by plain clothes crime squads to gather as much information about the suspect as possible, or as an officer told McConville and Shepherd:

Right, let's get to know him; he's at it, whatever. I'll stop him if I can and see what he's doing, see what he's about.

(McConville and Shepherd, 1992: p 156)

This statement tends to suggest that this use of discretion is arbitrary and not grounded in reasonable suspicion, a policy which may in some cases verge on harassment of the suspect at one level and organisational police deviance at another. Fitzgerald, (1999: iv–v), acknowledges 3 patterns of police stop and search activity, if they produce results. These patterns focus on targeting certain known individuals who have a higher likelihood of arrest, a so-called fishing trip, a measure of performance and as a means of proactively dealing with local crime and disorder problems. Fitzgerald further suggested that in some cases, a stop may lead to a search where circumstances had deteriorated as the encounter had become more confrontational. This implies that in some cases where due deference and respect has not been paid to an officer by the suspect or where suspects are particularly difficult, that 'failing the attitude test' as some officers call it may bolster arrest statistics, (Mooney and Young, 1999). It appears that mis-use of discretionary powers in stop and search practice where suspicion ends in arrest may absolve police because the ends justify the means.

Lustgarten's, (1986), view of discretion is at variance with this notion, and he adds:

> ...*where the exercise of discretion is possible, for the most part this is in the direction of lenience. The police choose not to exercise their powers fully in many situations and they may prefer to deal with matters informally for two main reasons. One is to avoid unnecessary conflict with the public, thereby investing in improved community relations in the context of their responsibility for keeping the Queens Peace. The other, more self interested incentive is to keep bureaucratic demands to a minimum, especially if officers think the eventual outcome will contribute little to meeting either their own personal objectives or those of the force.*
>
> (Lustgarten, 1986: p 95)

From the perspective of police culture this suggests two types of officer, as Reiner, (1997), makes clear; the first officer is 'the law enforcer' seen as proactive, resourceful and reckless whilst the other is 'the peace keeper, active, cautious and watches his back', (Reiner, 1997: p 1019). Both types of officer use discretion in differing ways, suggesting that this is a complex phenomenon and difficult to gauge. Mis-use of discretion and reasonable suspicion when bound together in stop and search practice present problems relating to high individual moral standards and the exercise of good judgement, essential elements for membership of the police service.

The rhetoric and understanding of 'stop and search' procedures show the use of the power is elaborate, complex and problematic.

Stop and Search Powers, Ethnicity and Public Dissatisfaction

In recent years the question of race has emerged as one of the critical issues in debates about crime and policing. Some critics argue that black communities are over-policed and that this attention results in the over representation of black people in crime data. To others high crime figures represent a black crime wave.

The issues of stereotyping, targeting and discrimination were raised at the Lawrence Inquiry, not only regarding stop and search practice but also in regard to police practice generally. The crux of the problem is what can be done in the event of justified public dissatisfaction? Public dissatisfaction with the police is dealt with through PACE and the police complaints system. Not surprisingly, the Lawrence Inquiry was told unequivocally that there was little confidence in the present system amongst minority ethnic communities. They found that the lack of confidence adversely affects the atmosphere in which racist incidents and crimes are addressed and that the importance of public disquiet must not be underestimated, (Macpherson, 1999: p 315). Lack of confidence in the complaints process leads to small numbers of complaints and ever growing public dissatisfaction, which in turn leads to alienation and calls for greater control of the police. This is often marked in times of crisis for the police with either the introduction of a Royal Commission or the implementation of regulating legislation like The Police Acts 1964, 1967, 1976, the Police and Criminal Evidence Act 1984, the Police and Magistrates Courts Act 1994 and the Police Act 1999. Each piece of legislation has tended to follow scandals or causes célèbres that have attempted to constrain and regulate police practice with a view to even greater external influence and control.

Substantiation

The police complaints system is an important indicator of public feeling towards the police and is a significant balance in the accountability of police. One of the major problems which has beset the complaints system is the apparent lack of credence it shows to public complaints. This is reflected in the very low numbers of public complaints upheld or substantiated. The legacy of low substantiation rates is a fact which has cast a shadow over the system since the Police Act 1976 established the Police Complaints Board (PCB); an independent element to complaints scrutiny. Complaints against police are a serious matter and low substantiation rates only fuel the argument that public redress through the complaint process is often futile.

A number of research studies have considered the element of substantiation. One such study of ethnic minorities and police complaints by Stevens and Willis for the Home Office in 1981 concentrated on the Metropolitan Police over a period from 1970–1979. They found that complaints against the police rose by 60 per cent, or 80 per cent if one considers that each complainant often made more than one complaint, in that time, even though the population within the Metropolitan Police District (MPD), declined during this period. More black and Asian complainants alleged assault in police custody than did white complainants, and this was as true at the beginning of the sample as it was at the end. Black and Asian complainants made more complaints per person and usually more than one complaint at a time. The age range for complainants was 15–24 years showing 28 per 10,000 population for black and Asian complainants, compared with 5 out of 10,000 for white complainants. On the basis of these statistics, a black or Asian complainant, aged 15–24 years old, with a criminal record, reported for an offence, alleging an assault whilst in police custody would have virtually no chance of substantiating the complaint.

Furthermore, the PSI report also found an ethnic disparity of its survey of Londoners in 1981. West Indians stated that they were less likely to make a complaint against police if they had a grievance, 79 per cent compared to 90 per cent of whites and 88 per cent of Asians.

Recent complaints' data drawn from PCA Annual Reports, (1994/7), indicate that black and Asian complaints account for between 16–18 per cent of all complaints handled by them. The Home Affairs Committee minutes of evidence, relating to the Police Complaints Authority dated 13th December, 1995, recognised that some, '18 per cent of complaints dealt with by the Authority came from members of minority ethnic communities', (Home Office, 1995: p 3). However, only 2.3 per cent of all complaints made to police were substantiated in 1996–7, (Home Office Statistical Bulletin, 21/97). The PCA regularly objects that this comment is misleading since it takes no account of the complaints which are withdrawn, informally resolved or dispensed with. They add that over recent years roughly one in four cases that are fully investigated has led to disciplinary action of some sort being taken against officers.

Low substantiation rates undermine public confidence in the police and the process itself. It follows that an ethnic disparity in rates also understates the differences in grievances. A lack of confidence in the complaints system causes dissatisfied people to either seek redress

elsewhere or to take no action whatsoever. Both of these courses undermine not only the whole complaint process but also the legitimacy of the police. The extreme of this of course leads to the withdrawal of consent to policing.

Dissatisfaction and stops

Dissatisfaction at police stop and search tactics has been evident since the early 1980s. The PSI report, (1983), found that black people were more likely to be stopped than whites and officers frequently had no reasonable suspicion for stopping suspects. The British Crime Survey, (BCS, 1993), data also confirmed black over representation when it revealed that there were six black searches for every white subject. The Metropolitan Police Service, (MPS), statistics for the same year revealed a lower ratio of 4:1.

Young, (1994), emphasises that there are ever increasing numbers of stop and search being carried out and that often they are grounded in prejudice and irrationality which is disproportionately weighted against young, working class, male and black people. He states further that:

> To stop 1 in 10 of the black population and, indeed over one in two black males is an extraordinary degree of discriminate focusing which has no justification in terms of prevalence of likely offenders.
>
> (Young, 1994: p 73)

A study of the Police Complaints system was undertaken by Maguire and Corbett with the co-operation of the Police Complaints Authority, (PCA), which highlighted a lack of confidence in the complaints process. They added that these questions drew:

> ...negative answers from significantly higher proportions of black and ethnic minority respondents than of white respondents.
>
> (Maguire and Corbett, 1991: p 159)

A recent Home Office report entitled *Statistics on Race and the Criminal Justice System*, (1998), show that black people are five times more likely to be stopped and searched than whites. The PCA expressed concern regarding stop and search complaints in 1995, 1996 and 1997. When the PCA produced its 1996 annual report they specifically focused on stops and searches, especially those which resulted in a complaint. They argued that:

> Complaints resulting from the use of stop and search powers amounted to 13 per cent of all cases considered

during the year. This was a fall of two per cent compared to 1994–5. However, the proportion of these complaints which were made by black people rose from 22 to 29 per cent. Stop and search accounted for a quarter of all cases involving black complainants.

(PCA, 1996)

The PCA analysis showed that the Metropolitan Police accounted for 51 per cent of all these stop and search cases during the year, or, put another way, 79 per cent of all stop and search complaints originated from black and Asian people. The indication here is that whilst complaints made by white people resulting from stop and search are on the decrease, there was a significant rise in black and Asian complainants.

Research appears to show that membership of minority ethnic groups attracts suspiciousness and young males are likely to attract most police attention. What determines over representation of stop and searches has more to do with who becomes a target, when this happens and what influences bring about their selection. Pre-determined perceptions or stereotypes that locate crime within the black community will inevitably mean that police attention is focused on many more innocent black people than guilty, and a greater proportion of black people will be targeted compared to whites. Suspicion, reinforced by intelligence, may, in this context, provide a legitimate cloak for harassment, (Fitzgerald and Sibbett, 1997). Confidence and satisfaction in the complaints process appears low and the time is ripe for taking a more proactive stance in respect of complaints against police so that the public are aware that when things go wrong, the police take these matters more seriously.

The following section considers the levels of contact that exist between police and public drawn from the Finsbury Park Crime Survey, (1994). Comparisons will also be made with findings from the 2nd Islington Crime Survey, (2ICS, 1990), Hammersmith and Fulham Crime Survey, (HFCS, 1988), the West Kensington Crime Survey, (WKCS, 1989), Police Complaints Authority Public Opinion Survey, (PCAOS, 1996), and Police Complaints Authority data.

The Finsbury Park Crime Survey (1994)

The survey was designed to obtain information regarding a wide range of factors which not only included criminal matters but also about other areas of concern and interest, police behaviour and public satisfaction levels. The survey questions asked for details of victims, offenders, the time and place of the incident, its impact, and its reporting and/or non-recording. Its purpose was to relate victimisation to factors that included age, race, gender, place of residence and so on. Consideration was given to the impact of victimisation on both attitudes and behaviour.

The survey sought to address two areas of concern, namely: the fear of victimisation in relation to the actual extent of crime and the response of the police, their behaviour towards victims of crime and other members of the public who come into contact with police. Furthermore, and perhaps more importantly, the survey also considered the attitudes of victims and the public towards the police.

Contacts

This survey explored rates of contact whether voluntary or otherwise, between members of the public and police. Results showed that there were 11 types of police/public contact, they were split into two categories: public initiated contacts and police initiated contacts. Public choice and police selectivity separated the two types of contact. The results of the analysis included proportionality between white and black respondents.

Complaints

Respondents were asked whether they were seriously dissatisfied with police behaviour, whether this had occurred within the last three years and if a complaint against police had been made. It was necessary to use the word 'seriously' simply to exclude those more 'trivial' or 'incidental matters' from the database. In so doing the results of general public dissatisfaction would be lower and perhaps fairer. Only those who answered yes to the question were permitted to answer the next three questions, although all respondents were asked the general questions on complaints procedures.

It was felt essential to try to count those who declined to complain even though seriously dissatisfied with police behaviour. Their reasons for not doing so were noted. This would give an insight into the figure of hidden complaints and levels of public dissatisfaction and confidence in the police. The figures for not complaining were taken as a percentage of those who were seriously dissatisfied with police behaviour.

Public initiated contacts

There are four types of public initiated contact. These are:

- a personal call to a police station
- approaching a police officer in the street
- making a 999 call
- reporting an incident to police

Police initiated contacts

On analysis there are seven types of police initiated contacts. These are:

- police calling at the home
- home searched by police
- stopped by police in street
- stopped in occupied car
- taken or detained by police
- searched occupied car
- stopped and searched in street

When compiled, collated and analysed the picture of overall contact with police could be examined. The analysis broke down contact levels into their ethnic groups in order to consider minority ethnic group representation. For this survey, the term white meant white European and the term black refers to black Caribbean, black African, black other, Pakistani and Indian.

Findings

Contacts with police

Black respondents were 50 per cent less likely than white respondents to contact the police of their own volition. Put another way white people appear to make twice as many contacts with police than members of the black community. In contrast, black people were more likely to be stopped in the street and three times more likely to be searched, and if stopped in a car three times more likely to be searched than white people. No proportional difference was found between blacks and whites reactively contacted by police with results weighted to house calls for arrests.

Complaints against police

30 per cent of respondents, 29 per cent white and 39 per cent black, were seriously dissatisfied with police behaviour with about a half of the respondents, 52 per cent white and 69 per cent black, indicating that the dissatisfaction occurred within the last three years. Only 16 per cent of dissatisfied respondents complained about that behaviour with two thirds, or 68 per cent, comprising 68 per cent white and 65 per cent black, wishing not to make a complaint on the grounds that complaining would have no effect.

Exactly eight per cent would not complain on the grounds that the police investigate themselves and these results reflect a lack of confidence in this procedure. Some nine per cent, eight per cent white and 13 per cent black, said they were afraid of either complaining or reprisals. Ethnic dissatisfaction was too small to count in respect of the other variables. About 28 per cent white and 26 per cent black, were aware of the new complaints procedure implemented in April, 1985. Some 72 per cent of respondents, 65 per cent white and 76.5 per cent black, were unaware of the new system of complaints. Seven per cent of respondents, six per cent white and 13.5 per cent black, had either used the new system themselves or a family member or acquaintance had done so. Some nine per cent felt that the procedures had improved the system of complaints although 38 per cent white and 53 per cent black, felt it was much the same, with roughly two per cent white and 0.5 per cent black, stating it was worse. Exactly half of the respondents, 52 per cent white and 35 per cent black, did not know if matters had been improved or had got worse.

Four sets of data were compared. Two sets have been drawn from surveys commissioned by the Centre for Criminology, Middlesex University and relate to victim surveys conducted locally in Hammersmith and Fulham, (1988), and West Kensington Estate, (1989). The remaining two sets of data were commissioned by the PCA in 1996 as part of a national attitude survey, with a booster sample drawn from ethnic minorities.

When the Hammersmith and Fulham and West Kensington Surveys were compared, the results showed that 79 per cent would complain in the event that there was any form of police behaviour which dissatisfied them. This represents, certainly as far as intention is concerned, a significant vote of confidence in the police complaints procedures. Roughly 15 per cent claimed they would not complain while about seven per cent did not know. When asked what body they would report any complaint to, an average of 17 per cent replied that they would report their grievance to Scotland Yard, while roughly 75 per cent would complain to a senior officer at the local police station. 48 per cent of respondents considered complaining directly to the PCA, the second largest response. Ten per cent of complainants wished to report their complaint to either their local councillor, their Member of Parliament, 13 per cent, the Home Secretary, five per cent, or a lawyer, 13 per cent. These results are consistent across all the surveys.

The main PCA sponsored survey reflected the responses from 2,000 people and the booster survey highlighted a sample number of 430 people drawn from ethnic minorities.

The PCA survey showed that 40 per cent of men and 35 per cent of women, and 35 per cent of men and 33 per cent of women drawn from ethnic minorities, would complain at a local police station. Some 12 per cent of respondents would complain to the PCA and four per cent in the case of ethnic minorities. There was a high proportion, 22 per cent, of people in the main survey and 36 per cent from ethnic minorities who did not know where they would complain. This represents the second highest response. Eight per cent of the main survey and eight per cent of the ethnic minority sample would write to the police, 18 per cent, 12 per cent of ethnic minorities, would contact a chief constable, 12 per cent, 5 per cent in the case of ethnic minorities, would contact a Member of Parliament while 11 per cent, 13 per cent in the case of ethnic minorities, would contact a solicitor.

The results indicate confidence by all respondents that they would complain at a police station in the event of dissatisfaction. This confidence is not reflected when actual behaviour is compared to intention, as some members of the public decline to complain whatever dissatisfaction against police behaviour there may be. A high proportion of people, particularly from ethnic minorities, were unsure of their response in such a situation. Furthermore, ethnic minorities were more likely to contact a lawyer/solicitor than their white counterparts.

Discussion

Public dissatisfaction through interaction with police was investigated. The analysis showed a great reluctance on the part of black people to contact police of their own accord. There was a slightly higher incidence of black people to white being stopped by police, but once they were stopped, they stood three times more chance of being searched compared to their white counterparts. Furthermore, if travelling in a car, white people were a third less likely to be stopped than black people. However, if black and travelling in a vehicle the incidence of being searched stood at three times the rate for white people.

Using national statistics there does appear to be an over-representation of black people amongst complaints. Nationally, the black and Asian group represent six per cent of the population, but in the PCA complaints data they represent, on average, 17 per cent of all complaints dealt with by that body. From this perspective these figures appear to indicate an over-representation of nearly three times the national average for recorded complaints.

The analysis considered a number of independent surveys that reviewed complaints against police and was able to compare this data against public dissatisfaction revealing a high level of public dissatisfaction with police generally, 29 per cent of white people and 39 per cent black. Dissatisfaction levels with police behaviour appear to be increasing with nearly one third of white people and two fifths of black people being seriously dissatisfied with police. Proportionally, a third more black people were dissatisfied with police behaviour than people from the white community. Some two thirds of black people and half of white people stated that their dissatisfaction arose over the last three years. However, only a small number of people who were seriously dissatisfied made a complaint, with 16 per cent of complaints being made over three years for both ethnic groups.

A high proportion of both blacks and whites, two thirds in both cases, indicated that making a complaint would have no effect. Black people were less confident in the complaints process with just over half of them stating that the new complaints system had not improved matters.

Only a very small section of the public knew about the improved procedures and half had no knowledge of them whatsoever. Twice as many black people had either used or had a friend or acquaintance who had used the new complaints process. Only 10 per cent of black people indicated that improvements had been made and therefore had confidence in the new system.

Conclusion

The research has found a significant lack of confidence in the complaints system not only from white complainants but more particularly from aggrieved members of the black community. Very high numbers of complaints originate from proactive use of stop and search powers. Mooney and Young, (1999), highlight the increasing numbers of stop and search activities being carried out and point to growing levels of dissatisfaction and alienation. When members of the public feel upset or dissatisfied with police behaviour or they resent being stopped, their choice of redress is limited. Aggrieved members of the black community tend to resort to civil redress rather than complain, as many of them are reluctant to contact the police, let alone make a complaint about police behaviour. Clearly what lies at the heart of this matter is police attitudes and a stereotypical assumption that roots crime in the black community. McConville and Shepherd emphasise this point thus:

> Complaints related to harassment of black people, unjustified stopping, searching and arresting and much less frequently brutality towards black people. Overlaying all of these comments was a persistent complaint about attitude of officers.
>
> (McConville and Shepherd, 1992: p 173)

The Tottenham Experiment, (1997), report showed a drop of 52 per cent in stops and searches and a reduction in arrests from those stops of 45 per cent. This meant that raising the profile and importance of stops and searches during any encounter had benefits because it required officers to be more individually accountable. This process required the police to justify and explain themselves more comprehensively than before and to provide people with information about their rights; in essence to have higher levels of discretion and suspicion before stopping someone. Previously, stops and search were unimportant, attracted little attention and could be done expeditiously. However, with the increased accountability, it follows that time implications occur resulting in fewer stops and a decline in arrest rates. Perhaps in this case quality prevailed over quantity?

High numbers of complaints attract comment and criticism. Even more positively, feedback regarding numbers and the types of complaint could prove invaluable for police managers responsible for supervision. It is also not necessarily the high profile complaints that cause the problems but the much higher volume of low-level matters that are not investigated or dealt with seriously, which can upset public opinion.

The police organisation is a performance culture, a factor which largely came about as a result of the Financial Management Initiative

(FMI) in 1982, Home Office Circular 114/83 and the Police and Magistrates' Courts Act 1994. The legacy of these measures require objective setting, devising and applying indicators and measuring inputs and outputs relative to those objectives. Some indicators include the counting of complaints and stop and search data. However, some have argued that the models of objective setting are inappropriate to the policing function, (Waddington, 1986), and measures of performance may actually conflict with the application of police work because of the need to produce 'figures'. The PSI report underscored this assumption but for opposite reasons, by stating that:

> ...it is believed that figures are a bad criterion of performance and that the use of such a criterion leads to unnecessary or unjustified arrests and stops.
>
> (Smith and Gray, 1985: pp 344–345)

It is strongly suggested that stop and search statistics are removed from the list of performance indicators for all police forces, not only at the level of the individual officer but also at station and force level. The Metropolitan Police placed a bar on counting stops and search as an indicator of performance in 1997. A more robust system of recording stops and searches should be implemented, which fairly and accurately provides a true picture. Additionally, some internal monitoring and further questioning research may also be necessary. This will remove the pressure on police officers to achieve quotas and produce quality rather than quantity.

There is a low success rate for stops and search within the Metropolitan Police which currently stands at 12 per cent, (Fitzgerald, 1999). The national figure is much lower. On the one hand civil libertarian concerns focus on the high numbers of innocent people who were not arrested and who may be dissatisfied, whilst on the other there is some evidence to suggest that not all arrests originating from stops and search are properly counted. This may also contribute to the low measure of success. What lies at the heart of this matter is the strict control, management and supervision of discretion, recording and monitoring of stop and search where improvements may only come about with enhanced education and training at all levels of the police organisation.

Complaints against police should also be removed as an indicator of performance. In doing so, this would allow for a more transparent and honest reporting system which as far as complaints are concerned would end the police obsession for number crunching. Whilst the police should not canvas for complaints, there should be a more appropriate internal police policy on 'resented stops' which allows for positive action so that they may be tackled quickly and robustly. Furthermore, a complainant should feel that their complaint is being taken seriously and that all complainants should be kept regularly informed of developments and not done in the ad hoc way as at present; in essence the whole system should be customer driven. True levels of public dissatisfaction are far from congruent with the number of complaints.

The issues of stop and search are clearly enjoined with public dissatisfaction and complaints. The Finsbury Park Survey established that stop and search is the litmus test of equality in policing and its frequency of use, and when compared to the proportion of minorities in the population allows some means by which police managers may assess its impact. The pernicious effects of the disproportionate use of stop and search, together with a lack of confidence in the complaints system are mutually compounding and magnify genuine resentment to the police amongst minorities. The police rely on inaccurate complaint statistics as a measure of performance, so by removing the barriers and obstacles to complaining, it may encourage more complaints, turning a negative input into a positive outcome. In this way they may win back some of the lost confidence and legitimacy in the police organisation. In summary, the ideal solution to policing by consent is, as Lea and Young suggest:

> *The accountable police force will be one that is trusted by the community, and, of course, this accountability must include a 'monitoring' element: an effective complaints procedure involving the public and the visitation of swift justice on officers who commit illegal acts. A force trusted by the community will be one which the community will be prepared to yield a high flow of information concerning crime.*
>
> **(Lea and Young, 1993: p 260)**

References

Alderson, J. (1979). *Policing Freedom*. Plymouth: Macdonald.

Ainsworth, P., and Pease, K. (1987). *Police Work*. London: British Psychological Society and Methuen Press.

Baker, M. (1985). *Cops Their Lives in Their Own Words*. New York: pocket series Simon and Schuster Inc.

Banton, M. (1973). *Police Community Relations*. London: Collins.

Barton, P.G. (1970). Civilian Review Boards and the Handling of Complaints Against Police. *University of Toronto Law Journal*, Vol. 1: p 449–469.

Bayley. D. (1977). *Police and Society*. London: Sage.

Bayley. D. (1994). *Police for the Future*. Oxford: Oxford University Press.

Bayley, D. (1983). *Future Policing*. New Brunswick: Rutger University Press.

Baxter, J. (1985). *Police. The Constitution and the Community*. Abingdon: Professional Books Ltd.

Belson, W.A. (1975). *The Public and the Police*. London: Harper and Row.

Black, D. (1980). *From Disputing to Complaining*. New York Press.

Box, S. (1971). *Deviance, Reality and Society*. UK: Cassell Press.

Box, S. (1983). *Power, Crime, and Mystification*. London: Routledge.

Bowling, B. (1998). *Violent Racism: Victimisation, Policing and Social Context*. Oxford: Clarendon.

Brake, M. (1995). *Public Order and Private Lives*. London: Routledge.

Brewer, N. (1994). *Psychology and Policing*. Australia: L.E.A. Press.

Brown, D. (1987). *The Police Complaints Procedure: A Study of Complaints Views*. Home Office Research Study No. 93. HMSO.

Brogden, M. (1982). *The Police Autonomy and Consent*. London: Academic Press.

Cashmore, W. (1991). *Out of Order: Policing Black People*. London: Routledge.

Christian, L. (1983). *Policing by Coercion*. GLC Police Committee.

Campbell, D. (1978). *Police: The Exercise of Power*. Plymouth: Macdonald and Evans.

Centre for Contemporary Cultural Studies, (1982). *The Empire Strikes Back*. London: Hutchinson and Co.

Coleman, C. (1996). *Understanding Crime Data*. Milton Keynes: Open University Press.

Crawford, A., Jones, T., Woodhouse, T., and Young, J. (1988). *Second Islington Crime Survey*. London: Middlesex Polytechnic, Centre for Criminology.

Farrel, A. (1992). *Crime Class and Corruption*. London: Bookmarks.

Fielding, N.G. (1991). *The Police and Social Conflict*. New Jersey, USA: Athlone Press.

Fielding, N. (1991a). Police Attitudes to Crime and Punishment. In *British Journal of Criminology*, 31:1; p 39.

Fitzgerald, M., and Sibbett, R. (1997). *Ethnic Monitoring in Police Forces*. Home Office Study 173. London: HMSO.

Fitzgerald, M. (1999). *Searches in London*. London: Metropolitan Police.

Francis P. (1997). *Policing Futures*. London: Macmillan Press.

Freckleton, I., and Selby, J. (1988). Piercing the Blue Veil. In Chappell, D., and Wilson, P. (1988). *Australian Policing*. Sydney: Butterworths.

Gifford, Lord (1986). *The Broadwater Farm Inquiry*. London: Karia Press.

Gilroy, P. (1987). *There Ain't no Black in the Union Jack.* London: Hutchinson.

Goldsmith, J. (1991). *Complaints Against Police: A Trend Towards Civilian Review.* Oxford: Oxford Press.

Hain, P. (1980). *Policing the Police,* Vol. 2. London: Calder.

Harrison, J. (1987). *Police Misconduct. Legal Remedies.* Wiltshire: Legal Action Group.

Haringey Community and Police Consultative Group (1997). *Policing Local Communities: The Tottenham Experiment.* London: NACRO.

Hewitt, P. (1982). *A Fair Cop: Reforming the Police Complaints Procedure.* London: National Council for Civil Liberties Press.

Hough, M., and Mayhew, P. (1983). *The British Crime Survey.* London: HMSO.

Holdaway, S. (1977). *The British Police.* London: Arnold Press.

Holdaway, S. (1983). *Inside the British Police.* Oxford: Blackwell.

HMSO (1962). *The Royal Commission on the Police.* London: Home Office.

HMSO (1981). *Crime Control and the Police.* London: Home Office.

HMSO (1984). *The Police and Criminal Evidence Act 1984 (Sec 66): Codes of Practice.* London: Home Office.

HMSO (1993). *Police Reform.* London: Home Office.

HMSO (1995). *Home Affairs Select Committee: Minutes of Evidence on The Police Complaints Authority,* 13th Dec.

HMSO (1995). *Police Duties and Responsibilities.* London: Home Office.

HMSO (1998). *Statistics on Race and the Criminal Justice System.* London: Home Office.

Home Affairs Select Committee (1997). *Police Disciplinary and Complaints Procedure,* Vol. 1–2. London: HMSO.

Home Office (1985). *Guidance to Chief Officers on Police Complaints and Discipline Procedures.* London: Home Office.

Humphry, D. (1971). *Police Power and Black People.* London: Panther Books.

Jones, T., Maclean, B., and Young, J. (1986). *The Islington Crime Survey.* Aldershot: Gower.

Keith, M. (1993). *Race, Riots and Policing.* London: UCL Press.

Kinsey. R., Lea, J., amd Young, J. (1986). *Losing the Fight Against Crime.* Oxford: Blackwell.

Lambert, J. (1970). *Crime Police and Race Relations.* London: Oxford University Press.

Lea, J., and Young, J. (1984). *What is to be Done About Law and Order?* London: Penguin.

Leishman, F., Loveday, B., and Savage, S. (1996). *Core Issues in Policing.* London: Longman.

Leonard, T. (1998). Change in Internal Complaints System Urged. In *Police Review,* 106 5462, 27th March

Lustgarten, L. (1986). *The Governance of the Police.* London: Sweet and Maxwell.

Mark, R. (1977). *Policing a Perplexed Society.* London: Allen and Unwin.

Mark, R. (1978). *The Office of Constable.* London: Collins.

McConville, M., and Shepherd, D. (1992). *Watching Police Watching Communities.* London: Routledge.

Macpherson, Sir W. (1999). *The Stephen Lawrence Inquiry.* London: HMSO.

Maguire, M., and Corbett, C. (1991). *The Study of the Police Complaints System.* London: HMSO.

Matthews, R., Young, J., and Lea, J. (1986). *Confronting Crime.* London: Sage.

Morgan, R. (1997). *The Future of Policing.* Oxford: Clarendon.

Mooney, J., and Young, J. (1999). *Social Exclusion and Criminal Justice.* Centre for Criminology, Middlesex University.

Oliver, I. (1987). *Police, Government and Accountability.* Basingstoke: Macmillan.

Painter, K., Lea, J., Woodhouse, T., and Young, J. (1989). *The Hammersmith and Fulham Crime and Policing Survey.* London: Middlesex Polytechnic, Centre for Criminology.

Painter, K., Woodhouse, T., and Young, J. (1990). *The Ladywood Crime and Community Survey.* London: Middlesex Polytechnic, Centre for Criminology.

PCA Annual Report (1995). *The 1994–5 Annual Report of the Police Complaints Authority.* London: HMSO.

PCA Annual Report (1996). *The 1995–6 Annual Report of the Police Complaints Authority.* London: HMSO.

PCA Annual Report (1997). *The 1996–7 Annual Report of the Police Complaints Authority.* London: HMSO.

PCA (1995). *Police Complaints Authority 10. The First 10 Years.* London: HMSO.

Polyvious, P. (1983). *Search and Seizure.* London: Duckworth.

Pope, D. (1981). *Modern Policing.* London: Croom Helm.

Reiner, R. (1978). The Police, Class and Politics. *Marxism Today,* March.

Reiner, R. (1991). *Chief Constables.* Oxford University Press.

Reiner, R. (1992). *The Politics of the Police.* Harvester Wheatsheaf.

Reiner, R. (1993). *Accountable Policing.* London: Institute for Policy Research

Reiner, R. (1997). Policing and the Police. In *The Oxford Handbook of Criminology,* 2nd edn: pp 997–1049. Oxford: Clarendon Press.

Russell, K. (1976). *Complaints Against the Police.* Leicester: Milltak.

Scarman, Lord J. (1982). *The Brixton Disorders.* HMSO.

Skogan, W. (1994). Contacts Between Police and Public in findings from *The 1992 British Crime Survey,* Home Office Research Study No. 134. London: HMSO.

Skolnick, J. (1986). *The New Blue Line.* New York: The Free Press.

Smith, D., and Gray, J. (1985). *Police and People in London.* London: Policy Studies Institute.

Stephens, M., and Becker, S. (1994). *Police Force Police Service.* London: Macmillan.

Stevens, P., and Willis, C. (1979). *Race Crime and Arrests.* Home Office Research study No. 58. London: HMSO.

Stevens, P., and Willis, C. (1981). *Ethnic Minorities and Complaints Against the Police.* Research and Planning unit paper No. 5. London: HMSO.

Taylor, I., Walton, P., and Young, J. (1973). *The New Criminology*. London: Routledge.

Tyler, T.R. (1990). *Why People Obey the Law*. New Haven, USA: Yale University Press.

Uglow, S. (1988). *Policing Liberal Society*. Oxford University Press.

Waddington, P.A.J. (1986). Defining Objectives: A Reply to Tony Butler. *Policing*, 2(1).

Waddington, P.A.J. (1991). *The Strong Arm of the Law*. Oxford: Clarenden Press.

Waddington, P.A.J. (1997). More than good citizens. In *Police Review*, 23rd January.

Waddington, P.A.J. (1999). *Policing Citizens*. London: UCL Press.

Wilson, J.Q. (1968). *Varieties of Police Behaviour*. Massachusetts: Harvard University Press.

Young J. (1994). *Policing the Streets: Stops and Search in N. London*. Islington Councils Police and Crime Prevention Unit publication.

Zander, M. (1985). *The Police and Criminal Evidence Act 1984*. London: Weidenfield.

Chapter 7

Policing Ethnic Minorities: Stop and Search in North London

Jayne Mooney and Jock Young

Background of the Project

This project forms part of a long-term study of stop and search in North London, particularly the Borough of Islington, and focusing, amongst other things, on the relationship between the police and ethnic minorities, (Jones *et al.*, 1986; Crawford *et al.*, 1990; Woodhouse *et al.*, 1991; Young, 1995). The advantage of such continuing research rather than one-off projects is that it allows ideas to develop and hypotheses arising out of one project to be tested in another. It also permits some measure of comparison over time.

The present study arises particularly out of a need to re-examine the findings of the 1995 study, *Policing the Streets*, which was based on a large scale high intensity study of the Finsbury park area in North Islington. This involved a survey of 1,000 individuals using a sample of 50 per cent of all households and a random selection of one person over 16 per household. It was funded by the Department of the Environment and was one of the most intensive studies of policing to occur in this country. It came up with some extremely interesting findings, not the least being the patterning of foot stops:

Table 1 – Prevalence of Foot Stops by Country of Origin, Finsbury Park Study

	%
All	8.6
African-Caribbean	12.8
English/Scottish/Welsh	5.8
Irish	14.3
Greek/Turkish/Cypriot	8.2
African	5.9
Asian	4.5

Where foot stops are police initiated and are specifically concerning an active suspicion of crime, social and service stops are specifically filtered out, unlike in many previous surveys, (see Young, 1995: pp 5–6).

The high level of Irish and African-Caribbean stops were of interest, as were the lower than average level of African stops. The fact that Irish stops were greater than African-Caribbean and African lower than English was of particular interest. The level of stops of English, Scottish and Welsh, (ESW), versus Irish was significant at the one per cent level, of ESW versus African-Caribbean significant at the 5 per cent level, the African data was too small to allow statistical testing (see Mooney and Young, 1999). The present study resolved to re-examine these findings, carrying out a series of qualitative interviews in order to put flesh on the bones of the data.

Lastly, we finished this study shortly after the publication of the Macpherson Report into the murder of Stephen Lawrence. The findings touch frequently on the concerns of this report and our concern has been to appraise and develop its conclusions particularly in terms of institutionalised racism and the practice of stop and search.

Aims of the Project

The overall theoretical aims of the project are to examine the following areas:

1. Disproportionality

A wide scale debate exists with regards to the 'disproportional' contact between ethnic groups and the criminal justice system, (for a good summary of the literature and research findings see Smith, 1997; Sanders, 1997). Much of this is focused on disproportionality at sentencing, (see Blumstein, 1983, 1993; Hood, 1992), and its subsequent effect on the structure of the prison population, but interest has also been extensive in terms of the 'entry' point into the criminal justice system, (see Fitzgerald and Sibbit, 1997).

Our present study's remit was to attempt an explanation of the patterning of stops. Three competing theories will be examined:

The incongruity thesis: that stops are a function of the conspicuousness of members of one ethnic group in an area predominantly made up of other ethnic groups;

The prejudice thesis: that stops are a simple function of police prejudices against particular ethnic groups; and

The class thesis: that the differential patterns of stops are largely a function of the police focus of suspicion on working class, young men. That is, the high focus on certain ethnic groups largely reflects the sizeable proportion of working class, young men in their population.

2. Institutionalised racism

Directly relating to the phenomenon of disproportionality is the notion of its mechanism being a function of institutionalised racism within the police service, (see Gilroy, 1987; Gordon, 1983; Macpherson, 1999). Both the incongruity thesis and the prejudice thesis clearly fit this conjecture, although both have different outcomes in terms of police focus of suspicion. Such discussions are obviously of considerable political significance particularly in the wake of the Lawrence Inquiry.

3. Actuarial justice

In the last ten years there have been repeated assertions as to a major shift in the orientation of Western criminal justice systems. That is, from a system which was neo-classicist, concerned with justice, evidence, individual guilt or innocence and clear cut crimes, to that which is managerial and administrative, concerned with control, balance of probability and categorical suspicion, and concerned with the management of actual and potential troublemakers, (see Feeley and Simon, 1992, 1994; Young, 1999). This assertion has to be put in the context of the rapid change in the use of stop and search in the present period. Several authors have pointed to the rise in the prevalence of stop and search since 1986, but a decline in the proportion of arrests, (e.g. Sanders, 1997; Fitzgerald and Sibbit, 1997). Thus, over seven times more people were stopped and searched on foot or vehicle under PACE in 1996 than in 1986, the first year of the PACE legislation, whereas arrests declined from 17 per cent to 11 per cent during that period, (Wilkins and Addicott, 1997). In the Metropolitan District searches rose by almost eight times, whilst the arrests declined similarly from 17 per cent to 11

per cent. There has recently been a decline in stops in the Metropolitan area which probably relates to the special circumstances centring around the impact of the Lawrence Inquiry, (see Fitzgerald, 1999).

From an actuarial point of view such a decline might be explained as a clear indication of a shift to a concern with disorder management, rather than criminal justice. That is, with moving undesirables along rather than being involved in the criminal justice process starting at arrest. This clearly links to the incongruity thesis detailed above.

The most recent national figures show the continuation of this trend with a 21 per cent increase in the last year, (1998), an overall nine times increase since 1986 and an arrest rate now reduced to 10 per cent. On the face of it such a remarkable deployment of police resources has strong actuarial overtones, particularly with the low arrest rate and the minor nature of many of the offences dealt with.

4. Social exclusion

The focus of policing on certain sections of the community raises the question of the degree to which the exclusionary forces emanating from the criminal justice system are exerted on those who are excluded from the labour force, or at least the secure, primary labour market. The compounding of social exclusion is an important area of investigation as is the extent to which this represents a criminalisation and scapegoating of poverty.

5. Categories

We are concerned in this paper as to the extent that the conventional categorisation by pigmentation, i.e. black compared to white, disguises important ethnic differentials, particularly those between the Irish and the English population, (see Hillyard, 1993; Hickman, 1998). Crucial here is whether the custom of deriving categories from the language of prejudice, (i.e. black compared to white), is adequate in understanding the actual lived realities of ethnic groups.

Explaining Differences

Let us look at the three explanations of ethnic discrimination one by one:

1. The incongruity thesis

> *Although the police seem to create a few 'safe spots' within 'bad neighborhoods', gang members report that the boundaries of neighborhoods are patrolled with great seriousness and severity. The police are seen as very hard on 'suspicious looking' adolescents who have strayed from home territory...Race thus becomes a particularly salient indicator of 'suspiciousness' when Negroes or Mexicans are found in white neighborhoods. Being a Negro per se (as being a Negro in a Negro neighborhood) is apparently not as important a criterion of suspiciousness as being a Negro who is 'out of place'.*
>
> (Werthman and Piliavin, 1967: pp 77–79)

Thus Werthman and Piliavin, in their pioneering study of policing gangs, first enunciated the theory of incongruity. Closer to home, Cohen, in his much cited study of policing in Islington in the first part of this century, developed the theory of incongruity in a fashion which widened the historical and contextual perspective of the phenomenon. Charting the development of policing, he notes:

> *Now initially, and at the time when large numbers of the so-called 'dangerous and perishing' classes still lived crowded together in close proximity to the citadels of power, the police attempted to apply the same norms of public order to these residential areas as to the central place itself. As the problems of enforcing these norms became apparent, and as the urban poor were evicted from the city centre, the policing strategy changed. The innovations consisted precisely in differentiating between the two urban contexts. While statutory norms were still routinely enforced in the centre, in the new heartlands of the working-class city they were increasingly used only as an emergency measure, to justify the last resort of physical repression. In their place, a system of informal, tacitly negotiated and particularistic definitions of public order were evolved which accommodated certain working-class usages of social space and time, and outlawed others. What were ratified were those practices which articulated the institutions of patriarchy and public propriety within the class habitat; what were outlawed were those practices of women and children which challenged the monopoly of those institutions over the working-class city and its legitimate usage. The new norms in effect imposed a system of unofficial curfew, informal out-of-bounds, to define what were the wrong people, wrong age, wrong sex, in the wrong place and the wrong time.*
>
> (Cohen, 1979: pp 130–131)

Such an analysis, applied to discrimination against blacks in the present period, has achieved wide currency, (e.g. Dixon *et al.*, 1989; Sanders, 1997). It is closely associated with the notions of social exclusion and the creation of barriers separating 'respectable' and 'non-respectable' sections of the population, in particular, the patrolling and sifting out of a posited underclass.

At first glance some of these figures give credence to the incongruity thesis. Thus, if we examine Table 2, the ratio in London as a whole, where the overall black proportion of the population is small, is much greater than in more central Boroughs such as Islington and Hammersmith and Fulham, where the proportion is comparatively higher. It is even further corroborated by the Leeds study of Walker *et al.*, (1990), which shows a very high ratio of stops in that part of Leeds with low ethnic minority populations, 2.7:1 in areas at less than 10 per cent, and even a reversal of the ratio in an area of Leeds where the ethnic minority population is high.

It falls down, however, when one looks at a breakdown within Islington. Thus the ratio in North Islington, with a higher black population, is much greater than in South Islington - the reverse of what should happen under the incongruity thesis. And this is corroborated by the Finsbury Park figures which show a ratio which, although not as high as North Islington overall, of which more later, is considerably greater than in the south of the borough.

Table 2 – Ratio of Black to White Stops: London Studies

Study	Area	Ratio	Author
PSI	Greater London	3.7:1	Smith, 1983
ICS2	Islington	2.1:1	Crawford *et al.*, 1990
HCS	Hammersmith and Fulham	1.2:1	Painter *et al.*, 1989
ICS2	North Islington	3.0:1	Crawford *et al.*, 1990
	South Islington	1.4:1	Crawford *et al.*, 1990
FPCS	Finsbury Park	2.2:1	Young, 1995

2. The prejudice thesis

The prejudice thesis would state that the explanation of the disparities in police stops is simply a function of police prejudice. If this is so, one might expect some uniformity of results in the various studies, particularly in the same area which presumably consists of police officers of roughly similar attitudes. The London studies simply do not show this. For example, within Islington, as a whole, there are clear and wide disparities, whilst in Hammersmith and Fulham in West London, surveyed in the same period, the differences are not substantial. One glance at Table 2 shows a wide variation in rates and, indeed, a remarkable difference between practices in the North and South of Islington.

3. The class thesis

The class thesis was first put forward by James Q. Wilson in his influential book *Varieties of Police Behavior*:

> Order maintenance means managing conflict, and conflict implies disagreement over what should be done, how, and to whom. Conflict is found in all social strata and thus in all strata there will be resentment, often justified, against particular police interventions (or their absence), but in lower-class areas conflict and disorder will be especially common and thus such resentment will be especially keen. It is hardly surprising that polls show young lower-income Negro males as being deeply distrustful of and bitter about the police; it would be a mistake, however, to assume that race is the decisive factor. No doubt race makes the potentiality for police-citizen hostility greater, but if all Negroes were turned white tomorrow the hostility, only slightly abated, would continue. Throughout history the urban poor have disliked and distrusted the police, and the feeling has been reciprocated; the situation will not change until the poor become middle class, or at least working class, or until society decides to abandon the

> effort to maintain a common legal code and a level of public order acceptable to middle-class persons.
>
> (Wilson, 1968: pp 296–297)

The line of argument is clear: disorderly behaviour is concentrated amongst the lower-classes and, therefore, that is the natural focus of police attention. Whilst blacks are unevenly concentrated amongst the poor then they will inevitably be at the receiving end of policing and, just as inevitably, be bitter about this bias.

The class thesis resurfaced in Britain in the work of Monica Walker and her associates, (see Walker, 1987), and has a radical spin in the reflections of John Lea on the Macpherson report, (1999). Race is a signifier of class, the true function of stop and search is the control of the dangerous classes.

Let us now look in detail at the class thesis. This states that what seems to be prejudice or incongruity is, in fact, class, coupled, as acknowledged by Wilson, (1968), with youth and masculinity. Thus black is merely a signifier for working class and that as the African-Caribbean community has a higher working class population than whites, it inevitably will have higher stop rates. Therefore, the reason why the ratios are so high in London as a whole is that the white population has a wide class spread, and why it is low in the inner boroughs is that the white population is much more working class— hence the differences between black and white begin to narrow. As we see, this fits well with the first three London studies in Table 2, and is generally congruent with findings elsewhere, but still has the problem of the divisions between the boroughs with the middle class South having lower rates than the more working class North.

What we wish to do in terms of this present study in Finsbury Park is look at the class, age and gender dimensions of the ethnic population there and see if this explains the differences in discrimination.

Table 3 – Ethnic Populations: Finsbury Park by Class

	Professional	Lower middle class	Working class
English/Scottish/Welsh	20.3	35.2	47.8
Irish	25.9	23.3	50.9
African-Caribbean	18.1	20.1	61.1

The main differences are the markedly working class nature of the African-Caribbean population, but note the comparatively high professional middle class population of the Irish, which makes it perhaps the most class varied of the ethnic groups.

Table 4 – Ethnic Populations: Finsbury Park by Age

Age	<24	25–44	>45
English/Scottish/Welsh	13.8	56.2	30.0
Irish	17.1	56.9	26.0
African-Caribbean	20.1	50.0	29.2

The Irish population is comparatively youthful, with a low population older than 45, the African-Caribbean has the widest spread of age, with the highest proportion under 24, yet almost a third over 45.

Table 5 – Gender Ratios and Ethnicity Finsbury Park.

	Male : Female
English/Scottish/Welsh	0.93 : 1
Irish	1.39 : 1
African-Caribbean	1.07 : 1

Note the strikingly higher proportion of men in the Irish community.

To summarise: the overall proportion of each of the above three groups is: English, Scottish and Welsh, 46 per cent, Irish, 14 per cent and African-Caribbean, 14 per cent. If we compare the two immigrant communities with the English, Scottish and Welsh majority, we could make the following distinctions: the Irish population has a wider class composition, a more youthful population, and a higher ratio of men to women.

The *class thesis* suggests that stops are related to the population of working class, young, males. On this score the more youthful and masculine nature of the population would, all things being equal, ensure a higher rate of stops.

Thus, the African-Caribbean population has a markedly more working class population, has a more youthful population, and has a fairly equal ratio of men to women.

In terms of the class thesis, then, we would expect a higher rate of stops because of the working class and youthful nature of the population.

The question now revolves around: is the higher Irish and African-Caribbean rate of stops merely a function of the differences in the demography of their communities when compared to the English, Scottish and Welsh, or is there something extra? Although it is difficult to be precise because of the exigencies of classification by the age groups used or contestable definitions of class, it can be surmised that we would need to hypothesise that all stops were solely directed at young, working class males and nobody else, which is clearly not true, to explain the higher African-Caribbean rate. Further, this would only at the most explain 75 per cent of the higher rate of Irish stops.

Foot stops by age and class

Let us look at the differences in the patterning of police contact by age and class to see if we can determine what makes for this extra level of stops. Although the numbers are small, some distinct differences can be observed:

1. English, Scottish and Welsh, (ESW), stops can be characterised as focusing predominantly on the young and the working class.

2. African-Caribbean stops do not have a working class focus: they occur irrespective of class. They also extend to a much wider age range, but drop off after 45.

3. The Irish stops have a working class focus, like the ESW, but they have an extremely wide age range, including those over 45.

The patterning of stops thus varies across these three dimensions by ethnic group. The class thesis in an undiluted form only works for the English, Scottish and Welsh; the focus on young working class males is, of course, also true for the Irish and African-Caribbeans, but age is of less relevance for the Irish, where the focus is less youthful, whereas class is of less relevance for the African-Caribbeans and the middle class are less immune from stops.

The Politics of Social Exclusion

Let us first delineate the level of concentration of the police on certain sectors of the population. The level of focus of foot stops is extraordinary, so that one in seven of the Irish population is stopped on suspicion of crime in a twelve month period and one in eight of the African-Caribbean, and, of course, each individual is liable to multiple stops in the year, perhaps seven to eight on average. Furthermore, if we hone down our focus by age and gender we find that over one in two African-Caribbean men between the age of 18–24 have been stopped and a slightly higher proportion of young Irish men. Yet even here we have not added class, and with working class put into the perspective, there is, in all probability, the fact of nearly all African-Caribbeans and Irish in this group having been stopped. Such a suspicion is universally corroborated by the interviewees.

It is necessary to spell out these findings because they assist the reader to realise that one is not talking about a police procedure which now and then, ever so slightly, impacts on the lives of people. This may be true of some, and the survey found no professional, white men over 55 who had been stopped on foot and only the occasional over 45 year old. In these instances it would be quite correct to say that such policing encounters have little or no effect on people's attitudes to the police: the occasional, rare stop on the way back home at night may lead to a one-off adverse or critical comment at most, but is soon forgotten. But for some people the constant attention of the police becomes a subject of continuing discussion and resentment. And this is, of course, particularly true of those, such as the Irish or African-Caribbeans, who consciously identify as part of an ethnic group and who in discussion come to realise that 'people like us' are a prime and regular target of police attention.

The compounding of exclusion

It is common to examine the level of stop and search as an entry point into the criminal justice system. This is, of course, important, and will obviously relate to disproportionalities in terms of sentencing and prison populations. But, just as important is the lateral effect: that is in terms of the general compounding of social exclusion.

It cannot be too strongly emphasised how the focus of foot patrols is, on the whole, proportional to the level of economic marginalisation of a social group. That is, the more a section of the population is economically in the categories of the structurally unemployed, or that part of the secondary labour market where work is casual and insecure, the more they are suspected in the street, and other public places, by police patrols. No one suggests that such a coincidence is necessarily purposive, although elements of such stereotyping undoubtedly occurs, but what is without doubt is that economic exclusion is compounded by what is perceived as a legal exclusion. Having being belittled in their economic citizenship such groups are then belittled in their citizenship as legal equals. Thus the effects of such gross focusing on certain groups in our population is not merely limited to the impact of the perceived injustice and indignity of interrogation but occurs in the already fragile circumstances of economic marginalisation. It has been noted elsewhere, (see *What is to be Done About Law and Order?*, Lea and Young, 1993), how such compounding of economic marginalisation and perceived harassment by the police is the standard component of riot situations whether it is in Brixton or Los Angeles. This, of course, is an extreme example of such compounding of social exclusion. The day to day gradual process we depict in this research has the more mundane effect of simple alienation from society and from the moral bind to law and order. It creates a situation of cops and outlaws where the extraordinary levels of focus of police attention create and constitute groups.

They're never there when you want them

A frequent criticism of the police by those stopped centres around not a critique of policing or a dislike of the police *per se* but on the lack of protection which the police provide when the interviewee has been victimised. There is a rational core to this. Certain ethnic groups, in particular, have extremely high victimisation rates in public places as well as a high rate of stops in public spaces. Thus if we look at Table 6, which analyses victims of street crime by ethnicity using the same Finsbury Park data base as the large scale study of stops, the Irish have the highest overall victimisation rate, and Irish women, in particular, the greatest victimisation rate by street robbery of any group. Such findings are reinforced when we examine in Table 7 victims of violence in public space by ethnic group, once again using the same data base.

Table 6 – Victims of Street Crime by Ethnicity and Gender. Prevalence in a Twelve Month Period (Percentages)

Ethnicity	Male	Female	All
English, Scottish, Welsh	5.8	7.5	7.0
Irish	9.0	13.4	11.2
African-Caribbean	4.9	2.6	3.3
African	10.5	10.5	10.5

(Source: *Islington Street Crime Survey*, **Harper** *et al.*, **1995**)

Table 7 – Violence in Public Space by Ethnicity and Gender. Percentage of Total Sample

Ethnicity	Women Per cent	Men Per cent
English, Scottish, Welsh	7	13
Irish	6	21
African-Caribbean	13	13
Other	6	7

n = 1,000 threats of or any form of physical violence

The Social Construction of Stop and Search Statistics

In our 1995 study we pointed to the fact that there are two major components which generate the stop and search statistics: The people selected by the police, and the people available to be selected. If one wants, the demand and the supply of the situation. We indicated how it was commonplace to ignore the second component although it is obvious that, for example, as 51 per cent of stops in Finsbury Park occur either at dusk or at night—those people who regularly go out at night are more likely to be stopped than others. This certainly would suggest men rather than women, the young rather than the old, in terms of on foot, working class rather than middle class and, given our knowledge of leisure patterns, members of certain ethnic groups (such as African-Caribbean and Irish) rather than others. Such an analysis was developed by Home Office research, (Fitzgerald and Sibbitt, 1997), in which it was suggested that to understand differences in rates of stops by ethnicity one must separate out a series of socio-economic factors other than ethnicity, for example, age or class, lifestyle factors which determine the *availability* for being stopped, as well as policing factors:

The triple compounding of exclusion

Our argument, so far, is that the economically excluded are most likely to be the focus of police attention and of criminal victimisation. The marginalised are harassed and then neglected. Let us now turn to the reasons why the police focus tends to be of this nature.

Table 8 – Factors Likely to Influence Ethnic Patters in PACE Data

Socio-economic factors	Lifestyle factors	Policing factors
Age	Car ownership	Patterns of stop/search within and between forces
Gender	Nights out per week	
Area of residence	School exclusions	Operational reasons for variations (e.g. response to crime reports targeted operations and surveillance of prominent nominals)
Employment and education status		Interpretation of powers
Marital status		Recording practices

(Source: Fitzgerald and Sibbitt, 1997: p 65)

Let us rejig this in terms of our notions of demand and supply: police suspicion and public availability.

Table 9 – The Demand and Supply Model of Stop and Search

Demand	Supply
Suspiciousness	*Availability*
Police stereotypes	Unemployment
Yield	Lifestyle
Spatial focus	School exclusions
(Clubs and pubs)	Poverty

It should be noted that in terms of the class thesis both demand and supply come together markedly. The police are suspicious of young, working class males as indeed they commit a high proportion of street crime and the yield from stop and search is presumably highest for this group. And precisely this section of the population are more likely to be out at night, to be on the street because of school exclusion etc.

Thus young working class men are the most frequent offenders and have the lifestyle, out at night and on foot, which makes them available

for stop and search. Our conclusion from our earlier study was that on a superficial level police suspicion would be rationally directed towards this group. Yet, in fact, only a very small proportion will be, and ever are, arrested for serious offences. Thus, although this may be the most sensible group to focus upon, the yield will be small, and is indeed falling, and the likelihood of alienating a significant section of the population is considerable.

Institutionalised classism?

As we have seen, the overwhelming focus of police attention is on the working class, young, male. And let us note that both police suspicion and public availability come together to produce this statistic. That is, these are the people the police suspect most and these are the very people most available to be picked up on the street, at night, or wandering the city in 'inappropriate places'.

Zygmunt Bauman, in his recent work, talks of 'the criminalisation of poverty', (1998a: p 125), and notes how 'poverty turns from the subject matter of social policy into a problem for penology and criminal law', (1998b: p 77). Indeed, these people are largely poor, lower working class rather than skilled, and this focus seems to have increased, facilitated by notions of 'underclass' and the belief that social problems can be solved, or at least contained, by multi-agency policing and the rhetoric and practice of community safety.

The criminalisation of poverty

The stereotypical division of the world by police officers into the vast majority of respectable people, and 'the dregs', 'the scum', the small minority of the unworthy and the disreputable has been pointed out by nearly every commentator on policing, (see Reiner, 1992; Smith, 1983). These people are, in Lee's, (1981), graphic phrase, 'police property', the 'true' object of police attention and concern. The rational core of this is, of course, that it is the poor who commit most street crimes such as mugging and burglary, with which police patrols are concerned, and conversely, that it is the rich and the middle classes who commit crimes such as fraud and insider dealing with whom patrols are, by definition, unconcerned. The focus upon the poor, the young and the male part of the population is not, therefore, at all odd. Yet, as only a tiny minority of the suspect poor are actually guilty of such an offence, the widespread use of stop and search inevitably results in a large number of innocent people being stopped and consequently alienated. Indeed, the proportion of searches which do not result in arrest has been rising rapidly since 1986. The problem, always there, has seemingly increased remarkably.

As numerous studies have shown, this section of the population which is the focus of police attention has the:

- Highest level of criminal victimisation (i.e. the greatest *need* for police services).

- Highest knowledge of illegalities (i.e. the potentially most useful *knowledge* as informants).

- Highest level of alienation and suspicion of the police.

- Lowest level of willingness to co-operate with the police.

The division of the society into two sections is dramatically indicated by Kennison's observation that the ratio of black to white police contacts is inverted when we compare police-public contacts in public spaces. That is, the disproportionate level of *police initiated* contacts

with blacks compared to whites becomes a similarly disproportional level of *public initiated* contacts with the police of white compared to blacks, (see Kennison, 1999). Thus one side of the line are perceived as the focus of police attention as potential criminals and demand less of a service from the police whilst the other are seen as the focus of police service provisions and demand a comparatively higher level of provision. Such a stereotypical division of the world is seen tragically in the events following Stephen Lawrence's death where the detectives seemed to view the dead teenager as part of a criminal incident rather than the victim and were extraordinarily unhelpful to the Lawrence family in the subsequent investigation, (Macpherson, 1999).

The focus of police attention on this group is, therefore, rational in direction but irrational in terms of the low yield. As we have seen, the degree to which ethnic groups have a high masculine or youthful or working class component will mean that in these terms they will inevitably have a higher focus upon them: the critique of this point is therefore not on the existence of disproportionality but the high amount of stops and the low level of yield. Furthermore, as we have argued earlier, the high stop rate of African-Caribbeans and the Irish is over and above that expected simply from a focus on the working class poor. It is here, locked on top of institutionalised classism that we will find racism both of an institutionalised and non-institutionalised variety.

Institutionalised racism

There is considerable disagreement and confusion in the literature as to what constitutes institutionalised racism, let alone whether it exists and what is its impact, (Solomos and Back, 1996). The clearest exposition of types of racism is that set out by Lea, (1986), which is of particular interest as it is developed in a discussion of policy. In this he uses two dimensions: whether the racism is direct or indirect, and whether it is based on individual or institutional practice. Thus:

Table 10 – Types of Racism

	Direct	Indirect
Individual	**A** Individual racist acts consciously intended	**B** Individuals behaving in ways which have racist consequences
Institutional	**C** Policies of institutions directly geared to racism	**D** Institutional practices having racist consequences

(Source: Lea, 1986: p 149)

Table 11 – Types of Racism and Types of Remedial Policies

'Bad apple'	Weed out these individuals
Unconscious stereotyping	Racial awareness training
Institutionalised racism at level of state	Political change
Institutionalised racism as a function of unintended practice	Organisational change

Lea's classification is of importance because it clearly distinguishes working practices from individual attitudes, and takes on board the fact that certain practices can have racist outcomes *whether or not* the overarching policy is racist in intent. The intended institutional racism, (type C above), and which is exemplified historically by the Apartheid regime in South Africa and the activities of some police departments in the South of the United States, has no clear parallel here, it is institutionalised racism of an unintended nature, (type D), which is of greatest relevance.

Thus racism can occur on all of these levels, but institutionalised racism which is locked into the *practices* of a bureaucracy is much more difficult to eradicate than that which is merely on an attitudinal level. With the right practices in place, as Lea indicates, even racist officers can act in a civilised fashion because it is in their interests to do so. On the other hand, when racist practices are institutionalised into the working practices of a police service, then racist attitudes are given legitimacy. In these instances those police officers with racist opinions will be encouraged to express them but, even more unfortunately, those perfectly decent officers of a fair minded disposition will find themselves bound into practices which have racist outcomes.

Occluded focus

By occluded focus we mean that police officers may put a particularly high pressure of surveillance on a community without realising that this is happening. For example, as the white population of Finsbury Park is considerably larger than the black population, from the point of view of the police officer, he or she is hardly singling out blacks given that five out of six foot stops are directed at whites. Yet, of course, from the point of view of young blacks what actually happens is that a very high proportion are multiply stopped. This is even more occluded in the cases of those of Irish descent to whom one in three of stops occur in Finsbury Park. This is a fairly high proportion of stops, yet because many second generation Irish have London accents with little or slight Irish lilt, it would not be obvious to the police officer in many instances that they were Irish, *although from the perspective of those stopped and their families it would be obvious that a very significant targeting was occurring.*

Furthermore, it is interesting what the effect is of including the Irish in the same category as English, Scottish and Welsh in the pseudo-scientific category 'white' when making comparisons. For, in fact, just over one half of stops are focused on African-Caribbeans and the Irish. Put this way, the bias of policing is obvious.

Lurking and larking: the spatial focus

The focus both of stops and searches was clearly focused. Some 71 per cent of all multiple stops were in the Finsbury Park area, rather than people being stopped outside of their area of residence, as were 70 per cent of searches. But the spatial focus was greater than this: it was outside of particular pubs and clubs, it was on specific areas of particular estates. It was surely targeted towards what were seen at certain times as hotspots of incivilities and crime. Places which deserved attention but perhaps, more significantly, places where it was easy to attend. The incongruity thesis clearly did not apply: the focus was on particular sorts of people in precisely those parts of Finsbury park, at those times that one would expect to find them. If anything, this corroborates the surmise of our earlier, 1995, study which used the metaphor of trawling. The police trawl in those areas where they can make some level of arrest, some possibility of result, even though the yield is low and consists largely of trivial crimes and misdemeanours.

Failing the attitude test

It is important to stress the hostility, more often unspoken but sometimes replete with racist epithets, which accompanies many a stop, particularly late at night. Interviewee after interviewee mentioned the bristling of resentment as one group of young men in

uniform confronted another walking the streets. Frequently, the individuals stopped eventually crack and quarrel with the police, sometimes on the edge of violence. The arrests which arise from such confrontations we called, in the last report, 'meta-crimes'—crimes created by the confrontation rather than crimes in themselves. It is difficult not to view these situations as an attempt to bolster arrest statistics or, as one police officer interviewed put it succinctly, the suspects had 'failed the attitude test'.

Institutionalised classism and racism

As we have seen, the notion of the class thesis, more precisely the focus on the young, the male and the working class, is frequently posited as an alternative to the notion of racist prejudice as the mechanism which explains away the ethnically disproportional focus of stops. In the marvellous phrase of the Macpherson Report, the host of factors which 'pray away' racism. But even if the disproportionality were to be explained completely by class factors, and as we have seen this is not so, this would not for a moment mitigate the racist *impact* of such disproportionality. Yet we have uncovered not only institutionalised classism but upon its back institutionalised racism: a double burden of prejudice and exclusion. This process has both a social and a spatial focus; it concentrates on certain ethnic groups and dwells upon the places, the pubs, clubs and streets, that they frequent. Its stereotype varies and differentiates between ethnic groups. Thus it sees *certain* South Asian groups as of low criminality, and others, such as African-Caribbean and Irish of high criminality, troublesome and uncivil. And, as we have delineated, it draws different parameters around groups. It focuses on all African-Caribbeans, regardless of class, with the exception of those over 45, as potential troublemakers. Perhaps this is because officers see black skin as equalling lower class and are unable to distinguish middle class African-Caribbeans, perhaps this is simply racism, but whatever the reason, it has a significant racist impact on the community, placing black people in the category of the targets rather than the 'consumers' of the police service. The events around the death of Stephen Lawrence were a tragic example of this. With regards to the Irish, the parameters cut differently: the focus is more upon the working class but there is little allowance made for age. 'They see us all as drunken Paddies', one interviewee said and this sentiment was echoed amongst the older people we talked to.

The Profligate Use of Stop and Search

We noted the extraordinary rise in stop and search which has occurred since the inception of PACE in 1986. This has been accompanied by a steady decline in those arrested, so that at present 90 per cent of those searched are innocent—and, of course, these are only those whose stop has been recorded. Our task must be to reduce these numbers and the method must be through control of the basis of suspicion.

If we look at the variation nationally we can find some clues as to the way forward in terms of returns in the Metropolitan Police Area.

In *Policing the Streets*, (1995), we argued that suspicion could be of three sorts:

1. Stereotypical: which is the present system where police stereotypes and practice focus upon certain groups creating alienation from the public yet producing a low yield;

2. Democratic: where every group, sub-group and individual within society is suspected equally. This is often the ideal against which stereotypical suspicion is found wanting but it would be costly to enact, be politically counterproductive and would in no time make the law look like an ass. It would be a nonsense to suspect old ladies of burglary, street robbery and the possession of ecstasy tablets. As stop and search is aimed at street crimes, and working class young men are the chief offenders, the focus is naturally upon them. In a way this is 'institutionalised classism' but the public prioritise these crimes, and in that the poor suffer more from these crimes than do the middle classes. The problem of such institutionalised classism is not the focus but the scale: enormous numbers of innocent people are suspected and stopped, causing widespread public disaffection. And, on top of such classism is an institutionalised racism which, as we have seen, both intentionally and unintentionally focuses on ethnic groups such as the Irish and the African-Caribbean in a discriminatory fashion.

3. Information-led: against both of the above models it was argued that the ideal use of stop and search would be where suspicion was information-led, that is, where stops only occurred where there was actual hard evidence as to the likelihood that the person stopped was an offender.

The Home Office Research Study, *Ethnic Monitoring in Police Forces: A Beginning*, follows this line of reasoning, concurring that democratic suspicion would be unfeasible and illogical and agreeing that stereotypical suspicion undoubtedly occurs. But the researchers note:

> This poses a real dilemma...also illustrated by reference to Young's study of stop and search ...the police cannot do their job effectively without being selective in their suspicions; and there are strong arguments that improved sharing and strategic use of 'intelligence' will contribute to more effective (and efficient) policing. Yet, in the context of concerns about police relations with ethnic minorities, two considerations need to be borne in mind. One is that, inasmuch as some proportion of those targeted will inevitably be innocent of any offence, a greater proportion of innocent black people will be targeted than whites. The other is that suspicion reinforced by intelligence may provide a legitimate cloak for harassment. This can only increase resentment, reinforcing the widespread perception that the police disproportionately pick on black people. Where forces are conscious of this dilemma, ethnic monitoring data may prove invaluable, not only in indicating whether they are achieving the right balance between the potentially conflicting demands of better targeting and improved community relations but also, as necessary, in pinpointing where the first of these objectives is putting the second in jeopardy.
>
> (Fitzgerald and Sibbitt, 1997: p 95)

This seems to mistake our position. The nature of the crimes upon which stop and search focuses makes it inevitable that there will be disproportionate focus by class, age and gender *and* because of this, ethnicity. That is, any group which has a higher than average working class population, such as the African-Caribbean and the Irish, or a higher male proportion, such as the Irish, will inevitably have a disproportionate police focus upon them. The problem is not the existence of disproportionality but its *level* and the *quantity* of people suspected. As far as level is concerned, we have seen how racist stereotyping and practice inflates the proportion of Irish and African-Caribbean compared to the English, Scottish and Welsh population. If this institutionalised racism were removed the class focus would still result in disproportionality but this would be of a substantially reduced level. But the problem of the high, and increasing, number of stop and searches would remain with the concomitant alienation of a large number of innocent people. This is the problem of institutionalised classism. What is necessary here is to fundamentally change the *practice* of stop and search so that the numbers are drastically reduced. This would be achieved by a shift from stereotypical to information-led suspicion. The Home Office study agrees with the notion of information-led suspicion but casts information in much too general a mode. It is not based on *specific* and *detailed* information about individuals and places but on much more general information of likelihood. Because of this it would not alleviate the problem of community relations as it quite correctly points out.

Stops to be judged in terms of yield

Stops must be judged in terms of yield, that is, in terms of:

- Quality and seriousness of crime: it is not impressive, for example, to net as in Hackney, 83 per cent of possession of drugs arrests for cannabis, a crime which is extremely low on public priorities, (see Jones et al., 1986; Crawford et al., 1990), and only five per cent for cocaine and four per cent for heroin, (Hackney Community Safety Partnership, 1999).

- Levels of arrest and ultimate successful prosecution, i.e. the present ten per cent arrest rate with perhaps three per cent found guilty must be raised considerably so that many less innocent people are harassed by the police.

To argue that police performance should be stringently tied to yield, of course, completely rules out the habit of making stops a register of performance in themselves. There can be no doubt that accountability demands that public bodies be subject to assessment by the application of agreed performance indicators. But the impact of an overburdening and ill-thought out performance culture is often counter-productive, (see Loveday, 1999). There is a point where rather than the indicator measuring the performance we have the performance being judged by the measurement of the indicator.

Dealing with practice rather than attitude

We have taken a position which maintains that in order to tackle institutionalised racism and classism one must tackle the institutionalised practices themselves, rather than hope that reforming individuals will achieve the task. In particular, this should be achieved through the assessment of results in terms of clearly specified yield, (see Smith, 1986). We wholeheartedly concur with the Macpherson Report that a central problem of current policing is institutionalised racism, and would add classism to this category, and that the disparities in the stop and search statistics relate to stereotyping. But these stereotypes are lodged and maintained in institutionalised practices, yet the Macpherson Report stops short of recommending any institutional change, (see Recommendation 60). Instead, by putting such a strong emphasis on racial awareness training, it focuses in upon individual mistakes in belief rather than tackling the institutional roots of the problem, (Type B rather than Type D racism: see Table 10 above).

Policy Recommendations

1. Reduction in levels of stop and search

The rate of stop and search should be drastically reduced and occur only in where there is suspicion based on concrete evidence. That is, the practice should be information-led and not based on generality or probability.

Our general argument is that stop and search as used at present is a massive and blunt instrument, costly to maintain and grossly inaccurate in its impact. Its effects are counterproductive, its yield largely of minor crimes and its necessity unproven. In its place we suggest a smaller, precision instrument, intelligence led and sharply focused.

2. Spatial targeting must be information-led

Just as the surveillance and searching of individuals must be based on hard evidence, so too must the focus on spatial areas whether it is clubs, pubs, or designated 'hotspots'. The danger of regular, indiscriminate surveillance is that it will generate hostility and bear down disproportionally on particular sections of the population. The fashion of identifying hotspots prevalent in recent crime audits is useful only if the targeting is honed down and temporary.

3. Stops must be judged in terms of yield

The reduced, more lean version of stop and search should aim at a much higher arrest rate. Furthermore, this rate should have highest 'quality' crimes. Crimes of a minor nature, e.g. cannabis possession, should be weighted very lightly in any measure and offences which are often the result of altercation resulting from the stop itself—should be regarded with suspicion. What should be looked for is a yield which is both high in productivity and quality. The number of stops achieved *per se* should cease to be used as a performance indicator.

4. Ethnic monitoring

In line with the Macpherson Report we stress the importance of the ethnic monitoring of stop and search by 'self-defined ethnic identity', (Recommendation 61). Important here is the inclusion of the Irish, not just Irish born, but self-identifying, and the separation out of figures for different South and South-east Asian ethnic groups, Turks, Cypriots, etc. The aim should be to discern patterns of discrimination, but although ethnic disproportionality should be substantially reduced, their elimination is an unlikely and undesirable goal as differentials in age, class and gender between ethnic groups will always result in variation. What is more important is the drastic reduction in the ratio and the quantity of stops so that such disproportionality does not have a large scale discriminatory effect as it does at present.

References

Baldwin, R., and Kinsey, R. (1985). Rules, Realism and the Police Act. *Critical Social Policy*, 4: pp 91–105.

Bauman, Z. (1998a). *Globalisation: The Human Consequences*. Oxford: Polity Press.

Bauman, Z. (1998b). *Work, Consumerism and the New Poor*. Buckingham: Open University Press.

Blumstein, A. (1983). On the Racial Disproportionality of the United States Prison Population. *Journal of Criminal Law and Criminology*, 73: pp 1259–1281.

Blumstein, A (1993). Racial Disproportionality of US Prison Populations Revisited. *University of Colorado Law Review*, 64: pp 743–760.

Cohen, P. (1979). Policing the Working-class City. In Fine, B., Kinsey, R., Lea, J., Picciotto, S., and Young J. (Eds.). *Capitalism and the Rule of Law*. London: Hutchinson.

Crawford, A., Jones, T., Woodhouse, T., and Young, J. (1990). *The Second Islington Crime Survey*. Middlesex University: Centre for Criminology.

Dixon, D., Bottomley, A., Coleman, C., Gill, M., and Wall, D. (1989). Reality and Rules in the Construction and Regulation of Police Suspicion. *International Journal of the Sociology of Law*, 17: pp 185–206.

Feeley, M., and Simon, J. (1992). The New Penology: Notes on the Emerging Strategy of Corrections and its Implications. *Criminology*, 30(4): pp 449–474.

Feeley, M., and Simon, J. (1994). Actuarial Justice: The Emerging New Criminal Law. In Nelken, D. (Ed.). *The Futures of Criminology*. London: Sage.

Fitzgerald, M. (1999). *Searches in London Final Report*. London: Metropolitan Police Service.

Fitzgerald, M., and Sibbitt, R. (1997). *Ethnic Monitoring in Police Forces: A Beginning*. London: Home Office Research Study 173.

Gilroy, P. (1987). *There Ain't No Black in the Union Jack*. London: Hutchinson.

Gordon, P. (1983). *White Law*. London: Pluto.

Hackney Community Safety Partnership, (1999). *Hackney Crime and Disorder Audit 1998/99*. London: Hackney Borough Council.

Harper, P., Pollak, M., Mooney, J., Whelan, E., and Young, J. (1995). *The Islington Street Crime Survey*. London: London Borough of Islington.

Hickman, M. (1998). Reconstructing Deconstructing Race: British Political Discourses About the Irish in Britain. *Ethnic and Racial Studies*, 21(2).

Hillyard, P. (1993). *Suspect Community*. London: Pluto.

Hood, R. (1992). *Race and Sentencing*. Oxford: Clarendon Press.

Jefferson, T. (1993). The Racism of Criminalization. In Gelsthorpe, L. (Ed.). *Ethnic Minorities and the Criminal Justice System*. Cambridge: Institute of Criminology.

Jefferson, T., Walker, M., and Seneviratne, M. (1992). Ethnic Minorities, Crime and Criminal Justice. In Downes, D. (Ed.). *Unravelling Criminal Justice*. London: Macmillan.

Jefferson, T., and Walker, M. (1992). Ethnic Minorities in the Criminal Justice System. *Criminal Law Review*, pp 83–95.

Jones, T., MacLean, B., and Young, J. (1986). *The Islington Crime Survey*. Aldershot: Gower.

Kennison, P. (1999). *Policing Black People: A Study of Ethnic Relations as Seen Through the Police Complaints System*. Middlesex University, Centre for Criminology.

Lea, J. (1986). Police Racism. In Matthews, R., and Young, J. (Eds.). *Confronting Crime*. London: Sage.

Lea, J. (1999). *The Macpherson Report and the Question of Institutional Racism*. Middlesex University, Centre for Criminology.

Lea, J. and Young, J. (1993). *What is to be Done About Law and Order?* London: Pluto.

Lee, J.A. (1981). Some Structural Aspects of Police Deviance in Relations with Minority Groups. In Shearing, C. (Ed.). *Organisational Police Deviance*. Toronto: Butterworth.

Loveday, B. (1999). *The Impact of Performance Culture on Criminal Justice Agencies*, Occasional Paper, No. 9. Portsmouth University, Institute of Criminal Justice Studies.

Macpherson, Sir W. (1999). *The Stephen Lawrence Inquiry*. London: HMSO.

Mooney, J. (1992). *Street Robbery and Snatch in Islington: A Study of Highway Robbery Today*. Middlesex University, Centre for Criminology.

Mooney, J., and Young, J. (1999). *Social Exclusion and Criminal Justice*. Middlesex University, Centre for Criminology.

Painter, K., Lea, J., Woodhouse, T., and Young, J. (1989). *The Hammersmith Crime Survey*. Middlesex University, Centre for Criminology.

Reiner, R. (1992). *The Politics of the Police*, 2nd edn. London: Harvester.

Reiss, A. (1971). *The Police and the Public*. New Haven: Yale U.P.

Sanders, A. (1997). From Suspect to Trial. In Maguire, M., Morgan, R., and Reiner R. (Eds.). *The Oxford Handbook of Criminology*, 2nd edn. Oxford: Clarendon Press.

Smith, D. (1983). *Police and People in London*, Vol. 1. London: PSI.

Smith, D. (1986). The Framework of Law and Policing Practice. In Benyan, J. *et al.* (Eds.). *Police Powers, Procedures and Priorities*. Oxford: Pergamon.

Smith, D. (1997). Ethnic Origins, Crime and Criminal Justice. In Maguire, M., Morgan, R., and Reiner, R. (Eds.). *The Oxford Handbook of Criminology*, 2nd edn.

Oxford: Clarendon Press.

Smith, D., and Gray, J. (1983). *The Police in Action*, Vol. 4. London: PSI.

Solomos, J., and Back, L. (1996). *Racism and Society*. London: Macmillan.

Walker, M. (1987). Interpreting Race and Crime Statistics. *Journal of the Royal Statistical Society*, A150, pp 39–56.

Walker, M., Jefferson, T., and Seneviratne, M. (1990). *Ethnic Minorities Young People and the Criminal Justice System*. Sheffield: Centre for Criminology.

Werthman, C., and Piliavin, I. (1967). Gang Members and the Police. In Bordua, D. (Ed.). *The Police*, pp 56–98. New York: Wiley.

Wilkins, G., and Addicott, C. (1997). Operation of Certain Powers under PACE. *Home Office Statistical Bulletin*, 27/97. London.

Wilson, J.Q. (1968). *Varieties of Police Behavior*. Cambridge, MA: Harvard University Press.

Woodhouse, T., O'Meachair, G., Clark, N., and Jones, M. (1991). *The Irish and Policing in Islington*. London: Islington Council.

Young, J. (1995). *Policing the Streets*. London: London Borough of Islington.

Chapter 8

Effective and Efficient Policing: Some Problems with the Culture of Performance

Stephen Hallam

Introduction

The public and the Police Services of the United Kingdom are justifiably proud of the tradition of an unarmed police service which polices with the consent of the public…[However] at present the confidence and trust of the minority ethnic communities is at a low ebb. Such lack of confidence threatens the ability of the Police Services to police by consent in all areas of their work, not simply in the policing of racist incidents and crimes.

(Macpherson, 1999: p 325)

Such comments would not have been out of context if Lord Scarman had written them in his 1981 report following the Brixton Disorders. The resounding message contained in that report could justifiably have been expected to produce an understanding and recognition of a much-needed change in policing and social policy in the United Kingdom. For such a paragraph to have been published in 1999 suggests that the clear lessons carefully expounded in Lord Scarman's report have gone unheeded by the government and police alike.

In November, 1981, Lord Scarman reported on his findings of an inquiry into 'The Brixton Disorders, 10–12 April, 1981', (Scarman, 1981). The report dealt with not just the disorders, but with social conditions within which the communities of Brixton and other similar inner city areas found themselves. A mixture of social deprivation, poor housing, unemployment, educational failings and discrimination was described. There were elements of police harassment, racism and a failure to protect a minority ethnic group from racist attacks. The report describes how the senior command in one district had 'not become sufficiently adjusted to the problems of policing a multi racial community', (Scarman, 1981: p 68). Furthermore, there was clear evidence that members of ethnic minorities were far more likely to be stopped and searched than their white counterparts. The report describes how ethnic minorities had lost faith in the police service and how the system to investigate complaints against the police compounded this lack of trust. Eighteen years later Part Two of the Stephen Lawrence Inquiry, (Macpherson, 1999), reported unmistakable similarities.

The latter report provides evidence of failings in housing and education, evidence of discrimination and racism and of a failure by the police to deal with racist incidents. There is a general lack of trust of the police and of the procedures adopted for the investigation of complaints against the police.

Wherever we went we were met with inescapable evidence which highlighted the lack of trust which exists between the police and the minority ethnic communities. At every location there was a striking difference between the positive descriptions of policy initiatives by senior officers and the negative expressions of the minority communities, who clearly felt themselves to be discriminated against by the police and others.

(Ibid.: p 311)

Such striking similarities between Lord Scarman's Report and that of Sir William Macpherson pose inevitable questions regarding the failure of social and policing policy.

New Public Management, the Police and the Emergence of the Crime Control Imperative

Interest in problems needs to be sustained if they are to pass successfully through the tortuous decision making processes of government.

(Benyon, 1984: p 16)

The outbreak of rioting in various cities in 1981 provoked condemnation from both sides of the House of Commons but, whereas opposition MPs pointed to a causal link to social deprivation, those in government dismissed this as in some way seeking to excuse the criminality which was clearly evident. Consequently, as a result of this denial of social causation, Lord Scarman's recommendations were subjected to 'emasculation, delay and political inaction', (Benyon, 1984: p 14). Almost certainly the failure of the police to take any action was inextricably linked to the failure of central government to recognise the pressing need for change. Central government was not to be deterred from its path of creating a market economy with an emphasis on moral regeneration coupled with an all-pervasive ability of the police not only to detect crime but also to somehow, through tougher policing, control it. Increases in recorded and actual crime were to lead to a concentration on law and order problems to the detriment of community welfare issues. For the Conservative government crime and policing efficiency and effectiveness were inextricably linked.

Morgan and Newburn noted that Mrs Thatcher and her ministers had, at the outset, two expectations as a result of an injection of capital into the police.

> First, that this would deliver a supportive police service and secondly, that the increased expenditure would result in reduced crime levels. Neither was to be so easily achieved.
>
> (Morgan and Newburn, 1997)

Initially the police were allowed to continue with a certain amount of autonomy. This was partially because the government, in order to succeed with its trade union reforms, needed the support of the police during the industrial disputes that took place in the early to mid 1980s. However, this did not stem the disquiet amongst Conservative ministers that the police were not fulfilling the promise of crime control.

> Perceived deficiencies in police management began to accumulate in the early 1980s, and were reinforced further as the decade progressed. They added urgency to the emerging influence of central government policy on public management which was to dictate the direction in which managerial change was to go.
>
> (Leishman and Savage, 1993: p 213)

Garland, (1996), stated that the change in management styles and its direct effect on policing has to be examined against the backdrop of the inability of successive 'law and order governments' to effectively deal with the law and order problem. It is not surprising therefore that there was a sustained effort to deflect criticism away from government by placing the police under increasing pressure to enhance performance. The attempted analysis of police performance led to an unprecedented scrutiny of police management and police roles and responsibilities and resulted in three separate reviews of policing in 1993. Reporting within just one week of each other, were: the Royal Commission on Criminal Justice, (RCCJ, 1993), the Sheehy Inquiry into Police Responsibilities and Rewards, (Inquiry into Police Responsibilities and Rewards, 1993), and the Home Secretary's *White Paper on Police Reform*, (Home Office, 1993). (See Newburn and Morgan, 1994; Jones and Newburn, 1997). A further Home Office *Review of*

Police Core and Ancillary Tasks, (Home Office, 1995), had the terms of reference:

> To examine the services provided by the police, to make recommendations about the most cost effective way of delivering core police services and to access the scope for relinquishing ancillary tasks.
>
> (Newburn and Morgan, 1994: p 144)

Reiner, (1994), takes a forthright stance in his commentary on the various reviews of police roles. In discussing the white paper that preceded The Police and Magistrates' Courts Bill he highlights a paragraph within the paper that states 'The main job of the Police is to catch criminals'. Reiner says this is 'Breathtaking in its audacious simple-mindedness'.

Furthermore, considering the government's drive towards 'New Public Management', (NPM), (Pollitt, 1993), in public services, Reiner's view that the *Review of Core and Ancillary Tasks*, (Home Office, 1995), was simply to flesh out what had already been decided, was well founded. The change brought about by the previous Conservative government, epitomised by the former Home Secretary's edict that the job of the police is to catch criminals, (Reiner, 1994), saw a new variation of the perceived role and management of the police. The simple ideological perspective that the police were not performing, were responsible for high crime rates and were in need of change fell neatly in line with the persuasive argument for the introduction of NPM within the service. This was to be achieved in part by a number of provisions contained within the Police and Magistrates Court Act 1994, in particular centrally set objectives.

The setting of objectives for the police and the measurement of success based on achievement of those objectives had become an issue as early as 1983. Home Office circular 114/1983, (Home Office, 1983), stated that there was a need for the effective and efficient use of resources. Consequently, Her Majesty's Inspectorate of Constabulary, (HMIC), would adopt an approach in their inspections regarding the setting, by chief officers, of realistic objectives and priorities, (Walker and Richards, 1996). Therefore, the Police and Magistrates' Courts Act 1994 merely reinforced the notion of objectives and priorities by giving the Home Secretary the power to set Key National Objectives and performance targets. NPM linked neatly with the ideas of the new right, which informed the agenda of the then Conservative government. It was not surprising that following the introduction of the Police and Magistrates Courts Act 1994, police forces, as a result of central government objectives and performance indicators, became more overtly concerned about recorded crime and detection figures. The relationship between recorded crime and detection rates was to become a dilemma that few were to resolve. The issues of community responsibilities in policing and effective partnerships outlined by the Morgan Report in 1991, (Home Office, 1991), were sidelined. Lord Scarman's report of 1981 was long forgotten.

Measurement of success became geared towards measurements of those things that were seen to be measurable and within the direct control of the police, more notably outputs rather than outcomes, (Garland, 1996). The direct control though, was not to be of crimes per se but of crime figures.

To this end a crime control model for policing emerged. However, it became policing to meet objectives and hitting hard targets in the pursuit of favourable performance indicators. Leishman and Savage, (1993), noted that the response in some forces to Home Office circular 114/1983 was the adoption of *Policing by Objectives*, (p 218), and this simply continued and was adopted by all as a consequence of the 1994 Act. Garland, (1996), sees the development of these performance indicators and the managerialist approach as a consequence of the overburdened crime system brought about by contemporary society. However, the Audit Commission and Her Majesty's Inspectorate of Constabulary openly subscribed to this model of policing. In describing the manner that the Audit Commission saw crime being dealt with by the police, Morgan and Newburn state:

> It is noticeable that the Audit Commission is employing military terminology, intelligence and field intelligence officers, which meshes closely with the Home Secretary's enthusiasm for the language of war against crime.
>
> (Morgan and Newburn, 1997)

This very idea regarding the war on crime epitomises the Audit Commission's notion that the police by a sound policing policy will control crime. The Audit Commission publication, *Helping with Enquiries: Tackling Crime Effectively*, stated:

> By adopting the recommendations in this report the police can help to prevent crime and raise clear-up rates significantly, which itself will help to deter would be criminals. The ultimate prize for the police, the criminal justice system and society is to break out of the current vicious circle into a virtuous circle in which the crime rate could be brought under control.
>
> (Audit Commission, 1993)

The Pathology of the Performance Culture

Central bodies, to indicate success or failure of police forces, have used a number of measurements of performance, most notably though is the heavy reliance by the Home Office, Audit Commission and HMIC on recorded crime and clear-up rates as an indication of individual force performance.

Over a period of four years the Government's Key Objectives and Key Performance Indicators (KPI) were consistent and also tended to be quantitative. The objectives generally involved a reduction in crime and a maintenance of or increase in detection rates, (clear-up rates), with the KPI being the number of crimes detected per 100 officers in each crime category. The indicators in the Audit Commission report of 1996/97, (Audit Commission, 1998a), and previous reports concentrated on five areas. These were the number of recorded crimes per 1,000 population; the percentage of all crimes detected by primary means; the percentage of violent crime detected by primary means; the percentage of burglaries detected by primary means and the number of crimes detected by primary means per police officer. The indicators for the year 1997/98 were in the categories of all crime per 1,000 population, violent crime per 1,000 population and burglaries per 1,000 households. This was coupled with the measurement of crimes detected by primary means in those categories, (Audit Commission, 1998b). This can only be described as signalling that the Audit Commission's thinking continued to be based, as it was in 1993, on the fact that more offenders processed through the criminal justice system had a direct causal effect on the reduction of crime.

In order to achieve these centrally set objectives and performance indicator targets, forces inevitably pushed the responsibility downwards to the extent that it affected the way that front line officers policed. It is, after all, the performance of frontline officers that contributes to the overall detection rate in objective crimes. The consequence of this is that officers have often been set individual performance targets that in any other environment would be considered to be counter productive. These targets generally tended to be quantitative rather than qualitative, such as the number of intelligence reports submitted, often resulting from stop searches carried out, or the number of crimes detected. In some cases benchmarking occurred whereby officers are set targets based on other groups of officers' achievements. Officers concentrated on crimes that gave the greatest yield in detections such as domestic violence or violence on the street. Where possible, crimes were downgraded to allow for alternative methods of detection with a minimum amount of work. As Leishman and Savage, (1993: p 219), noted… 'To impose upon the organisation a priori aims and objectives is at best unrealistic and at worst damaging to the flexibility on which policing responses depend'. Discretion was rarely exercised with a consequence that the results produced in the name of performance have not always been in the interests of justice or reflected a credible service to the public.

Loveday, (1995), is equally critical of the 'government's strategy of encouraging the public to judge police effectiveness in terms of league tables, ranking and performance measures'. Furthermore, he concludes that the indicators used fail to recognise real measures of performance such as the police service's ability to integrate with its local community and the degree to which the local community has confidence in its police.

Reiner gives forth a more pointed message:

> …concentrating more efforts on 'catching criminals' might boost clear-up rates a little, but will not significantly cut crime. What it will do, however, is divert resources from a variety of jobs which the public call upon the police to do…
>
> (Reiner, 1994: p 156)

Despite this, the recent Home Secretary's Letter, (Home Office, 1998), and the Audit Commission's performance indicators continue to push police forces into concentrating on reducing crime by catching criminals. The 1999/2000 Indicators, (Audit Commission, 1998c), are a repeat of the previous year save that there is a concession to repeat victimisation in the burglary of domestic premises.

In a letter addressed to 'The Chief Officer of Police' and 'The Chair of the Police Authority', (Home Office, 1998), the Home Secretary stated that he no longer intended to keep the existing objectives for the detection of violent crimes and domestic burglary as he wished to 'start shifting the emphasis towards crime reduction overall', (p 2). But, in the same letter, he states that both the Audit Commission and Her Majesty's Inspector of Constabulary will continue to monitor and publish these figures, therefore, it is apparent that as such they remain inter alia indicators of performance. What seems clear is that the only effect of such indicators has been to

make police forces less effective by virtue of their enforced inflexibility.

This apparent intransigence in the use of indicators and objectives is likely to be founded on the fact that modern 'sound bite' politics relies upon a simplification of the social world. Therefore, uncritical linkages between police activity and crime rates, increases political reputations and provides comfort and reassurance where perhaps on occasions the fear of crime far exceeds reality. The fact that these political messages are constructed on little more than exercises in creative accounting are as irrelevant as is the notion that the police have little or no control over crime.

Community Safety and Policing Plural Communities

> The consistent message given to us was that the police and other agencies did not or would not realise the impact of less serious, non-crime incidents upon the minority ethnic communities.
>
> (Macpherson, 1999: p 313)

The Audit Commission publication *Safety in Numbers: Promoting Community Safety*, (1999), discusses how peoples fears for their safety are affected by a number of factors of which crime is merely the 'tip of the iceberg'. The term disorder is used to describe a myriad of incidents or events such as vandalism, noisy neighbours, domestic violence, speeding and nuisance youths. Each of these has an impact on the feelings of individuals in the community and more often than not the police have given these low priority, preferring to give precedence to those offences that form part of national objectives. The fact that ethnic minorities complained that the police were inactive on these types of issues is therefore unsurprising. With the advent of crime desks, advocated by the Audit Commission publication *Helping with Enquiries: Tackling Crime Effectively*, (1993), whereby minor crimes are reported and 'investigated' over the phone, the impact of minor crimes on the community or individuals is somehow lost in the statistics. Common vandalism such as a brick through the living room window is seen simply as yet another minor crime to be filed away. No officer is required to visit the aggrieved, there is no contact with the aggrieved or community at large and to all intents and purposes the perception of the public is that there is no interest in what for them is an important event. Minor crime is not measured and is therefore not addressed. Garland, (1996), describes the use of crime desks as a defining down of deviance which has 'met criticism from victims of the many offences which now fall below the threshold of police interest'.

The problems of performance measurement and performance indicators manifest themselves in other ways. The Stephen Lawrence Inquiry, (Macpherson, 1999), described how black people were far more likely to be stopped and searched than white people. Brown, (1997), reaches the same conclusions but is cautionary in explaining how this phenomenon might arise. Maddock and Marlow, (1997), state that 'The influence of the Audit Commission report that proposed intelligence led offence detection and the Home Office key performance indicators should give added impetus to the frequency of the exercise of [search] powers'. Further comments suggest that forces have increased the use of stop and search powers which may be 'linked to the advent of the explicit and comparative monitoring of performance'. The increase in performance in this area coupled with any stereotypical behaviour by front line officers is undoubtedly problematic in terms of police and ethnic minority relations. The act of stop and search can by its very nature be confrontational, the fact that such practices have increased as a result of a performance culture has brought about a less consensual type of policing with a resulting rise in tensions between the police and certain social groups.

Smith, (1995), describes the impact of performance measurement and in particular focuses on public sector managerial behaviour. In doing so he provides an insight into a number of areas he considers prevalent when performance indicators are over used. One such insight he characterises as 'tunnel vision' and describes it as a 'Concentration on areas included in the performance indicators to the exclusion of other important areas'.

This 'tunnel vision' or concentration on single factors as indicators of success has recently been recognised by the Audit Commission as one of the failings of the previous system of Key Objectives and Key Performance Indicators. National-level performance indicators do not currently sufficiently reflect the emphasis on community safety. 'Police forces still feel under pressure to increase detections per officer rather than to reduce crime', (Audit Commission, 1999: p 37).

The requirements to fulfil national top-down require-ments may thus inadvertently weaken the link between

community safety work and the concerns of local communities.

(Audit Commission, 1999: p 30)

The HMIC report *Winning The Race: Policing Plural Communities Revisited*, (HMIC, 1999), noted that there was evidence that the performance culture adopted by forces had a direct detrimental impact on quality of service delivery. Inevitably with a concentration on performance indicators the police have failed to react to the need for community policing. This has been so for all communities but has had an even greater impact on those that have to cope not only with 'disorder' but also with prejudice and discrimination.

A Question of Priorities

The publication of an action plan by the Home Secretary, (Home Office, 1999), as a result of the recommendations contained within the Stephen Lawrence Inquiry report, (Macpherson, 1999), provides some indication that there is a willingness, at least on the face of it, to ring the changes within the police service. However, the nature of national and local politics when coupled with public expectation and media hype inevitably means that the crime agenda is unlikely to abate. Headlines such as 'Muggings soar as police tread softly', (*The Daily Telegraph*, 1999), and 'Violent streak in new crime figures', (*The Daily Telegraph*, 1999b), are unlikely to reduce public anxiety. It is notable that the media have made much of the post Macpherson Report reduction of the use of stop and search in and around London. The reporting of this alongside a reported rise in street robbery brings about a correlation that fuels the imagination of the public and adds to its fear of crime. The much publicised expected rise in property crime over the next few years, (Field, 1998), is also unlikely to diminish central governments and the media's appetite for more favourable crime statistics.

The consequence of a rise in crime coupled with an unerring push for 'Best Value', (Leigh *et al.*, 1999), means that crime and policing efficiency and effectiveness will remain as a main political agenda for the foreseeable future. A consequence of this is that forces will inevitably react to the most pressing objectives and associated performance indicators. The previous reaction to performance indicators relating to crime has been a manipulation of data, (HMIC, 1999), to produce a thin veneer of respectability in the crime figures. It is unlikely that any other performance indicators will be treated any differently.

There can be little argument against the fact that any organisation's performance needs to be measured if only to gauge whether it is successful in carrying out its aims. It could be argued that to fail to measure is a failure to accept that there may be scope for improvement. The inherent problem with performance indicators is that unless chosen carefully and managed effectively, the achievement of an acceptable result in an indicator becomes the objective in its own right. This has a detrimental effect on the real objective that the indicator was initially designed to gauge. As Rouse, (1997), noted 'The danger is that accountability becomes reduced to the meeting of pre-stated PIs and that activity is manipulated to show that these have been met whilst real priorities are neglected'. The adage 'what gets measured gets done' is an inevitable reality, but it fails to take into account that the measurement is often of what is perceived to be have been done rather than what has actually been done. Consequently, results are based not on reality but on the ability to present a set of statistical outcomes that are pleasing to management and political masters. Thus the performance indicators supporting the new Ministerial Priority which has its basis in the Stephen Lawrence Inquiry, (Macpherson, 1999), may well be subject to the same thought processes and manipulation that has occurred in crime figures. In order for the Ministerial Priority to succeed its associated performance indicators, whether they be the existing indicators or a variation of those contained within the reports recommendations, cannot be allowed to befall the same fate as all the other indicators used to measure police performance. Somehow, a notion of quality rather than quantity has to win through.

Loveday, (1997), stated that community participation in the 'policy process of policing' might be an effective way of reducing crime. There is a valid argument that such processes if managed effectively may be the vehicle to producing the achievement of the Ministerial Priority. The Crime and Disorder Act (1998) provides such a framework for public consultation and community partnerships. However, community safety and any other meaningful reforms such as those espoused within the Home Secretary's action plan need to evolve over time. 'Even in favourable circumstances there are likely to be grounds for scepticism about the penetration and durability of reform, especially as changing culture, and therefore values, attitudes and behaviour, can be a protracted process', (Painter, 1997: p 57).

The police have the unenviable task of producing results instantaneously to soothe the anxieties of the public and to please their political masters whilst at the same time building for the future by virtue of community partnerships. The police are required to do this with what are transparently diminishing resources and in an effective and efficient manner in line with the 'Best Value' ideology. Pollitt, (1993), sums it up best by stating that 'quality and consumer responsiveness sit alongside a fierce and continuing concern with economy and efficiency. It is not clear which group of values will take priority when a trade off has to be made', (p 189, quoted in Painter and Isaac-Henry, 1997: p 290). If past performance is any indication then reforms to achieve the outcomes expected from the Home Secretary's action plan are likely to be very slow if they occur at all. If crime continues to rise as predicted, (Field, 1998), then it will not be the 'values, attitudes and behaviour' of the police that will dictate what the trade off will be, it will be the values of government which will hold sway. Put simply, it is a matter of political expediency as to which objectives will succeed.

History has shown that the police and central government have had an opportunity since 1981 to turn the tide. The problems were clear and lessons were there to be learnt. Instead, the government concerned itself with pursuing a market economy and espoused the ideology of a moral rejuvenation backed up by hard policing and tough sanctions on those that failed to conform. Inevitably this led to some sections of the community becoming increasingly marginalised. As crime rose the government blamed the police for managerial failures and imposed on the police a role from which they have yet to recover; that of having the sole aim of catching criminals.

In 1992 Robert Reiner wrote:

> *For the most part, however, the fashionable languages of managerialism and consumerism overlook the fact that policing is not about the delivery of an uncontentious service like any other. Their business is the inevitably messy and intractable one of regulating social conflict. They cannot control, but rather are buffeted by, the prevailing currents in that temporarily banished concept, society.*
>
> (Reiner, 1992)

Policing is not about achieving predetermined crime targets or being at the top of a league table, nor is it simply about controlling crime. It cannot be measured in simple monetary terms and until central government and police management recognise this, the policing of 'plural communities', (HMIC, 1997), cannot move on from the lessons of 1981, let alone those of the last decade of this century.

References

Audit Commission (1993). *Helping with Enquiries: Tackling Crime Effectively*, Police Paper No. 12. London: HMSO.

Audit Commission (1998a). *Local Authority Performance Indicators 96/97: Police Services*. London: Audit Commission.

Audit Commission (1998b). *Direction '97: Performance Indicators for the Financial Year 1998/99*. London: Audit Commission.

Audit Commission (1998c). *Direction '98: Performance Indicators for the Financial Year 1999/2000*. London: Audit Commission.

Audit Commission (1999). *Safety in Numbers: Promoting Community Safety*. London: Audit Commission.

Benyon, J. (1984). *Scarman and After: Essays Reflecting on Lord Scarman's Report, the Riots and their Aftermath*. Oxford: Pergamon Press.

Brown, D. (1997). *PACE Ten Years On: A Review of the Research*. Home Office Research Study No. 155. London: Home Office.

Field, S. (1998). *Trends in Crime Revisited*. Research Development Statistics. London: Home Office.

Garland, D. (1996). The Limits of the Sovereign State: Strategies of Crime Control in Contemporary Society. *The British Journal of Criminology*, 36:4; pp 445–465.

HMIC (1997). *Winning the Race Policing: Plural Communities*. London: Home Office.

HMIC (1999). *Winning the Race: Policing Plural Communities Revisited*. London: Home Office.

HMIC (1999). *Police Integrity: Securing and Maintaining Public Confidence*. London: Home Office.

Home Office (1983). *Manpower, Effectiveness and Efficiency in the Police Service*. Circular 114/83, 30 November, 1983.

Home Office (1991). *Safer Communities: The Local Delivery of Crime Prevention Through the Partnership Approach*, (The Morgan Report). London: HMSO.

Home Office (1993). *The White Paper on Police Reform*. London: HMSO.

Home Office (1995). *Review of Police Core and Ancillary Tasks*. London: HMSO.

Home Office (1998). Letter dated 4 Nov, 1998, from Home Secretary Jack Straw to Chief Officers of Police and Chairs of Police Authorities: *Ministerial Priorities, Key Performance Indicators and Efficiency Planning for 1999/2000*. London: Home Office.

Home Office (1999). *Stephen Lawrence Inquiry: Home Secretary's Action Plan*. London: Home Office.

Inquiry into Police Responsibilities and Rewards, (The Sheehy Inquiry), (1993), *Final Report*. London: HMSO.

Jones, T., and Newburn, T. (1997). *Policing After the Act:*

Police and Magistrates Court Act 1994. London: Police Studies Institute.

Leigh, A., Mundy, G., and Tuffin. R. (1999). *Best Value Policing: Making Preparations*. Police Research Series Paper 116. London: Home Office.

Leishman, F., and Savage, S. (1993). The Police Service. In Farnham, D., and Horton, S. (Eds.). *Managing the New Public Services*. Houndmills: Macmillan.

Loveday, B. (1995). Reforming the Police: From Local Service to State Police? *The Political Quarterly*, 66:2.

Loveday, B. (1997). Management Accountability in Public Services: A Police Study. In Isaac-Henry, K., Painter, C., and Barnes, C. (Eds.). *Management in the Public Sector: Challenge and Change*, 2nd edn. London: International Thomson Business Press.

Macpherson, Sir W. (1999). *The Stephen Lawrence Inquiry*, Cm 4262-I. London: The Stationary Office.

Maddock, J., and Marlow, A. (1997). *A Study of the Use of Stop and Search Powers in Bedfordshire*, unpublished. University of Luton.

Morgan, R., and Newburn, T. (1997). *The Future of Policing*. Oxford: Clarendon Press.

Newburn, T., and Morgan, R. (1994). A New Agenda for the Old Bill. *Policing*, 10:3; pp 143–150.

Painter, C. (1997). Managing Change in the Public Sector. In Isaac-Henry, K., Painter, C., and Barnes, C. (Eds.). *Management in the Public Sector: Challenge and Change*, 2nd edn. London: International Thomson Business Press.

Painter, C., and Isaac-Henry, K. (1997). Conclusion: The Problematical Nature of Public Management Reform. In Isaac-Henry, K., Painter, C., and Barnes, C. (Eds.). *Management in the Public Sector: Challenge and Change*, 2nd edn. London: International Thomson Business Press.

Pollitt, C. (1993). *Managerialism and the Public Services: Cuts or Cultural Change in the 1990s*, 2nd edn. Oxford: Blackwell.

Reiner, R. (1992). Fin de Siècle Issues: The Police Face the Millennium. *The Political Quarterly*, 63: pp 37–49.

Reiner, R. (1994). What Should the Police be Doing. *Policing*, 10:3; pp 15–17.

Rouse, J. (1997). Resource and Performance Management in Public Service Organisations. In Isaac-Henry, K., Painter, C., and Barnes, C. (Eds.). *Management in the Public Sector: Challenge and Change*, 2nd edn. London: International Thomson Business Press.

Royal Commission on Criminal Justice (1993). *Final Report*, Cm 2263. London: HMSO.

Scarman, Lord J. (1981). *The Brixton Disorders, 10–12 April, 1981: Report of an Inquiry*, Cm 8427. London:, HMSO.

Smith, P. (1995). Outcome-related Performance Indicators and Organisational Control in the Public Sector. In Holloway, J., Lewis, J., and Mallory, G. (Eds.). *Performance Measurement and Evaluation*. London: Sage.

The Daily Telegraph (1999). Muggings Soar as Police Tread Softly, 24 April.

The Daily Telegraph (1999). Violent Streak in New Crime Figures, 13 October.

Walker, D., and Richards, M. (1996). A Service Under Change: Current Issues in Policing in England and Wales. *Police Studies*, 19:1; pp 53–74.

Chapter 9
The New York Policing Revolution and Old Tensions: A View from Abroad

Eli B. Silverman

Introduction

For the United Kingdom and most of the world, the New York City Police Department, (NYPD), particularly in the last five years, has embodied the successes and failures of a distinct brand of policing.

On the positive side, the NYPD has received considerable kudos as a significant factor in the City's remarkable crime reduction. Between the end of 1993 and the end of 1999, crime declined by a remarkable 55 per cent. This drop in serious crime is quite astounding: murder, 65 per cent; rape, 35 per cent; robbery, 58 per cent; assault, 37 per cent; burglary, 59 per cent; larceny, 41 per cent; and auto theft, 55 per cent. While most of the world has erroneously attributed zero tolerance policing as the animating force in the NYPD's anti crime efforts, (Silverman, 1998), the NYPD's best efforts actually represent the great strides policing has made in recent years, (Silverman, 1999). Specific police strategies that work best under particular conditions are more widely known and shared than at any time in history. Situational crime prevention, problem solving, crime analysis, computerised crime mapping, community policing, 'hot spot' policing and 'intelligence based policing' have all been offered as paths to crime reduction. Indeed, a central criminological debate today is how to explain the unprecedented reduction in New York and other American cities crime rates during the last several years. While scholars and the media debate various explanations, all agree that the police deserve a vast proportion of the credit. Controversy swirls around how much is due to policing as opposed to declining drug use and improved social and economic conditions.

As valuable as the focus on effective policing has been, it rarely addresses the vital concomitant question of 'at what price to public confidence and trust?'. On both sides of the Atlantic, there is great interest in the 'Broken Windows' approach, which champions police strategies to prevent low-levels disorder, such as public drunkenness, gambling, and prostitution, from escalating into fights, robberies and shootings, (Wilson and Kelling, 1982). Many

believe, however, that sustained police efforts, sometimes mislabeled 'zero tolerance policing', designed to curtail spiralling disorder inevitably generates police harassment and a rise in citizen complaints, particularly from the minority community. When violent crime in the UK, for example, declined by 17 per cent in 1998, an end of the year government report stated that 'black men are still five times more likely than white men to be stopped and searched', (Campbell, 1998).

Recent events in America's largest city dramatically underscore the prominent issues of justice and due process. In New York City, the prime adherent of the crime control model, controversy erupted in August, 1997, when four NYPD officers were charged with torturing, sodomising and brutalising Abner Louima, a Haitian immigrant, inside a police precinct where a wooden stick was shoved in his rectum and then in his mouth. In the first of at least two trials, one officer pleaded guilty and was sentenced to 30 years while a second officer was convicted of assisting the first officer. Passions were further inflamed after the February, 1999, killing of an unarmed West African street peddler in the foyer of his New York Bronx apartment building. Four members of the New York City Police Department's elite Street Crime Unit (SCU) fired 41 times, with 19 bullets striking Amadou Diallo who had arrived from Guinea almost three years before and had no criminal record.

While City, State and Federal investigations are under way, outrage has rekindled numerous protests against police racism and brutality and triggered demonstrations outside City Hall and Diallo's Bronx residence. Protesters claim the four white street crime officers judged Mr Diallo a criminal because of the colour of his skin. Columnist Jack Newfield represents this view: 'There has always been a famine of justice in communities like Soundview in the Bronx. Nobody I've spoken to can name a case where cops killed an unarmed, innocent white person', (Newfield, 1999). To compound racial sensitivities, an appeal court transferred the trial of the four officers from the New York's Bronx's minority white population to the upstate city of Albany with its majority white population. The court maintained that sustained adverse publicity emanating from widespread media coverage prevented the officers from receiving a fair trial.

Supporters of the NYPD laud its SCU, which has expanded threefold since 1997 to over 400 officers, as being the key to the confiscation of guns from New York City's streets. Yet, in the eyes of some critics, this 'elite force quells crime, but at a cost', (Roane, 1999). The NYPD later announced the improved training of all its members and a decentralisation of the SCU while others called for its disbanding.

In the United Kingdom, the Lawrence case and the Macpherson Report's sweeping impact has also strained the bond between police and the public. *The Times* of London reported that 'Many in North London's black community have once more come to see the enforcers of law as their enemy. The Metropolitan Police finds itself in the dock; society's protectors are accused not just of indifference to minorities but a callous hostility which requires radical reform', (*The Times*, January, 1999). The 'mood in London's Tottenham section' is 'so tense that the police have stopped patrolling alone, for fear of ambush'. 'Irate young blacks' have halted peaceful community vigils and rowdy public meetings between police officials and citizens with cries of "Police are the Murderers!" ', (ibid.). Nearly half of Londoners now say they have less trust in the police following the inquiry into Stephen Lawrence murder, (*BBC News*, 1998).

Declining confidence in the police has spread throughout Great Britain. A *Guardian* survey found that 25 per cent of Britons view most police officers as racists. One third of the public suspects that police forces are afflicted with 'institutional racism', (*The Guardian*, January, 1999). A Gallup survey for *The Telegraph* found public satisfaction with the police dropping to less than 60 per cent from 74 per cent ten years ago. The number of people declaring themselves 'very satisfied' declined to eight per cent from 26 per cent in 1989. More than a third, 38 per cent, considered police officers 'racists', (*The Times*, February, 1999).

Investigations of the New York and London episodes accuse the police of clinging to the 'blue wall of silence' as a protective device. Unbridled policing is rightly criticised when peace keeping and minority rights are downgraded and subordinated to the primacy of law enforcement. These issues are of vital concern because even under the best of circumstances, as John

Alderson states, there may be a 'permanent state of conflict' between order maintenance and 'protection of freedom', (Alderson, 1998).

The NYPD's Post Revolution Blues

In New York City, the tension between order maintenance and the freedom of all its citizens has entered centre stage. Public confidence in the NYPD's ability to protect minority rights while addressing crime is under intense scrutiny.

Determining the level of public confidence in the police is often fraught with difficulties and controversy. Clarity and consensus is difficult to unearth. This is perhaps no more applicable than in New York City where the evidence is often conflicting and subject to numerous interpretations. There is sufficient data, however, to strongly suggest a widening chasm between police and citizens, particularly the minority community.

Polls

A 1999 *New York 1* television poll found that the vast majority of African Americans and Latinos believed that police misconduct was a serious problem. A *New York Times* poll in March, 1999, conducted just weeks after the Diallo killing, found that 72 per cent of blacks, 62 per cent of Hispanics and 33 per cent of whites polled believed that most officers used excessive force.

A Quinnipiac College poll surveyed over a thousand city voters from June 8 to June 14, 1999, in the midst of intense publicity about the police torture of Abner Louima for which two officers were convicted and three acquitted. The poll found that 84 per cent believed police brutality was a 'very serious' or 'somewhat serious' problem. Among whites, 25 per cent believed police brutality was very serious compared to 81 per cent of blacks and 59 per cent of Hispanics. While a large majority believed the city has become safer, 45 per cent said governmental policies have led to an increase in police brutality, an opinion held by 28 per cent of white voters, 70 per cent of black voters and 51 per cent of Hispanic voters. At the same time citizens approved 'of the jobs the cops in their community are doing and approve of the way their mayor is handling crime, but they turn thumbs down on the current police commissioner', (Bowles, 1999).

On the other hand, a poll commissioned by the NYPD at the end of 1999 to measure the effectiveness of a recent advertising campaign found that most residents respect the police, including a solid majority of the blacks and Hispanics interviewed. Some 73 per cent of blacks and 83 per cent of Hispanics agreed with the statement 'I respect the New York City Police Department and its officers', whilst the proportion of whites that agreed was 83 per cent. Yet black and Hispanic support for the police dropped off when they were asked whether the police were trying to improve their relationship with members of minorities. 51 per cent of blacks and 58 per cent of Hispanics believed the police were making an effort, (Flynn, 1999). At the minimum, there is enough evidence to urge the NYPD to strive for stronger community relations.

Civilian complaints

The record of civilian complaints against the police also divulges a murky view of public trust. Those critical of the NYPD point to disturbing evidence. Amnesty International, for example, released a report in June, 1996, that raised questions regarding the department's use of force and the rise in complaints against NYPD officers for the use of force. In 1997, the New York Civil Liberties Union contended that only one per cent of 16,327 police officers charged with complaints were disciplined. Another review at the same time found the department cleared or dropped 70 per cent of the police officers charged with brutality by the Civilian Complaint Review Board, (McQuillian, 1997). One year later, in June, 1998, The Human Rights Watch Organization's report found a steady rise in civilian complaints since the NYPD began its heightened drive on quality of life offences. In November of the same year, an American Civil Liberties' report condemned the police commissioner for failing to act on a substantial number of civilian complaints. These charges were echoed the following year, in September, 1999, in a report by the Office of the New York City's Public Advocate, (1999). The Public Advocate's preliminary report claimed that the police commissioner handled cases in a disciplinary manner in only one third of the cases when the CCRB substantiated citizen charges of police abuse, (Gonzalez, 1999).

The evidence regarding civilian complaints, however, is also fraught with contradictory findings. In 1997, for example, Mayor Giuliani reported that civilian complaints plunged 21 per cent compared with the same period the previous year. This decline followed a more modest 0.4 per cent decline in 1996 compared to 1995. At the end of 1999, Commissioner Safir noted that the number of civilian complaints of excessive police force fell 12 per cent from the previous year, the culmination of four consecutive years of decline. This decline occurred at the same time the number of police-citizen contacts swelled as the size of the police force increased from just over 30,000 in 1996 to almost 40,000 in 1999, (Safir, 1999). A spokesman for the Civilian Complaint Review Board, however, challenged these figures as inconclusive since they did not include the last four days of the year, (Raymond and Gardiner, 2000).

Regardless of the level of downturn in civilian complaints from 1994 to 1999, these findings contrast with the earlier years of 1993 to 1995 when, according to the CCRB's semi annual report, there was a 57 per cent increase in civilian complaints, (CCRB, 1998).

Yet even encouraging signs are subject to differing interpretations. While the Mayor and Commissioner praised the department's CPR, (Courtesy, Professionalism, Respect), Program for cops, the executive head of the New York Civil Liberties Union charged that 'Complaint numbers have declined but that doesn't mean police misconduct is on the decline. It might mean CPR is working, but it also could mean people have lost confidence in the CCRB and don't go there anymore to complain', (Feiden, 1997).

At the same time, particular minority communities experienced a rise in civilian complaints. Complaints rose 11.8 per cent in the predominately minority Bronx for the first six months of 1999. In the Bronx's minority community of Soundview, where street peddler Amadou Diallo was killed by police officers in February, there was a doubling of citizen complaints during the month of June, 1999, when the trial was attracting much attention, (Kappstatter, 1999).

Similarly, when Police Commissioner Safir announced that 68 fewer citizens had lodged complaints concerning police abuse discourtesy in 1999 compared to 1988, the NYCLU Director responded that the Commissioner used selective numbers, (NY1 News, 1999).

Stop and frisk

Other agencies have joined some city officials in their reproach of the NYPD. In December, 1999, the New York State Attorney General released a 170 page report that reviewed 175,000 'stop and frisk' forms filled out by police officers between January, 1998 and March, 1999. Stop and frisk is the lawful practice of temporarily detaining, questioning, and, at times, searching civilians on the street. A 1968 US Supreme Court decision, (Terry v. Ohio), held that an officer must be able to articulate a 'reasonable suspicion' that criminal activity is 'afoot'.

The report determined that one of every seven stop and frisk forms, that is, over 15 per cent, did not state facts sufficient to meet the legal definition of 'reasonable suspicion'. Less than one quarter of the forms did not provide the Attorney General's office with enough information to determine if a stop was legally supportable.

The report's most controversial finding was that: 'The perception that minority residents have been disproportionately stopped and frisked by the police is based on reality'. The Attorney General contended that blacks constitute 26 per cent of the city's population while accounting for 50 per cent of the people stopped; and Hispanics make up 24 per cent of the population but account for 33 per cent of the stops. Whites, in contrast, who make up 43 per cent of the population, account for 13 per cent of the stops, (Attorney General, 1999). The disparity in 'stop' rates is most pronounced in precincts where whites are in the majority. In these precincts in which blacks and Hispanics represented less than 10 per cent of the total population, 'individuals identified as belonging to these racial groups nevertheless accounted for more than half of the total "stops" during the period examined', (ibid.). Nor did differing crime rates among various groups, the report declared, account for the disparate police practices. 'After accounting for the effect of differing crime rates, blacks were "stopped" 23 per cent more often than whites, across all crime categories. In addition, after accounting for the effect of different crime rates, Hispanics were "stopped" 39 per cent more often than whites across crime categories', (ibid.).

As expected, the NYPD took issue with the report. A deputy commissioner maintained that the report was flawed because the analysis relied on arrest data from 1997 but used stop and search figures from 1998 and 1999. The department defended the use of street searches as part of an effort to catch criminals as they prepare to commit crimes or flee crimes. Search and frisk has often been cited as one of the ways

the city has been able to reduce the number of illegal guns on the street. Furthermore, according to the police commissioner, 'The basis for stop and frisks is not the race of the individuals as determined by the police officer but the race of the individuals as determined by the description from the victim', (Flynn, 1999).

Whither community policing

Not only do some people depict the New York Model as inherently repressive, but they characterize it as the antithesis of community based policing, a convenient but misleading dichotomy. No less a respected observer than Fox Butterfield commented in April 1999, two months after the Diallo shooting:

> *A question many law enforcement officials around the country are asking is how much of this was self-inflicted after Mayor Giuliani and Police Commissioner Safir abandoned efforts by their predecessors to establish community policing, scorning it as social work. Whether police officers can do it all by themselves is at the center of the debate between New York City's approach, which relies on the massive use of officers to suppress crime, and the strategy of community policing and a related approach called problem solving policing.*
> **(Butterfield, 1999)**

Butterfield points to Chicago and San Diego as examples of cities where 'community policing, in which citizens are allies of the police, is thriving', (ibid.). Yet a 1999 national government study of police in 12 cities, which includes New York, Chicago and San Diego, notes that Chicago has a higher percentage of residents fearful of crime (48 per cent) than does New York (42 per cent), (Bureau of Justice Statistics, 1999). And while San Diego has a considerably lower percentage of residents fearful of crime at 30 per cent, one may well wonder how much can be attributed to its widely recognised community policing. When asked if police are doing community policing, 57 per cent of San Diego residents said yes while 51 per cent of New Yorkers responded affirmatively- hardly a yawning gap given the publicity heaped on San Diego's community policing. And while Chicago's fear of crime exceeds New York's, it had a higher percentage of residents, than did New York and San Diego at 67 per cent, who think police are doing community policing. It is difficult to extract an undisputed meaning from this, but it certainly does not lend credence to the position that New York lies at the far end of a bipolar spectrum.

Seeking Explanations

How does one explain specific evidence of public dissatisfaction, particularly by some members of minority communities, with NYPD practices in the midst of high approval for declining crime? Zero tolerance policing frequently emerges as the readily facile and overly simplistic response. In many nations, including the United Kingdom, New York City style policing is unfairly characterised as predominantly round the clock 'in your face' aggressive policing which is at the heart of the downturn of the city's crime rate. This is, as I have argued elsewhere, a grossly unfair misrepresentation of the nature of the New York success story, (Silverman, 1997).

The zero tolerance explanation is deficient in two fundamental aspects. Firstly, it assigns too much credit to zero tolerance and, more importantly, misunderstands the concept. Secondly, it understates the more vital ingredients of the New York NYPD revolution and the extent to which some of these reforms have been recently blunted. This chapter's remaining tasks are to address these two principal areas.

Misconstruing zero tolerance policing

Zero tolerance has been portrayed as leaving the police little or no discretion. Nothing could be further from the truth. Short of unlimited police resources and the complete absence of community opposition, zero tolerance is more easily viewed as a catchy political slogan than an illuminating concept. Zero tolerance, therefore, cannot mean 24 hours, 7 days a week, perpetual enforcement of all quality of life offences. Practitioners may be excused for having zero tolerance for the phrase.

Zero tolerance policing can, however, mean selective enforcement, as part of overall strategies, targeted to specific problems whether it relates to drugs, guns, youths or social clubs, etc. Strategies may include a vast array of tactics including car searches, warrant checks, and a range of community and social agency involvement. All, however, are directed towards particular problems based on their geographic and temporal crime distributions that we know generally falls into clusters. These approaches often include team led enforcement operations which entail co-ordinated plans of action with transit and housing divisions, special posts, observation posts, plainclothes, narcotics teams,

sting operations and intensive debriefing by detectives. Today's NYPD is far more focused on a holistic integration of generalist beat officers with the specialists units.

Thus, it is not only not viable, but undesirable to practice zero tolerance everywhere all the time. A substantial body of literature suggests that the real question is not zero tolerance policing; it is smarter policing allied with problem solving. Yet we have anti-NYPD polemics positing New York policing as the antithesis of problem policing. For example, the Thames Valley Chief Constable is quoted in the *Police Review* as saying, 'Zero tolerance implies that there is just one solution, tougher policing, for all crime problems', (Pollard, 1997). Smarter policing, however, is flexible and may simultaneously address short run problems and long range solutions. In America, for example, there is a federal funded program in which the police, in conjunction with local governments and social agencies, address specific community problems. It is known as 'weed and seed'. As the name implies, one needs to aggressively weed out the outgrowth before one cultivates long term growth. Many NYPD precincts, with the most intensive and directed policing, also have key programs in which community activists design and are involved in the distribution of governmental funds. In reality, there is more systematic problem solving going on in the NYPD than ever before, for example, closing down store fronts, called nuisance abatement through civil enforcement. This is based on a strategy to target an illegal activity, usually some narcotic or gambling activity. This permits the NYPD to sue landlords renting to these criminals. It requires the documentation of three incidents of criminal activity. This documentation is forwarded to the NYPD's Civil Enforcement Unit attorneys who prepare cases brought to court as legal actions against landlords who rent space to criminals. The judge signs an order closing the location for one year and the police lock up the location. No one is allowed back unless attorneys approve legitimate tenants. This action reduces public perceptions of revolving door justice not to mention shootings, robberies and other crimes that surround these core problem locations.

The real revolution in blue

Not only is zero tolerance policing misunderstood, it is also accorded too much weight in the NYPD revolution. Let us summarise the core ingredients of the NYPD's reforms and critique their staying power. In 1994, the new mayoral and police administrations significantly reformed the department to dramatically reduce crime. These reforms were based on:

Precinct autonomy.
The long sought goal of providing precinct commanders greater control over their own personnel was impressive. Resources were placed closer to the precinct delivery level. Rather than allow headquarters to determine staffing and deployment on a city wide basis, it was decided that reductions in crime, fear of crime, and disorder would flow from precinct co-ordination of selected enforcement and community efforts. The precinct became the key delivery level for tactical deployment and strategies. Precincts are held accountable for their performance at headquarters' innovative Compstat crime strategy meetings.

Geographic reorganisation.
Geographical based teams (such as the Street Crime Unit) would now operate in defined precinct areas supported by precinct-wide special resources. Precinct and borough commands were provided resources that formerly were the exclusive province of headquarters. For example, precinct commanders could now use their anti-crime units to perform decoy operations, a function that had previously been left to the citywide Street Crime Unit. The new arrangements replaced cumbersome reporting systems that hampered the precincts' ability to respond to and anticipate problems.

Decision making shift.
The above factors moved the organisation away from headquarters serving as the department's nerve centre whereby operational police tactics were solely conceived and disseminated on a 'city wide basis'. The department realised that standardised city wide crime fighting decisions were not as effective as strategies tailored for particular communities.

Dulled reforms

For the NYPD and its minority communities, the problem is that several of these reform

foundations have been eroded since early 1996, steadily widening the gap between police and the public. The greatest build-up in personnel has occurred in units that either do not report to the precinct commander or are directed either by headquarters or the boroughs. The large growth of borough narcotics officers is symptomatic of this expansion of specialised nonuniform units. Narcotics officers have increased from 2,138 in April, 1997, to 3,284 in January, 1999. On the other hand, according to the New York City Council, the number of uniformed officers assigned to neighbourhood precincts between 1997 and 1990 declined from 17,619 to 16,5759 in January, 1999, despite the fact that the total number of uniformed officers grew by more than 2,000, (NY City Council, 1999).

Street Crime Unit

The travails of the NYPD's Street Crime Unit, (SCU), spotlighted since the Diallo tragedy, embodies the turmoil and quandary that the NYPD faces today. The question over SCU searches fuels much of the public discomfort with the NYPD. The plainclothes SCU's assertive operations has accounted for more than 40 per cent of the guns police remove from the streets even though this unit represents less than 2 per cent of the force.

Since four unsupervised SCU officers fired 41 shots at Diallo in February, 1999, however, critics warn that success comes with a price tag. For example, in 1998, 27,061 people were frisked by the unit and 4,647 were arrested, meaning that more than 22,000 people were searched because they were mistakenly thought to be armed, dangerous and either had, or were about to commit a crime. In 1997, 18,023 people were searched and 4,899 were arrested. Citizen complaints of improper searches increased from 470 in 1996 to 531 in 1997 and to 565 in 1998, (Cooper, 1999).

The New York State Attorney General's report, cited above, observed that the SCU stopped 16.3 blacks, 14.5. Hispanics and 9.6 whites for each stop that resulted in an arrest and that blacks comprised 62.7 per cent of all persons stopped by the unit, (Attorney General, 1999).

Since the Diallo shooting, the SCU has been embroiled in controversy. Shortly after the shooting, it was revealed that two of the officers had 'troubling civilian complaint records'. One officer was the recipient of three complaints between March of 1996 and 1997 when he was accused of punching, kicking, beating and pepper-spraying suspects. The complaints were unsubstantiated by the Civilian Complaints Review Board but one law enforcement official was quoted as saying, 'Three complaints in one year is a red flag, no matter what'. The other officer had two complaints of excessive force, both of which were closed because the complainants did not co-operate with the CCRB, and one of verbal abuse that was declared unfounded. In two of the incidents, he was accused of using racial slurs, (O'Shaughnessy, 1999). Two months later, a newspaper investigation revealed that almost 18 per cent of the SCU officers 'accumulated so many civilian complaints that they exceeded warning levels set by department programs that monitor abusive officers'. According to this account, not all 65 members of the SCU's 374 officers eligible for one of three monitoring systems were actually being monitored. The NYPD responded that police who join the street crime unit tend to be more active cops and that seven officers, of the 32 monitored and evaluated, were removed from the unit, (Marzulli and Rashbaum, 1999).

A month after the shooting, the Police Commissioner ordered a sweeping reform of the SCU. The officers would now patrol the streets in full uniform rather than in plainclothes to increase their accountability to the public and lessen the chance of confusion on the part of the public. Furthermore, Commissioner Safir announced the addition of 50 minority officers to increase their representation in the overwhelmingly white SCU. Safir said that 50 white SCU officers would be transferred to precinct robbery units to make room for the incoming minority officers. A week earlier, the Commissioner transferred a black police captain to the position of SCU second in command.

Within a few months, however, the conversion of all Street Crime officers to uniform was diluted when the Commissioner announced that two members of each four or six person SCU team would be in plainclothes with the rest in uniform. The plainclothes would work undercover while uniform personnel would make the arrests. Months later, in September, the rules changed again—supervisors of each team could decide on their own mix of uniform and plainclothes officers. As a result, virtually all SCU personnel were shifted to plainclothes, provided a uniformed street crime unit cop was present at the scene of an arrest to avoid confusion about the identity of the undercover cops.

The following month, in October, 1999, the SCU was, in the view of many, dismantled: the SCU central command and headquarters closed down. SCU units were broken down, ('reorganised', the SCU had been centralised again in 1997—moving away from precinct direction) and assigned to the NYPD's eight patrol boroughs as a means of 'decentralisation'. A white flag was raised outside the unit's newly defunct headquarters after the changes were announced. At this stage, it is too early to tell how the new assignments are working out although there very well may be great variance in assignments and activity depending on the patrol boroughs involved and the nature of supervision.

This SCU's shifting fortunes, in reality, are not surprising since the earlier conversion to a total uniformed unit conflicted with the SCU's basic rationale. The Mayor's and Commissioner's Strategy 97 document, written in 1996, for example, praised the 'simple concept behind the street crime unit: highly motivated and experienced officers not assigned to the local precinct, patrolling in plainclothes in unmarked vehicles and not known to local criminals', (Giuliani and Safir, 1996).

In addition to lauding the SCU's record, the Strategy 97 document announced the unit's expansion from 138 to 438 officers. This hurried, centralised, less selective growth of the street crime and other specialised units drains precincts, which are still held accountable for crime reduction but with diminished resources.

The SCU has been highly successful in harvesting guns from the street, an approach that has no doubt decreased violent crime. But more intensified action is now necessary to recover dwindling numbers of street guns. Ratcheting up the pressure leads to more searches at the margins and possible mistakes, which rob the public of its sense of security and trust.

This 1997 rapid expansion of the undercover SCU inevitably affected quality control. Specialised units often develop their own distinct culture and require close supervision. In 1994, for example, when 20 officers were added to the small veteran dominated SCU, the arrests per officer tripled. But after the 1997 tripling in size, arrests per officer declined. The rush of rapid expansion impairs training, cohesiveness, and co-ordination. Many of the new officers were less experienced in tactics and verbal skills compared to the original small SCU whose officers had some plainclothes experience. When a new officer entered the original unit, he was paired with an older officer who would act as mentor and guide him on proper tactics and verbal persuasion skills. The hurried expansion of the SCU interrupted this process and decreased the officers' supervision.

Conclusion

The NYPD's visible police force has been drained in many ways. In addition to precinct patrol officers, a substantial number of precinct community police officers, key citizen connectors, have been shifted to narcotics and other specialised units further diminishing police visibility and public confidence. As the number of precinct officers steadily shrinks, police response times to crimes in progress have increased as daily police-citizen interaction diminishes. Yet the public is yearning for more of this type of contact which frequently spurs community organisations to reclaim and maintain their neighbourhoods. Like many American citizens who hold Congress in low esteem but highly value their own representative, many New Yorkers have the same attitude toward the NYPD: they resent the institution but seek more contact with their own beat officer.

Policing involves both negative and positive citizen contact. When the negative, as with the Street Crime Unit, far outweighs the positive, local police officers, then public confidence declines. We expect a lot from our police: enforce the law, reduce crime, and honour the rights of all citizens.

There have been a series of studies that demonstrate that there does not have to be a trade off between crime reduction and citizen satisfaction with the police. The Vera Institute of Justice study of two south Bronx precincts, where crime and civilian complaints simultaneously declined, explored numerous explanations including changing demographics. The researchers concluded that the key factor was the willingness and ability of precinct commanders to maintain a dual focus on departmental changes aimed at crime reduction *and* community satisfaction. Although they employed different management systems, both precinct commanders enhanced precinct training and improved personnel supervision and community interaction, (Davis and Mateu-Gelabert, 1999). These types of findings have been replicated elsewhere. In a study of policing in Oakland, Los Angeles and Chicago, a New York University psychology professor found that 'being treated properly, with respect and dignity and fairness, is two to three times more important to people than what happens to the crime rate in their neighborhood', (Tierney, 1999).

In the last several years, the NYPD has been quite innovative in navigating these often-conflicting currents of crime reduction and citizen satisfaction. If reform dimensions are properly attended to, citizen complaints will decline while police effectiveness and public satisfaction increases. New times require a new commitment to innovative policing. Fear of police should not replace fear of crime.

References

Alderson, J. (1998). *Principled Policing: Protecting the Public with Integrity*. Winchester: Waterside Press.

Attorney General of the State of New York. (1999). *The New York City Police Department's 'Stop and Frisk' Practices*. New York.

BBC News (1998). Lawrence Inquiry Shakes Trust in Police, internet ed., July 16.

Bowles, P. (1999). Poll Cites Fears Over Cop Abuses. *Newsday*, June 18.

Bureau of Justice Statistics, US Department of Justice (1999). *Criminal Victimization and Perceptions of Community Safety in 12 Cities, 1998*. Washington: Printing Office.

Butterfield, F. (1999). Citizens as Allies Rethinking the Strong Arm of the Law. *New York Times*, internet ed. April 3.

Campbell, D. (1998). Dark Side of the Force. *The Guardian*, internet ed., December 15.

City Council, Public Safety Committee, (1999). *Overview of the New York Police Department Staffing*. New York.

Civilian Complaint Review Board (1998). *Semi-Annual Report*, New York, January–June.

Cooper M. (1999). Street Tactics by the Police Draw Inquiry. *New York Times*, internet ed., March 18.

Davis, R.C., and Mateu-Gelabert, P. (1999). *Respectful and Effective Policing: Two Examples in the South Bronx*. New York: Vera Institute of Justice.

Feiden, D. (1997). Complaints Against Cops Drop 21 Per cent. *New York Daily News*, internet ed., June 20.

Flynn, K. (1999). Police Poll Finds Strong Support from Blacks and Hispanics. *New York Times*, internet ed., December 11.

Flynn, K. (1999). State Cites Racial Inequality in New York Police Searches. *New York Times*, internet ed., December 1.

Giuliani, R., and Safir, H. (1996). *New York City Police Department 'Strategy 97'*. New York.

Gonzalez, J. (1999). Abusive Cops Roam Free. *New York Daily News*, internet ed., February 16.

The Guardian (1999). The Legacy of Lawrence, internet ed., February 19.

Johnston, P. (1999). Police to Have Ethnic Quota System. *The Times*, internet ed., February 18.

Kappstatter, R. (1999). Call for CCRB Reforms. *New York Daily News*, internet ed., July 22.

Marzulli, J., and Rashbaum, W.K. (1999). Warning Signs Lit as Elite Cop Unit. *Daily News*, internet ed., April 12.

McQuillian, A. (1997). Bad Apple Cops Rarely Punished. *Daily News*, internet ed., July 10.

New York City Public Advocate, (1999). *NYPD Response to Civilian Complaints.*

NY1 News (1999). Safir Says Police Complaints Have Dropped, internet ed., January 14.

Newfield, J. (1999). Starving for Justice From Police. *New York Post*, February 12.

O'Shaughnessy, P. (1999). Red Flags on Two Cops. *New York Daily News*, internet ed., February 13.

Pollard, C. (1997). *Police Review*, April 4: p 17.

Raymond, G., and Gardiner, S. (2000). Board Disputes Police Complaint Figures. *Newsday*, internet ed., January 7.

Roane, K.R. (1999). Elite Force Quells Crime But at a Cost, Critics Say. *New York Times*, February 6.

Safir, H. (1999). Complaints of NYPD Force Still Dropping. *New York Post*, December 7.

Silverman, E.B. (1997). Crime in New York: A Success Story. *The Public Perspective, Crime and Punishment*, 8:4; pp 3–5.

Silverman, E.B. (1998). Below Zero Tolerance: The New York Experience. In Burke, R.H. (Ed.). *Zero Tolerance Policing*. Leicester: Perpetuity Press.

Silverman, E.B. (1999). *NYPD Battles Crime: Innovative Strategies in Policing*. Boston: Northeastern University Press.

Tierney, J. (1999). After Victory in the War on Crime. *New York Times*, February 25.

The Times (1999). Black and Blue: Growing Divisions from the Death of Stephen Lawrence, internet ed., January 30.

The Times (1999). Murder Taunts Plunge Police in Race Crisis, internet ed., January 10.

Wilson, J.Q., and Kelling, G. (1982). Broken Windows: The Police and Neighborhood Safety. *Atlantic Monthly*, March: pp 29–38.

Chapter 10

Can Macpherson Succeed Where Scarman Failed?

Michael O'Byrne

Introduction

The essence of the argument to be presented, in this chapter, is, that since both inquiries examined essentially the same issue, if Scarman had succeeded, then Macpherson should not have been necessary. What then are the factors that will ensure a different outcome? In examining this question the issue will be approached by looking at three factors:

1. The two inquiries; examining the differences of approach and outcome.

2. The sustainability of the solutions; the usefulness and dangers of targets and a performance-management led approach.

3. The political climate; the effective implementation of the recommendations which is crucially dependent on the presence or lack of political will.

The Inquiries

Both of the inquiries were set up by the Home Secretary in order to report on what was essentially a breakdown in confidence between the black community and the police. With the Scarman Inquiry it arose out of the riots which occurred in Brixton in April, 1981 together with similar disturbances in the same year in Liverpool, Manchester and the West Midlands. The Macpherson Inquiry examined the investigation of the racist murder of Stephen Lawrence which occurred in April, 1993, only 12 years after the Brixton riots and the Scarman Report. The Scarman Report was lauded at the time as being ground-breaking. It set the agenda for the development of a better relationship between the police and the black community. It also made a significant number of recommendations for other social agencies whose policies impacted upon life in the inner-city. In theory therefore, the successful implementation of the Scarman recommendations should have prevented the need for the Macpherson Inquiry.

Methodology of the inquiries

Both inquiries used essentially the same methodology. Part One looked at the facts of the case: in Scarman the riots, in Macpherson the investigation of the murder. Part Two examined the issues which underpinned those facts, taking evidence on the causes and effects of racism, discrimination and the policies which were in place for dealing with them. Both inquiries also invited any interested party to submit written evidence. A key difference was that Sir William Macpherson used a panel of three lay advisers whose participation he clearly valued; he stated that:

> ...*their contributions to the report and to the conclusions and recommendations made have been imaginative, radical and of incalculable worth. Without their advice and support the Inquiry would have been infinitely less effective.*

> (Macpherson, 1999)

Advantages enjoyed by Lord Scarman

The key advantages enjoyed by the Scarman Inquiry were:

- Speed. The riots took place in April, 1981; both parts were completed and the report submitted to Parliament by November in the same year. This meant that memories were fresh and the recommendations had a nexus to the events which gave them additional weight and relevance.

- The absence of other litigation. At the time of this inquiry society was significantly less litigious than now and there were no criminal or civil cases being pursued against potential witnesses. This meant that witnesses to fact and policy could be examined rigorously and there was a greater expectation for openness.

- It was easier for the inquiry to focus more objectively on the facts as there were no deaths resulting from the riots and there was not that highly personal focus faced by the Macpherson Inquiry.

- The unchallenged authority of Lord Scarman. He had carried out the Red Lion Square Inquiry to general acclaim and was a Law Lord of considerable standing.

Advantages enjoyed by Sir William Macpherson

The key advantages enjoyed by the Macpherson Inquiry were:

- The Kent police investigation. Sir William Macpherson had available to him the inquiry carried out under the supervision of the independent Police Complaints Authority by the Kent police. This provided a solid foundation for the examination of the witnesses and its findings of fact were not questioned.
- Mr and Mrs Lawrence. There is no doubt that the way that both of these intelligent and articulate parents were able to describe the way that they had been treated by the police, and other agencies, and to put that experience into a black context, had a significant, if not the most significant, impact on the overall outcome of the inquiry.
- Immunity for witnesses. The fact that the Attorney General granted a general immunity to witnesses for evidence given to the inquiry significantly helped to remove barriers to witnesses being open and honest. The pity was that key witnesses did not take up the challenge that this presented.

Key issues

As already stated, the fundamental issue was a breakdown in the relationship between the police and the black community and the way that this was reflected in the lack of confidence which that community had in how it was policed. In comparing the effectiveness of the outcome of both inquiries it is necessary to look at how this issue was expressed.

Scarman

Two views have been forcefully expressed in the course of the Inquiry as to the causation of the disorders. The first is that of oppressive policing over a period of years, and in particular the harassment of young blacks on the streets of Brixton. On this view, it is said to be unnecessary to look more deeply for an explanation of

the disorders. They were 'anti-police'. The second is that the disorders, like so many riots in British history, were a protest against society by people, deeply frustrated and deprived, who sought in a violent attack upon the forces of law and order their one opportunity of compelling public attention to their grievances. I have no doubt that each view, even if correct, would be an over-simplification of a complex situation. If either view should be true, it would not be the whole truth.

(para 1.4)

...the policing problem is not difficult to identify: it is that of policing a multi-racial community in a deprived inner-city area where unemployment, especially among young black people, is high and hopes are low. It is a problem which admits of no simple or clear-cut solution.

(para 1.6)

I identify the social problem as that of the difficulties, social and economic, which beset the ethnically diverse communities who live and work in our inner cities.

(para 1.7)

Lord Scarman was clearly a creature of his time and saw the problem as being one which was shared equally between the black community and the police rather than one in which the police carried the major responsibility in creating conditions where change could come about. It took little or no account of the fact that those agencies which had the power and resources to bring about change had the consequential responsibility to ensure that the conditions were created which would guarantee that those changes would occur. This is shown in his description of discrimination, its effects and his proposals for a remedy:

...much of the evidence of discrimination is indirect rather than direct; but I have no doubt that it is a reality which too often confronts the black youths of Brixton... It was alleged by some of those who made representations to me that Britain is an institutionally racist society. If by that it is meant that it is a society which knowingly, as a matter of policy, discriminates against black people, I reject the allegation. If, however, the suggestion being made is that practices may be adopted by public bodies as well as by private individuals which are unwittingly discriminatory against black people, then this is an allegation which deserves serious consideration, and, where proved, swift remedy.

(paras 2.21–2.22)

He was later to reject the allegation that institutionalised racism existed and his remedy was in the main an exhortation to make better use of the existing law and procedures.

Changes in legislation are not the principal requirement if discrimination is to be rooted out. What is required is a clear determination to enforce the existing law, and a positive effort by all in responsible positions to give a lead on the matter.

But again he goes on to show that he thinks that the need for change is an evenly shared responsibility rather than one in which government agencies have the major responsibility by stating:

> *Pride in being black is one thing, but black racialism is no more acceptable than white. A vigorous rejection of discriminatory and racialist views is as important among black people as among white if social harmony is to be ensured.*
>
> (para 6.35)

Macpherson

> *Unwitting racism can arise because of lack of understanding, ignorance or mistaken beliefs. It can arise from well-intentioned but patronising words or actions. It can arise from unfamiliarity with behaviour or cultural traditions of people or families from minority ethnic communities. It can arise from racist stereotyping of black people as potential criminals or troublemakers. Often this arises out of uncritical self-understanding borne out of an inflexible police ethos of the 'traditional' way of doing things. Furthermore, such attitudes can thrive in a tightly knit community, so that there can be a collective failure to detect and to outlaw this breed of racism. The police canteen can too easily be its breeding ground.*
>
> (para 6.17)

> *The failure of the first investigating team to recognise and accept racism and race relations as a central feature of the investigation of the murder of Stephen Lawrence played a part in the deficiencies in policing which we identify in this report.*
>
> (para 6.21)

> *It [institutional racism] persists because of the failure of the organisation openly and adequately to recognise and address its existence and causes by policy, example and leadership. Without recognition and action to eliminate such racism it can prevail as part of the ethos of the culture of the organisation. It is a corrosive disease.*
>
> (para 6.34)

> *There is no doubt that recognition, acknowledgement and acceptance of the problem by police services and their officers is an important first step for minority ethnic communities in moving forward positively to solve the problem which exists. **There is an onus upon police services to respond to this.***
>
> (para 6.48, author's emphasis)

> *Things [in the investigation] obviously went wrong from the start, and **it was a duty of the senior officers in particular to take their own steps to ensure that**

> **alternative methods were followed** *in order to see that the family were kept properly informed and that their relationship with the investigation team was a healthy one. This they signally failed to do. Whatever the difficulties and **whatever their cause the onus clearly lay upon Mr Weeden and his officers to address them**.*
>
> (para 14.74, author's emphasis)

The essential difference between the Scarman approach and that of Macpherson is that Scarman saw the responsibility for change as being shared more or less equally between the black community and the police. Macpherson is clear that the responsibility lies with the agency which has the power, resources and legal accountability for the equal delivery of services to all of the communities, and that this responsibility lies with them totally, regardless of their views and perceptions of the responses and reactions of those communities. This reflects a sea change in the way in which the police and other agencies will be held accountable in the future.

Proposed remedies

There were two major differences in the recommendations which the inquiries made.

In Scarman, the allegation of institutional racism was rejected and he focused his major attention on changes to the police discipline code and system; the strengthening of the independent element in the investigation of complaints against police; lengthening of police training with a clearer community relations element and changes in tactics in dealing with public order. It can be said that he dealt with the system issues very effectively but that he avoided, or failed to deal with, the underlying cultural issues. As far as discrimination is concerned he merely called for a determination to enforce the existing law and for all in responsible positions to give a lead on the matter. His belief clearly was that the existing law was adequate and that exhortation was enough to bring about the necessary cultural changes.

Macpherson on the other hand puts cultural issues at the heart of his recommendations. There is a clear implicit acceptance of the fact that there were reasonably good systems in place and that the major failure in the Metropolitan Police investigation was that these systems had not been applied. This strengthens the impact of the report as far as other forces are concerned as they too would have been critical of the Metropolitan Police investigation, and would have been confident that the same approach, in terms of the investigation, would not have been taken in their force. Crucially, exhortation has been replaced by prescription. Key issues such as recruiting, the exercise of powers to stop and search, strategies for the prevention, recording, investigation and prosecution of racist incidents, multi-agency co-operation and training are now to be monitored and measured in terms of their implementation and effectiveness. The probable effect of this approach will now be covered in detail.

Sustainability

In the last ten years the police service, and public service as a whole, have been slowly but surely introduced to performance management systems which require the setting of hard targets. The effectiveness and efficiency of forces are increasingly judged by their ability to achieve these targets. At the time of the Scarman Inquiry this was not accepted practice in the public sector although it was well-established in commerce.

The key difference that target-setting makes is that it is no longer possible to disguise or hide failure, or to live with failure by ignoring the lack of success. For example, Scarman advocated increasing the number of police officers to be recruited from the visible ethnic minorities. The idea was accepted in principle by the government of the day and by the Association of Chief Police Officers, (ACPO). However, no targets, no matter how general, were set and the fact that the numbers increased by very small amounts over a very long time was not a matter for review or apparent concern. This has been fundamentally changed by the fact that the Home Secretary has now set targets, not just for the police but for all the major agencies in the criminal justice system. Whether or not all of these targets are achievable, and what can be done if they are not, will be a matter of debate later in this article. The crucial issue is that failure will be public and the agencies will need to account to their political masters for it and come forward with proposals to correct the situation.

Performance management is, however, a triple-edged sword. The effect of the first edge is as described above. The second edge is best encapsulated by the old maxim, 'what gets measured, gets done'. The difficulty that this presents it is that the corollary is also true, i.e. what is not measured is ignored. This means that any approach must be broadly based and ensure that *all* of the factors which can contribute to the

success or failure of an approach to major issues are subject to both measurement and management: too often measurement alone is mistaken for management. It is not enough to know what is going on. It is also necessary to have in place a positive management ethos which seeks to use that information to make a difference.

The second element of this factor is that the selection of priorities becomes critical to overall success. It is a truism that there can only be a limited number of priorities, but it is a truism which tends to be ignored in the heat of the debate whilst politicians are being forced to deal with a complex situation on an issue by issue basis and where the soundbite rules supreme. A classic example of this is the current debate around NHS waiting lists. The priority being given to time has led to treatment for serious and even life-threatening conditions being delayed in favour of patients with less serious conditions who have been on the waiting list for longer than the targeted period.

To put this in a police context, it is clear that the government is now nervous about the coincidence of a predicted upswing in crime, especially property crime, and the timing of the next general election. Pressure on the police to improve crime reduction and crime detection could easily lead to a willingness to be less demanding on the way that issues such as 'stop and search' are managed if there is a possible penalty in the growth of crimes such as burglary, theft of and from motor vehicles and street robbery. A large number of forces still have relatively primitive information systems and fairly crude approaches to performance management. It is not clear if they have the capacity to quickly develop this into the sophisticated performance management systems required to deal with the complexity that the problem presents.

The third edge is the general experience that when performance management comes in the door, ethics go out the window. Where targets are difficult or impossible to achieve there is a tendency, in the first instance, to massage the figures rather than work on the problem. There are examples in recent police history where forces have engaged in exactly these practices. The danger is that these forces will be tempted to go further than mere massaging and will actually engage in corrupt practices in order to achieve targets. In order to avoid this, it is necessary that everyone concerned, from the constable to the Home Secretary, is aware of these dangers and is committed to the development of effective systems working within a corruption-intolerant culture.

Political Will

The Scarman Report could not have been published in a less favourable political climate than was the case in 1981. The economy was about to enter into the deepest and longest recession since the 1930s, during which manufacturing industry would be decimated. This made many of Scarman's recommendations on housing, education and employment in the inner cities difficult, if not impossible, to implement for a government committed to the reduction of public spending. Michael Heseltine was the honourable exception to this while in government as he did try to target resources on inner cities, especially Liverpool. In addition, this was a government which denied the connection between crime and social conditions and put an emphasis on individual rights and responsibilities whilst trying to minimise the role of government, both on grounds of dogma and of fiscal necessity.

The debate on the issue, such as it was, was soon displaced by the overwhelming concerns that the public had with the economy and then by the country's engagement in a war. As the 1980s developed, both the government's approach to crime, and its role in sustaining society became more and more focused on the individual and less on the community. It became more and more committed to reducing the tax burden, gradually transferring the responsibility for issues such as health and education from the state to the individual. In addition, the prolonged involvement with the miners' strike led to the politicisation of the police and the whole issue of changing the nature of the relationship between the police and the ethnic minority communities was allowed to effectively wither on the vine.

In comparison, Macpherson has both the wind and the tide behind it. Jack Straw agreed to do what at least two previous Home Secretaries had refused to do by the setting up of the inquiry itself, and, as discussed above, he has set targets in most of the key areas and has put his personal weight and the considerable weight of his office and that of other cabinet ministers behind the issue.

That said, this is also a government which appears to be committed to at least contain and perhaps reduce public spending as a proportion of GDP. This means that there is no commitment to additional resources should they be required. This tempts the commentator into stating that whilst talk is cheap the real test of commitment is shown by action and that is most clearly shown by the commitment of resources, be it the ring-fencing of current resources or the promise of additional resources where they are proved necessary.

The litmus test on commitment will be recruiting, where the government has required the service to significantly increase the number of police officers recruited from the black and Asian communities. This requirement must be seen in the light of the government's current approach to police spending. The Comprehensive Spending Review is committed to providing the police with a 2.7 per cent increase in the current year and 2.8 per cent in 2000/2001. Actual police inflation runs at between four and six per cent. This means that a large number of forces are suffering year-on-year cuts. Since most of the budget where cuts are possible involve staffing, it is inevitable that they will be reflected in reduced police numbers. For some forces this has already meant a freeze on recruiting with the prospect for the coming year being just as bleak.

It is a statement of the obvious that if there is no recruiting there can be no improvement on the overall position in terms of black and Asian officers. For those forces with large ethnic minority communities the existence of targets will mean not only a continuing failure but that the scale of failure must increase as the proportions to be recruited will increase year-on-year as a result of recruiting generally being reduced. It is difficult to see how this circle can be squared other than by some form of additional funding specifically to support recruiting. The money committed by the Home Secretary for an additional 5000 officers does not seem to be the answer as its real effect is questionable and the promise has been rightly described as a trick with 'smoke and mirrors'.

It is inevitable that the black and Asian communities will use this very visible measure to gauge the seriousness of the police intention. No matter what improvements are made elsewhere in issues such as the use of stop and search powers, improved effectiveness in dealing with racist crimes and incidents, it is likely that the views of the ethnic minority communities will be heavily influenced by progress in the area. It is important that the government realises that the visibility created by targets and monitoring also applies to them and that the debate will encompass their willingness to fund the changes that they have demanded.

Conclusion

The persistence of the Lawrence family and the courage of Jack Straw led to the setting up of the Macpherson Inquiry. Its conclusions and recommendations gave a clear direction and focus to all public agencies, but especially the police, on what must be done in order to change the underlying and undermining attitudes, processes and procedures which sustain racism and create and sustain inequality in England today. The problem is now clearly defined, the beginnings of a solution are clearly described, the creation of targets means that success and failure will be visible and that a continuing and informed debate on how best to progress the

issues is now possible. In this light it is clear that Macpherson can succeed where Scarman failed. The police service and other agencies must now show that they have both the commitment and the imagination needed to translate this into a more equal future. For its part the government must deal with the issue as one which is complex and which cannot be resolved by soundbite policies. It, too, must be willing to 'walk the talk' by providing the support and resources necessary for success.

References

Macpherson, Sir W. (1999). *The Stephen Lawrence Inquiry*. London: Home Office.

Scarman, Lord J. (1981). *The Brixton Disorders, 10–12 April, 1981*. London: HMSO.

Chapter 11

An Intelligent Use of Intelligence: Developing Locally Responsive Information Systems in the Post-Macpherson Era
Robin Fletcher

Introduction

In the aftermath of the death of Stephen Lawrence and the subsequent public inquiry, (Macpherson, 1999), a number of criticisms have been directed at the Metropolitan Police Service, (MPS), concerning the adequacy of the criminal investigation and allegations of corrupt practice and institutional racism. Whilst it is right and proper to focus on these issues, hidden in the report's recommendations was one all too familiar criticism. It concerned the inability of the police to collect and analyse information that appeared to have been available to the community and other agencies, (recommendations 15,16,17), prior to this tragic incident. It is a criticism with which the police have been trying to come to terms for a number of years.

Information exchange is not a new concept, having been raised in 1981 by Lord Scarman; Home Office memos 54/1982 and 2/1985; S105 PACE, 1984; the Morgan Report in 1991; S96 Police Act, 1996; and more recently *Winning the Race*, 1998; the Macpherson Report; and finally the Crime and Disorder Act. It has also been a major driving force in the adoption of community orientated policing styles, like Neighbourhood Policing, Sector Policing, Problem Orientated Policing, Community Orientated Policing, etc. and the move toward social crime prevention programmes, as the police sought ways to re-establish community ties which would enable them to deliver the type of service demanded by a more demanding citizenry. The traditions of policing have always assumed the support of the public and indeed boast that it is only with their consent that the police can achieve their objectives. Objectives, hitherto determined by central policies, often failed to recognise the full diversity of communities that demand a service capable of solving problems, rather than merely reacting to incidents.

The post modern era

We are entering a 'post-modern era' of societal fragmentation, (Fletcher, 1999), which is challenging centralised philosophies that tend to imply a commonality of need. There is also a demand for a more positive judicial response that recognises the cultural diversity of individuals and groups and which is capable of delivering local solutions to local problems. Society in the latter half of the 20th century has undergone a number of major changes, which need to be recognised and understood if societal control, whether it be formal or informal, is to be re-established.

Changes in employment status, (Harvey, 1989), increased leisure facilities and expectations as to how personal lives are lived have created a more flexible workforce. In turn, policing has to be more flexible.

The increased mobility of peoples, both nationally and internationally, has also challenged many local cultural practices as communities absorb the differing standards, morals and values of new populations. These groups rightly demand equitable status and recognition of their individuality, (Stanley, 1995). These factors render notions of state standardisation in provision outmoded. We are now witnessing challenges to the 'meta narratives', (Harvey, 1989; Lyotard, 1984), of the modern era which are no longer seen as being able to deliver an acceptable service to the local communities.

For many, the arrival of a New Labour government after 18 years of conservative radicalism, was the first step toward re-establishing welfarism as a central theme of urban regeneration. Nothing less than a return to 'welfare statism, Keynesian economic management, and control over wage relations', (Harvey, 1992: p 135), would satisfy traditional supporters. The fact that such measures failed to materialise is considered by some as a betrayal of the roots of the British tradition of socialism. But worse was to follow, for not only did 'New Labour' not support re-centralisation and re-nationalisation they actively promoted ideas of de-centralisation and free enterprise, (HMSO, 1999: p 38). Concepts that have been demonstrated by the devolution of power to Scotland and Wales, the lobby for regional assemblies across England, the creation of a Mayor of London and increasing the involvement of business partners in such 'Holy Grails' as transport, the National Health Service and even education. All these developments have provided templates in which diversity flourishes.

Human rights

Since November, 1998, the Human Rights Act has been incorporated into UK law and is a guarantee of citizen's rights. It contains 59 Articles setting out principles which place human rights at the centre of policy and practical decision making. The convention provides rights to individuals against interference of the state and public authorities that must be a consideration when developing processes that collect information about individuals. It is a principle of this legislation that the action taken must be the least intrusive or damaging to the individuals rights.

As a result of this Act, all future policy making decisions which affect the community, and the individuals who reside therein, must be tested against the various Articles and Principles to ensure that the rights of individuals are not abused by excessive interference of the state.

Policing diversity

The tradition of 'policing by consent' is perhaps a rather outdated concept and should now be reconsidered as one that has been achieved through a public complacency towards the policing institution. A complacency which has now been shattered, not least by the Macpherson Inquiry. A public mood now exists that is challenging the ability of state agencies to reduce crime, create a safer environment and deal with issues that matter to the micro communities as opposed to the meta concept of the nation state.

In 1998, the Metropolitan Police published their strategy document *The London Beat*. In this document they acknowledge policing diversity as an issue that required additional effort and understanding from their officers, if the citizens of London are to rebuild their wavering trust of the police. This is a poignant statement in the aftermath of the Lawrence investigation. To improve relationships between the police and the public there needed to be a dialogue which would enable information to be exchanged and police action to result from public consultation, as opposed to imposition by the police

organisation. During the Macpherson Inquiry, Michael Mansfield, The Queen's Counsel representing the Lawrence family, included the following in his recommendations to the Inquiry:

> There has to be a compendious and effective local intelligence gathering operation in existence that can be accessed by local officers at anytime, day or night, especially when those officers may be unfamiliar with the locality.
>
> (Macpherson, 1999)

Recommendations 15, 16 and 17 in the Macpherson Report have taken these comments further and clearly established the need to develop a multi agency process that pulls together all relevant information and make it accessible.

If we accept that information sharing is a vital element of community safety and recognise that previous efforts have failed, it is imperative a system is developed that can deliver the 'right information to the right people at the right time', an adaptation of the MPS principle 'the right people, doing the right thing, the right way'. The introduction of the Crime and Disorder Act heralds a new approach to community safety issues, making crime reduction a compulsory element of all local strategies by insisting due regard for crime and disorder be considered when dealing with all matters, (Home Office, 1998). The requirement for local crime audits, partnership co-operation and community consultation confirms the need to exchange information, which, in turn, should inform action plans.

The Crime and Disorder Act has identified the police as the most experienced of the partners in collecting and analysing crime and crime data. It would seem a reasonable first step to see how the police define the meaning of 'intelligence' and 'information' and then review the mechanisms that are in place to collect and collate data and then identify models that can progress the exchange of information.

Communication Breakdown

From my own research I have found that the 'inter' agency activity, which should have been generated by various government directives, often failed to materialise because of a lack of understanding as to the various partners' expectations. One reason for this is language conflict, as the various agencies demonstrate basic misunderstanding of phrases used to promote the ideas of partnership. 'Negotiation', 'consultation', 'two way flow', 'information exchange' and 'intelligence led', mean different things to different people and to different agencies.

Within the intelligence gathering process there are three words that can be a source of particular conflict:

- **Community:** Although this term is open to debate, most agencies would consider 'community' to be geographically or ethnically based. At the very least there would be some degree of unity, which would enable a response to a recognised problem. When dealing with serious disorder, the police would redefine 'community' to include football fans, extremist political or highly vocal minority groups and is directly linked to their understanding of the phrase 'disorder', and those who participate in such activity.

- **Intelligence:** For the police it is the analysis of internally generated information gleaned from limited community sources, mostly consisting of historical data focused on 'tactical' interventions. For others it is the analysis of information supplied directly by the community about issues that do not necessarily involve crime or criminal activity and is responsible for the creation of 'strategic' interventions.

- **Disorder:** The Crime and Disorder Act has introduced a new dimension to this word. Previously, disorder had a juridical definition, related to public displays of violence that required a robust police response. The new Act has extended this meaning to include any anti social behaviour, however minor, that affects the quality of life within a community and has a closer association to philosophies of actuarial justice.

Information

There are fundamental differences in the way information and intelligence are used by the various organisations and agencies who influence crime and anti social behaviour within our communities. Most organisations collect information, which is analysed for strategic purposes, to set objectives, assess value for money and to determine resource allocations for the future. Such information would not be

considered by the users as 'intelligence', which has a more sinister meaning of covert intrusion into personal space. The police are almost exclusive in collecting information for 'intelligence' purposes, because their main function, (see the White Paper preceding the Police and Magistrates Courts Act 1994), is to target individuals involved in criminal activity.

In response to the Macpherson Report, the Metropolitan Police created a Racial and Violent Crime Unit and a manual of instruction to assist officers in the investigation of race/hate crime. It includes a section on 'Intelligence Approaches' as a guideline to the capture of information from a variety of sources which can be converted into intelligence, defined as 'the organisation of verifiable information, known in advance and based on assumptions drawn from various sources, which can initiate a course of action', (MPS, 1999: p 27). Using this as a starting point we can say that intelligence is the rearrangement of specified passive information into something more active, which usually means a plan to arrest an individual(s), or the disruption of illegal activity. This process is referred to as the gathering of 'tactical intelligence'.

There is, however, a call for another type of intelligence, 'community intelligence', which differs in two ways to that described above. Firstly, it is the collection of more generalised non-crime data, which helps to build a picture of community tensions and secondly, in how that information is used. The broader process of 'Community Intelligence', is a product of similar information analysis but with a focus on the community, as opposed to the individual and concerns such activity as racism or anti-social behaviour. It looks toward a problem solving activity and is based on information learnt *'about'* the community from internally generated (police) sources.

To add to the confusion there is now demand for a third product we shall call 'Community Information'. It is something most likely to be used by 'non police' agencies, as it is a passive process of planning out crime and anti social behaviour by using information collected 'from' the community. When added to other collected data it will assist in creating 'Strategic Intelligence', which is a new phenomena and one that will gain more prominence with the arrival of the Crime and Disorder Act as the partners seek total intervention and holistic resolutions.

Strategic Intelligence

The need to develop all encompassing 'Strategic Intelligence', through information sharing, will gain added impetus with the introduction of 'Freedom of Information' legislation, which will require organisations to declare information they hold. Organisations have been reluctant to indulge in frank information exchanges, preferring to work to their own agendas and thereby jeopardise the potential to provide holistic solutions to community problems. It will not be difficult to understand the anger of communities if they become aware of any agency that fails to make the environment safer by not sharing relevant information. The Crime and Disorder Act has already taken the first step toward sharing information in a wider domain through its audit process.

Such is the importance of the information exchange concept, that Chapter 5 of the Home Office Guidelines, (1998), is dedicated to this one topic stating 'Confident and effective information exchange is the key to multi-agency working…', (para 5.1), and that 'One of the first tasks that the partners will face is putting in place a mechanism for ensuring effective information sharing', (para. 5.3). Not content with merely stating the need to pass on information, the government has even prescribed the groups with whom this interaction must take place in the Crime and Disorder Strategies (Prescribed Descriptions) Order, 1998.

Having made a case for exchanging information the government then loses sight as to how this can be 'practically' achieved. The failure to identify a single lead agency, (Morgan Report, 1991), prevents the gathering and analysis of community information to one point. As a result, there is a danger partners will develop their 'intelligence and information' systems in isolation, to an internal agenda rather than the need to achieve a common goal. Furthermore, performance criteria, which will in turn influence success and final outcomes, may also reflect insular objectives. The measurement of success, or failure, often relies upon the type of data available, irrespective of its importance to the final outcome, and all too often organisations undertake activity simply because they can measure it, (see chapter by Hallam in this volume). Having failed to give the lead to one agency the government mirror many of the mistakes made by Home Office memoranda 54/1982 and 2/1985, which failed to create the necessary conduits for the 'two way flow of information' suggested by Lord Scarman in 1981.

Despite the legal provisions of the Crime and Disorder Act, it does not override any existing legal restrictions, (Data Protection Act, 1984 and 1998; European Data Protection Directive 95/46/EC; and Common Law duty of confidence). Although the Act allows for the 'passing on' of information, it requires the data to be sanitised in such a way so as not to identify individuals. A seemingly perverse process, that requires answers to problems, which are often focused around individuals, to be tackled so long as they are not identified.

The Act also acknowledges some partners, (para 5.6), have no experience exchanging information and previously had no power to do so. Section 115 of the Act changes this position. Agencies are now encouraged to share their knowledge, but are told '[although] organisations have a power to disclose; it does not impose a duty to disclose'. Having placed emphasis on the exchange of information as a key to improving community safety and the quality of life, we now discover an opt out clause which reduces the impact of this important function. In reviewing 32 Crime and Disorder Act audits almost none contained any data from the NHS, even when the emerging strategy called for such information. Even if these problems can be overcome, as they surely must, the next problem to be addressed is how this exchange will take place.

Intelligence Gathering

Of all the agencies involved in reducing crime, the police are unique in being the only organisation to collect, as a matter of course, crime data through a dedicated intelligence system. Other agencies undoubtedly collect large quantities of information, but it is not stored in a manner that allows for useful crime analysis, hardly surprising as their role has never been seen as an agency of crime or social control. Police expertise in crime analysis is elucidated by the Home Office observation that 'The police obviously have a crucial part to play here, given their long experience in analysing crime data', (Home Office, 1998: p 4), although the findings of Greenaway, (1998), are not so conclusive.

Police 'crime intelligence systems' are a relatively new phenomena, (Greenaway, 1998). Having previously been the province of specialist units, it was not until the mid 1980s that the use of intelligence to direct street level policing became a realistic proposition. In 1994 the Metropolitan Police Service created a computerised local CRIMinal INTelligence system, (CRIMINT), which aimed to bring to 'front line' policing the experience and professionalism of the elite squads.

Its function was identified by the Commissioner, Sir Paul Condon, when he said '…we have had to quite rightly develop new professionalism's to do with surveillance, intelligence and informants, things that will give us a better chance of *catching criminals in the act*' (their emphasis), (MPS, 1994). The object of this process was to create policing styles that were more efficient, intelligence led and provided value for money, (Grieve, 1996), by concentrating resources on the few individuals who were disproportionately engaged in criminal activity. From a victim perspective this is not an ideal theory of intelligence, as it relies upon patterns of criminality, rather than victimisation, in order to develop potential solutions.

Data collection models

Following the Brixton riots, in 1981, a number of innovative practices were developed in an effort to bypass first level gate-keepers who were thought to have hampered the information flow. Community Liaison Officers (CLOs) were created to establish direct contact with the community, community leaders and various influential organisations, although their exact function was unclear, (Phillips and Cochrane, 1988). The Metropolitan Police had created a Community Affairs Branch in 1968. Creating a specialist community department had both positive and negative aspects. On the one hand closer ties were made with minority groups on an individual basis. On the other it allowed non-community officers to abrogate this responsibility, (Dixon and Stanko, 1993). Other attempts at gathering community information through consultative groups like Neighbourhood Watch and Police/Community Consultation Groups (PCCG)

were also doomed to fail and are discussed below.

The police intelligence process takes place within a Divisional Intelligence Unit (DIU) and works on a 'sponge' principle, (see Figure 1), soaking up all information provided by the 'street' officers who act as gatekeepers, only passing into the system that information they believe to be relevant. Data collected in this fashion is unfocused and determined by the knowledge and understanding of community problems, and is directly related to the adopted policing style. (For a discussion of the merits of community policing see Lea and Young, 1993; Dixon and Stanko, 1993.)

During any given period the DIU will receive vast amounts of relevant and irrelevant data, which needs to be processed, evaluated, analysed and disseminated, (Greenaway, 1998), and turned into a Collection Plan for action, being a tactical plan created to secure the arrest of a target criminal. As this process relies upon an influx of non structured information, analysis in this model tends to be historical and reactive.

A second, more focused process of intelligence gathering, adopted by specialist operation police units, overcomes the problems described above. These units concentrate on specific problems and only seek out information, (see Figure 1) which is specific and relevant. This process tends to apply to the 'higher grade' intelligence cells, which target organised criminal activity.

Both processes are concerned with developing 'tactical intelligence', which is focused on incident solving, through police action. Neither model fulfils the criteria of the Crime and Disorder Act, which calls for the creation of mechanisms to assist in the development of long term strategic interventions through sharing community information.

Figure 1 – Basic intelligence models

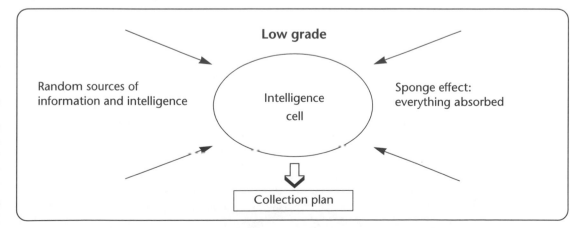

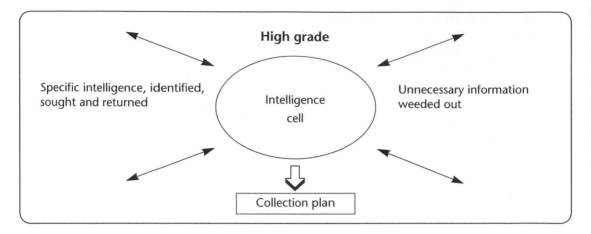

Assuming relevant agencies can be persuaded to fully exchange their information, further problems arise due to the lack of a single agency leader who will:

- Undertake the necessary strategic and tactical analysis on behalf of all the participating agencies.

- Identify the potential solutions and decide which is the most appropriate.

- Monitor and evaluate accepted strategies.

- Be in a position to task the various agencies with the necessary pro-activity.

And how will communities, in particular the 'hard to hear' groups, be fully consulted? An activity which is accused of being '...little more than routine', (HMIC, 1998/99).

Information exchange models

Using the experience of the last 25 years, four models of information exchange are identified, which reflect the changes in developing social, as well as situational, crime prevention programmes. The changing prominence of the police as the key agency for crime prevention becomes obvious as they are joined by other organisations now engaged in addressing broader community safety issues.

The first example to consider is the 'Police Model', which follows the traditional role of being 'incident driven' and recognises the police as the primary agency for crime prevention. The second is a 'multi agency' model, which reflects the growing realisation that the police cannot tackle community problems alone. The third is a community based model and shows the

movement away from the 'multi agency' toward an 'inter agency' programme of problem solving, and the last, an 'Integrated model' which reflects the hopes of the Crime and Disorder Act.

The police model

The first attempt at reintroducing information flows came in the early 1980s, driven by the Scarman Inquiry, (1981), which saw the need for a 'two way' exchange of information between the police and the policed. It was assumed this could be achieved through community policing, and by the more mechanical processes of enforced consultation with community leaders. The Police and Criminal Evidence Act 1984, requiring the police to consult influential members of the community, (Police and Community Consultation Groups or PCCGs), created a statutory duty. This was at a time when 'new victims' of visible and invisible minority groups were being recognised, and the police were being challenged to respond positively to their needs.

Acknowledging their earlier failings, the Police opened up other conduits with the community to encourage a two-way flow of information. Neighbourhood Watch was an attempt by the police to engage in social engineering and positive non-confrontational interaction with ordinary members of the community. But the flow of information from these schemes has failed to materialise in any useful way. The police have since discovered NHW demands a continual flow of information outward and this relationship has become a means of testing police accountability. Scarman's PCCGs are similarly failing to produce meaningful information to such an extent that the Crime and Disorder Act comments, 'police consultative groups…can attract a rather narrow range of people, who often pursue sectional interests', (HMSO, 1998; 3.51), calling into question the worth of PCCGs.

Figure 2 is a representation of the 'Police Model' and shows how the police dominated the information exchange process in the early 1980s. It reflects the police assumption that 'incident focus' is their first priority and that community involvement is a minimal intrusion. This is an accountability model, as the variously constituted groups called for more and more information of how the police conduct their business. Although police managers maintained their autonomous position in dictating tactics it was, and still is, conducted with one eye on the likely repercussions of the consultative groups.

Figure 2 – The police model: one way exchange

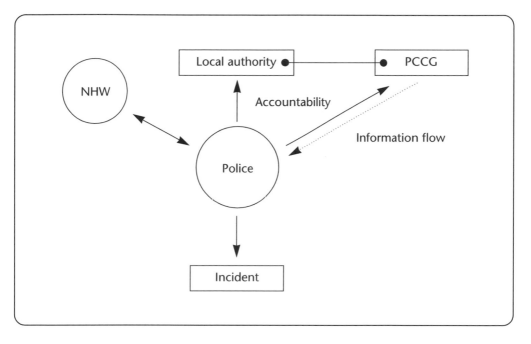

The multi-agency model

With the circulation of Home Office memorandum 4/84 came recognition that many influential factors in crime causation and social control went beyond the remit of the police, (Koch, 1998). It called for closer co-operation between those governmental departments and other agencies that could impact the more obvious causation factors of unemployment, bad housing and low educational standards. At a time when many 'new' crimes were being 'discovered', like domestic violence, race and homophobic discrimination, it was singularly the most important directive to be issued by the government, causing a fundamental shift from

the focus on property protection, to one that sought to improve 'community safety' and personal protection, (Graham, 1990; Graham and Bennett, 1995).

With the concept of social crime prevention taking hold, a model developed that saw the police, local authorities and identified voluntary agencies listening to the needs of the community, or to sections of the community, and reacting in any way their organisation could manage. Conflict was created between the various groups and agencies who saw solutions based within their own ideology. Despite new skills being developed, which enabled some organisations to take an holistic view of the various community problems, any activity remained 'incident' focused.

Figure 3 – The multi-agency model

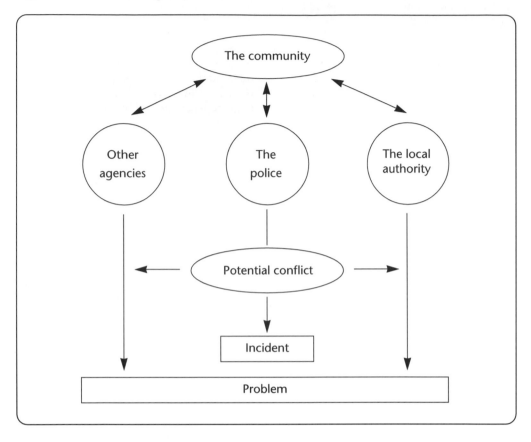

The inter-agency model

During the mid 1980s the government extended its commitment to social crime prevention by introducing the Five Towns Initiative and the Safer Cities programme. The uniqueness of these initiatives lay in the concerted efforts of delivering crime prevention/reduction activity in a focused manner, reflecting the needs of the local community. More importantly, this was to be achieved through an outside agent acting as a neutral co-ordinator, de-politicising local authority influence and bringing fresh ideas to community problems.

The benefit of having a 'neutral' co-ordinator supported by government finance, was its ability to enter the parochial territory of each partner and obtain data that could be used to build a profile of activity that went beyond the normal analysis of crime, often overcoming internal organisational politics and achieving what parent organisations could not. They also had different views of success. Being able to use a broad analytical base of information to devise strategy, meant the success of initiatives was not necessarily measured through input or output, but by outcomes, a challenge to the quantitative measures of the police and other partners.

Figure 4 – The inter-agency model

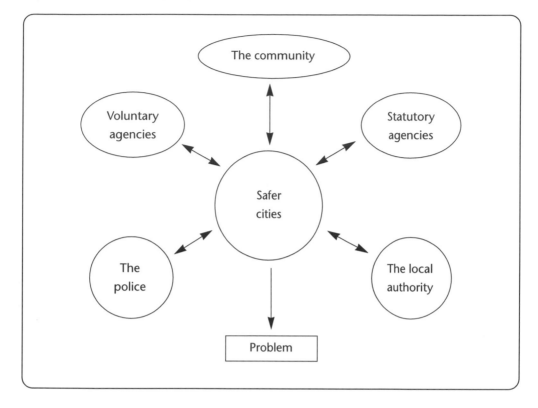

Integrated agency model

In time, multi-agency partnerships slowly gave up their fixed boundaries of expertise and came toward each other in an attempt to develop integrated solutions, overcoming political and ideological prejudices and focusing on the reason for their existence, to serve the community. This philosophy was expanded in *Modernising Government*, (HMSO, 1999), a paper which calls for closer co-operation of all agencies to deliver policy which is 'more joined up and strategic' in order to 'involve and meet the needs of all different groups in society'. This is a clear directive that crime reduction policies must now be driven by problems and solutions, not by organisation structures and hidden performance targets.

This final model idealises the concepts of the Crime and Disorder Act, which requires an absolute sharing of knowledge in both information as well as practical expertise. It suggests this can be achieved by creating an independent body to collect and analyse information from a variety of sources, without succumbing to organisational priorities. Such a body will have to acknowledge problems are complex issues, to be solved though activity, and which will tackle causes and not just symptoms.

The development of Child Protection teams, and more latterly Paedophile Risk Assessment Panels, have pulled together a variety of organisations with the intention that they pool information, resources and solutions. These are practical examples of this model which developed before the Crime and Disorder Act and reflect a 'new' socio/criminological issue, the management of potential offenders and social deviants, as practitioners move from a juridical to an actuarial philosophy of social control.

Figure 5 – The integrated agency model

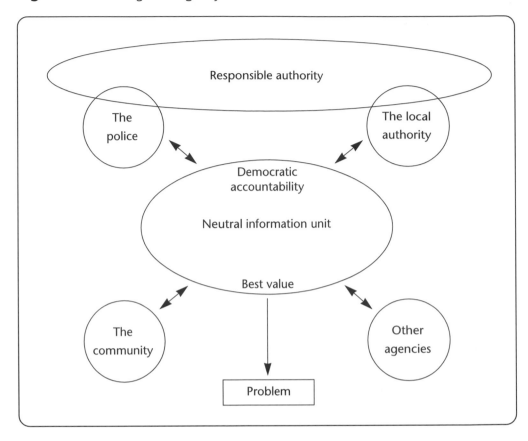

Overcoming Mistrust

It is clear that the last three decades have seen great inroads being made by many agencies to address the needs of local communities. It becomes imperative that successful solutions are contextualised by all parties who have an understanding of what can be achieved practically. Success must be defined locally in a number of qualitative ways, and not just through statistical crime data. The use of centralised statistical measures as a means of establishing success will therefore have to be reviewed. The successful progression of local autonomy will depend upon the ability of those with power to continue the decentralisation process, enabling the delivery of solutions appropriate to local needs.

What became clear from the Macpherson Inquiry is that sections of the community continue to mistrust the police, and the whole judicial process, because it remains largely unresponsive to cultural differences. This air of mistrust was compounded by perceived inaction of the police against neo-nazi racists who were known to many sections of the community and to some organisations. The problem lay in organisations each having part of the overall picture, but not having the confidence in others to share what information they had. It may also have assumed that because one agency knew what was happening, all other agencies must be in a similar position. What is required is a process that enables all parties to exchange information, air their views and thereby understand the rationale behind action, or inaction, as the case may be.

Analysis Options

To fulfil the implications of the Crime and Disorder Act, and the needs of the community, requires a completely new process of information exchange. It must be capable of identifying problems that are of most concern to the community, solutions that are acceptable to the community and the agencies and organisations that are capable of achieving these functions. To meet these needs three options are considered which have the capability of delivering community intelligence at a strategic level.

Option 1

Create a permanent, neutral intelligence unit staffed by members of key agencies who are skilled in the collection and analysis of raw data collected from existing sources, supplemented through public surveys and focus groups. This unit should be located at a site accessible to all and will require a 'pooling' of resources.

Its function will be to:

- Collect information from all organisations and the community.

- Identify future trends through the use of 'predictors'.

- Raise those issues which need to be tackled through strategic intervention.

- Identify lead agencies to co-ordinate activity through fully researched Action Plans.

- Evaluate and monitor all crime prevention/reduction activity, with a view to ensuring that objectives are being achieved and that it is 'value for money'.

Predictors, in this context, are warning signals raised by any agency, which has identified a potential problem, as opposed to a warning 'flag' that identifies a current problem. The more predictors identified by a variety of agencies, the higher the level of concern.

Option 2

Create a 'multi-agency tasking unit' whose function will be to focus activity on identified 'hot spots'. It will be a relatively small team staffed by key agencies, supplemented whenever necessary by personnel on secondment from other organisations/agencies, who have identified specialist skills.

This team will concentrate on one issue at a time, which could be offender, victim, crime type or geographically focused. It will collate information pertinent to the identified problem and through analysis raise a number of possible solutions. This unit will then be responsible for either implementing a solution until the problem is solved or identifying a multi-agency tasking team who will be responsible for implementing an identified solution. Having solved the immediate problem this unit will then move onto the next 'hot spot'.

Whichever method is preferred there will be an expectation of an exit strategy that contains a monitoring and evaluation process, which will be reported back to the Responsible Authority Information Group.

Option 3

Create a geographically based multi agency team (i.e. Estate Action Team, Neighbourhood Team, Sector Team) which may either focus on multiple issues pertinent to the designated area or concentrate on one issue, (as Option 2).

Because this model is geographically based it is likely to revolve around one agency which has already established a rapport with the community. This agency should take the lead in co-ordinating activity by bringing together those partners necessary to tackle a specific problem.

There is a danger with this model that problems and solutions are identified from a biased perspective, a result of which may be that not all agencies who could positively impact the problem become involved. Although solutions are more likely to be localised and fit the needs of the immediate community, the broader picture may show high levels of displacement beyond the geographical area.

Conclusion

The information exchange process is a multi layered activity, which requires the participation of all partners in a variety of ways. For the police this is best achieved by a locally based community policing style, as it enables officers of all ranks to interact with the community at several levels, a key element of the Crime and Disorder Act. The right policing style is the first, and probably most important, of the communication 'mechanisms' and must be built upon with other structures, which encompass all of the active partners.

Undoubtedly cost will be a major issue in establishing an information exchange process and should be viewed in the long term. One element of crime reduction, all too frequently missing from the equation, is a lack of financial evaluation by any of the affected agencies. The use of the 'Integrated Agency Model' will enable full cost benefit analysis to be undertaken and how far localised project savings can be reinvested in other key strategic areas. As we move into a 'Best Value' regime, (Home Office, 1999), it is essential partners pool their knowledge and resources to achieve meaningful outcomes. The provision for this radical approach is made in the Governments Local Authority Bill (s14) and also discussed in the Department of the Environments Transport and the Regions paper, (1998: paras 7.14 and 7.24), which discusses the sharing of IT and *'pooled service delivery'* and could become a fact of life, if it is considered expedient for the improvement of local services.

In a post modern world it is certain that information exchange, storage and analysis will become dependent upon computerised systems. There will be a need to ensure agencies become compatible so that the exchange can be achieved electronically. The government has expressed its intentions with the publication of its document *Modernising Government*, (Home Office, 1999), identifying the need for 'joined up thinking', and compatible technology.

When looking at the current method of exchanging information and drawing again on the Home Office Guidelines, (1998), some key questions to ask are:

- Who is able to monitor the views of the community throughout the delivery of the three year strategy? (para 1.32)

- How will performance be monitored against 'local (and national) benchmarks?' (para 3.26)

- Who is reviewing all of the 'partners' policy strategies to ensure they 'complement each other…a gradual process that should be achievable over the course of the next year or two?' (para 1.27)

- Is a continuing 'policy analysis' taking place over the next three years? (para 3.11)

- Do the overall strategies support the 'virtuous circle' concept of investment/re-investment? (see Audit Commission, 1998: p 76)

- Do all policies comply with the basic fundamentals of the Human Rights Act by ensuring proportionality of action?

- Do all crime prevention strategies support the rights of the individual?

One final thought to consider when establishing an information exchange process, is the comment made in the Home Office Guidelines, which compares the 'Umbrella Strategy' and 'Safety Net Strategy', (para 3.56), as processes for pulling together the future plans and objectives of partner agencies and organisations. There is a clear anticipation that partnership activity must move beyond rhetoric and deliver a tangible product, which overcomes the 'inefficiencies of fragmentation'. Using these comments as a steer, option 1 is the preferred model, as it will encourage full partnership integration.

For the police, such a move may be seen as an attack on their independence, with crime reduction activity being taken away from them and placed in the hands of other strategic thinkers, who may see solutions based in non policing tactics. As such, it becomes a further threat to those who view decentralisation as undermining their power base rather than an embracing of diverse cultures, practices and standards.

Option 1 enables independent analysts to view behaviour that is not yet criminal, and therefore not recorded by police, and seek positive intervention before a serious crime occurs. All of which moves policing further toward an 'actuarial justice' model of people management, recognising the need to classify groups according to their 'levels of dangerousness', (Feeley and Simon, 1994: p 173). Had such systems been in place in 1993, it is possible that information concerning those responsible for the death of Stephen Lawrence would have been available at the right time, in the right place, for the right people to take appropriate action, in sufficient time to prevent an unnecessary waste of a young life.

References

Audit Commission (1998). *Safety in Numbers*. London: HMSO.

DETR (1998). *Modern Local Government in Touch with the People*. London: HMSO.

Dixon, B., and Stanko, B. (1993). *Sector Policing and Public Accountability*. Islington: Islington's Police and Crime Prevention Unit.

Feeley, M., and Simon, J. (1994). Actuarial Justice: the Emerging New Criminal Law. In Nelken, D. *The Futures of Criminology*. Sage: London.

Fletcher, R. (1999). *Understanding Communities; Creating Strategies Through Mechanisms and Information Sharing*. Middlesex University (PhD thesis) forthcoming.

Graham, J. (1990). *Crime Prevention Strategies in Europe and North America*. Helsinki Institute for Crime Prevention and Control, Finland, HEUNI No. 18. United Nations.

Graham, J., and Bennett, T. (1995). *Crime Prevention Strategies in Europe and North America*. Helsinki Institute for Crime Prevention and Control, Finland, HEUNI No. 28. United Nations.

Greenaway, K. (1998). The Power of Information. *Policing Today*, 4(3).

Grieve, J. (1996). *Systems for Intelligence and Detection.* Metropolitan Police internal document.

Harvey, D. (1989). *Flexibility: Threat or Opportunity?* Socialist Review.

Harvey, D. (1992). Social Justice, Postmodernism and the City. *International Journal of Urban and Regional Research*, 16: pp 588–601.

HMIC (1997). *Winning the Race Policing; Plural Communities.* London: HMSO.

HMIC (1999). *Winning the Race Policing Plural Communities; Revisited.* London: HMSO.

HMSO (1998). *Guidelines on Statutory Crime and Disorder Partnerships.* London: HMSO.

HMSO (1999). *Modernising Government.* London: The Stationary Office.

Jessop, B. (1993). Towards a Schumpeterian Welfare State? Preliminary Remarks on Post-Fordist Political Economy. *Studies in Political Economy*, 40: pp 7–39.

Koch, B.C.M. (1998). *The Politics of Crime Prevention.* Aldershot: Ashgate Publishing Commissioners Library.

Lea, J., and Young, J. (1993). *What is to be Done about Law and Order?* Pluto Press.

Lyotard, J. (1984). *The Postmodern Condition: A Report on Knowledge.* Minneapolis: University of Minnesota Press.

Macpherson, Sir W. (1999). *The Stephen Lawrence Inquiry.* London: HMSO.

Metropolitan Police Service (1994). *Commissioner's Annual Report.* London: Metropolitan Police Service.

Metropolitan Police Service (1998). *The London Beat.* London: Metropolitan Police Service.

Metropolitan Police Service (1999). *Action Guide to Race/hate Crime.* Metropolitan Police, unpublished.

Morgan, J. (1991). *Safer Communities; The Local Delivery of Crime Prevention Through the Partnership Approach.* London: HMSO.

Phillips, S., and Cochrane, (1988). *The Role and Function of Police Community Liaison Officers*, Research and Planning Unit paper 51. Home Office.

Stanley, C. (1995). Teenage Kicks: Urban Narratives of Dissent not Deviance. *Crime Law and Social Change*, 23: pp 91–119.

Scarman, Lord J. (1981). *The Brixton Disorders, 10–12 April, 1981; Report of an Inquiry by the Rt. Hon. The Lord Scarman OBE.* HMSO.

Chapter 12
Principled Policing: Searching For Integrity

John Alderson

Introduction

Societies in which principled policing operates, it is contended, will be less likely to suffer from policing injustices than those where policing is driven by political opportunism, professional caprice, or just bad law. There has to be a robust moral objectivity in the way in which policing operates if it is to avoid the worst misuses and abuses of power. To seek rationalisation of the police mission, and to give it coherence and form in both theory and practice, has always presented a personal challenge. When leading and managing a major police organisation by what is commonly called the 'seat of the pants', a good deal of luck or over-weaning power is required to avoid the worst results of such professional sin. On the other hand consistency demands that command of policing and formation of policies be based on some coherent formula or framework. Such a formula provides not only consistency and objectivity, but is also available to others for their understanding of the rationale of behaviour behind policy making. My own tried and tested formula was as follows:

1. **Philosophy:** through cogitation and reasoning to acquire myself an understanding of the police idea.

2. **Ideas:** the product of 1 above.

3. **Policies:** through the combination of 1 and 2 above, and through consultation, to fashion the directives, both operational and administrative, for the functioning of the organisation.

4. **Performance:** through the use of power, and persuasion, to implement the product of 3 above.

The main thrust of this chapter will seek to follow this simple formula, beginning with a review of some relevant philosophical theories.

Philosophy and Policing

I write on the reasonable assumption that philosophers have something important to teach those who work in the wider world of practical affairs and people. However, one ought not to underestimate the risks taken when engaging in critical comment on philosophical theories.

Recourse to some philosophical justification of policing is essential in order to give a robust confidence to the command, and thereby to the function, of the organisation. Although it is easy to express this view, it is less easy to select and operate such principles in practice. The mysteries of philosophy sometimes resemble a moveable feast, during which philosophers appear to be in permanent dispute, but the high police command has to bring to bear the experience and knowledge of practical worldly police affairs which have their own unique legitimacy and strength.

I shall suggest that the high police should initially seek a philosophical basis for police work in order that their thinking and their actions may be rational. They will be aware, that as the coercive arm, they are part of government. They are therefore serving a political purpose, in which case political philosophies have direct relevance to their function. It goes without saying that in a liberal democracy whichever philosophy seems most apt, should be moral and just even at the expense of efficiency. The commander should of course seek efficiency, but not at any cost.

The commander is in search of a set of values of which he and all his officers should be aware, and what it is they are supposed to be protecting or defending. It is unlikely, though not impossible, that the values being sought are those already held by the commander, but in the main they are waiting to be discovered.

An extreme example of this would have been found in the work of the powerful political commissars under the communist system, whilst on the other hand, the police commander in a liberal democracy would be exposed to constant evaluation and criticism from any quarter.

In the first place those values which are exemplified by the political form of government and the social mores of the society which the police commander serves, leave little room for novelty or idiosyncrasy, but this is not to say that the police cannot seek to ameliorate harsh injustice under any system. In totalitarian systems it would be axiomatic to eschew the idea of freedom as a social value, even though there may be a certain amount of altruism. In a communist system the ownership of private property (for the police to protect) would not be regarded as high in value as state property. To steal from the state is to steal from the people. It is the noted experience in liberal democracies that theft of government property, whatever the law may say about it, is not regarded, as a general rule, so seriously as is theft of private property, e.g. 'It was only Government cash', said a Scottish villager when he heard that his local Laird, an accountant at New Scotland yard, had stolen £5m! (*Today*, 1995).

The French Declaration of the Rights of Man and the Citizen (25th August, 1789), provides at Article 2, 'the final end of every political institution is the preservation of the natural and imprescriptible rights of man. These rights are those of liberty, property, security and resistance to oppression'. At Article 17, the Declaration describes property as, 'an inviolable and sacred right...' On the other hand, the Constitution (Fundamental Law) of the Union of Soviet Socialist Republics, (1936), Chapter 10: Fundamental Rights and Duties of Citizens, makes no mention of ownership of private property; it does provide at Article 131, 'It shall be the duty of every citizen of the USSR to safeguard and fortify public, socialist property, as the sacred and inviolable foundation of the Soviet system'. Thus a high police commander in the Soviet system would have cause to assess the values which by his office he was obliged to protect, somewhat differently from his French counterpart.

But then what of conscience? It may be that the political system in question, or part of it, seems to be unjust or unfair, or morally deficient, in which case a high police commander with equally high personal moral ethical standards would have to lower those standards to remain and serve the police organisation, or fight against it from within, though there are obvious limits in confronting the political power behind the organisation, or to resign.

It is a matter of record how the police are able to adjust to serving amoral political institutions, and this in turn reflects police culture and its reflexes to authoritarian command. Such a case is meticulously researched and portrayed by Christopher Browning in his book *Ordinary Men*, (1992). This is a story of a battalion of German Order Police recruited in Hamburg from the ranks of regular police officers and various

tradesmen and skilled workers. In 1942 they were in Poland and under the high police command of Heinrich Himmler and his SS lieutenants. They were non-combatants whose task was to police territory over-run and captured by the German Wehrmacht. As Browning says in the title of his book they were, 'ordinary men' and unlikely to represent a high concentration of men of violent predisposition. Yet the high police command was able to motivate more than eighty per cent of these men to engage in mass shootings of Jewish children, women and old men. Young men were used as slave labour. As its first operation the battalion was ordered to round up 1,800 Jews in Jozefow, 'the women, children and elderly were to be shot on the spot'.

Reflecting on his part in the massacre, one policeman, formerly a metal worker from Bremerhaven said, 'I made the effort, and it was possible for me, to shoot only children. It so happened, that the mothers led the children by the hand. My neighbour then shot the mother and I shot the child that belonged to her, because I reasoned with myself that after all without its mother, the child could not live any longer. It was supposed to be, so to speak, soothing to my conscience to release the children unable to live without their mothers', (ibid.: p 73). This is rationalisation of human brutality in the extreme.

We must now consider those theories of government which may give a rational meaning to the policing function. On the face of it, the principle that policing would contribute to 'the greatest happiness of the greatest number' of the people, would seem to be very attractive. But let us see what relevance the political theory of utilitarianism might have for our study of policing.

Utilitarianism and Policing

I began to think about utilitarianism, following a conversation I once had with a respected lawyer who is a friend of mine and a clerk to a Magistrates' Court. He came upon me when I was reading a book and asked me what it was. I told him it was about capital punishment. He supported such punishment and asked whether I did. I told him that I opposed it because there was always the possibility of executing a person innocent of the crime. His reply was, 'Yes, but it doesn't happen often'! Something similar was allegedly said by a senior member of the English judiciary. He expressed the opinion that capital punishment reduced the number of enquiries into miscarriages of justice; which, if they are not checked could undermine public confidence (happiness) in the legal system!

In both those cases injustices to individuals were being justified, or at least tolerated, to make society at large feel better, or happier. Now, was that so morally right?

Since my earliest studies of law I have been intrigued by the case of R v. Dudley and Stephens, (14 QBD 273, 1884). This well known incident is often cited as a test case for the defence of *necessity* in criminal law. Dudley, Stephens, and someone else called Brooks, who all had families, along with a 17-year-old cabin boy, had been shipwrecked 1,600 miles from the Cape of Good Hope. Having gone eight days without food, they realised that their only hope of survival was for one of them to be killed and eaten by the others. It is said, although it takes some believing, that the hapless cabin boy offered himself for this purpose, and so was killed by Dudley and Stephens. They fed on the boy for eight days before being rescued and taken to Falmouth. Eventually, their case came up at the 1884 Devon and Cornwall Assizes and was then transferred for trial at the High Court before five judges.

During that trial Lord Coleridge, Chief Justice, quoting legal precedent, reminded the court that mere necessity was not in law defence. He said: 'if a person, being under necessity for want of victuals or clothes, and shall upon that account clandestinely steal another man's goods, it is felony, and a crime by the laws of England, punishable with death'. He went on, 'Though the law and morality are not the same, and many things are immoral which are not necessarily illegal, yet the absolute divorce of law from morality would be of fatal consequence: and such divorce would follow if the temptation to murder in this case were to be held by the law to be an absolute defence of it'.

Dudley and Stephens were sentenced to death, but this was then commuted by the Crown to imprisonment for six months.

These incidents raise the question of the morality of deeds done to individuals with a view to the general happiness. My friend the clerk to the magistrates, and the Law Lord at the High Court, and the sailors who survived, conveniently thought that it was all right in certain circumstances to sacrifice one person's life if thereby you were saving the lives of some other people. But I find that hard to accept not only in cases such as those to which I have referred, but as a general moral principle. This is a very live issue in contemporary philosophy, (Hudson, 1980).

Critics it seems, share the opinion that when a plain man consults his conscience, he will often find its deliverance at variance with those who are of the view that an act is right provided only that it will effect the greatest happiness of the greatest number. As the philosopher, Gertrude Anscome, pointed out, in certain conceivable circumstances utilitarianism could prescribe the execution of an innocent man, (in Hudson, 1983: p 384). It might be expedient that one man should die for the people. But, as she says, 'If someone really thinks…that it is open to question whether such an action as procuring the judicial execution of the innocent should be quite excluded from consideration—I do not want to argue with him; he shows a corrupt mind'.

The high police leader should be aware that the ethical theory of utilitarianism has its economic and political dimensions described as, 'the view of life presupposed in most modern and political and economic planning, when it is supposed that happiness is measured in economic terms'. But if police are not concerned with economic planning, what aspects of the doctrine are of their direct concern? The Oxford Dictionary of Philosophy records that 'the doctrine that applies utilitarianism to actions directly, so that an individual action is right if it increases happiness more than any alternative, is known as direct or act utilitarianism', (1994, p 388). In enforcing laws and restricting freedoms, it is not always immediately obvious that police activity is likely to increase anybody's happiness, though their protective role may, and often does reduce fear, and that is good; so in this sense it does increase happiness. Furthermore, in a society without some form of police, or with a form of police which is only concerned to serve and protect the freedoms of an elite or privileged hegemony, the control of crime would undoubtedly add to the general happiness, though not at any price.

It is in the indirect sense that police action may meet utilitarianism's demands because, 'Indirect versions apply in the first place to such things as institutions, systems of rules of conduct or human characters: these are best if they maximise happiness, and actions are judged only insofar as they are those ordained by the institutions, or systems, or rules, or those that would be performed by the person of optimal character', (Hudson, 1980). Police therefore will have to be of the highest standards if they are to fulfil this demand of indirect utilitarianism, but we still need to reconcile the doctrine with concepts of justice and morality, and this seems to be no easy task.

Police after all need to have regard for the common good, and may at times therefore be required to make the greatest number unhappy in order to serve or protect a very small number, e.g. ethnic minorities, and religious or political groups. In recent times the minority nationalist community in Northern Ireland perceived the police to favour, support, and to serve the political majority, even where that majority perpetrated political and social distributive injustices upon them. In this way the greatest number were happy, but a perceived denial of justice created such a high degree of unhappiness in the minority, that their violent reaction grew into a widespread terrorist campaign '…we may know of the general impact institutions, rules, and character have on the happiness of those affected by them'. Making the greatest number of people happy through their feeling safe and free from the fear of crime, seems on the face of it to offer a reasonable enough police objective. But this says nothing about morality, and does the morality of policing not have anything to say?

The founder of the school of the political philosophy of utilitarianism, Jeremy Bentham, (1748–1832), paid little heed to the work of Kant, (1748–1804), and in particular Kant's reputation as 'the philosophical defender par excellence of the rights of man and of his equality…', (in Hare, 1981).

Russell tells us that Bentham had a great contempt for the doctrine of the rights of man, (Russell, 1961). 'The rights of Man', he said, 'are plain nonsense; the imprescriptible rights of man, nonsense on stilts'. But of particular interest to the high police is that, 'Bentham's ideal, like that of Epicurus, was security not liberty'. I acknowledge that liberty is diminished when people feel afraid to exercise it, but to stress security to unnecessary extremes at the price of fundamental freedoms, plays in to the hands of would-be high police despots.

Such despots are quick to exploit fear in order to secure unlimited power. This seems to have characterised much of the rise of Hitler and his National Socialist Party in Germany in the 1930s.

The Nazi propaganda spoke of the Communist Party of the Weimer Republic as the 'Red terror'. Police raids were carried out on offices, and the Communist HQ in Berlin, on the 24th February, 1933. A purported discovery of plans for a communist revolution was calculated to strike apprehension in the minds of thinking people.

When the Reichstag building 'mysteriously' went up in flames on the night of 27th February, 1933, it only intensified public fear, and provided the pretext for government by decree, in order to assuage public desire for security. The day after the fire, on 28th February, Hitler promulgated a decree signed by the President 'for the protection of the People and the State'. The decree was described 'as a defensive measure against communist acts of violence', (Bullock, 1963). It began by suspending the guarantees of individual liberty under the Weimar constitution: 'Thus, restrictions on personal liberty, on the right of free expression of opinion, including freedom of the Press; on the right of assembly and association; violations of the privacy of postal, telegraph, telephonic communications; warrants for house searches; orders for confiscation as well as restrictions on property are permissible beyond the legal limits otherwise prescribed'.

In addition to the decree, very heavy penalties of life imprisonment and execution were provided for political crimes. This cameo of calculated political tyranny plays on fear, and then takes away liberty. This is not to suggest that utilitarianism intends such behaviour, but that the central place of human rights in modern politics may not be compatible with the doctrine. Protective security has still to grapple with the conundrum of maximising freedoms whilst at the same time controlling disorder, and this calls for great skill and determination.

If the modern high police leader needs to understand a more contemporary view of utilitarianism in relation to morality, he must seek out the more recent pronouncements on the subject. Writing in his book *Morality: An Introduction to Ethics*, Bernard Williams, (1972), after considering the theory, concludes devastatingly, '…if utilitarianism is true and some fairly plausible empirical propositions are also true, then it is better that people should not believe in utilitarianism. If, on the other hand, it is false, then it is certainly better that people should not believe in it.' So, either way, it is better that people should not believe in it. Sabine wrote of 'the grim egoism of utilitarian ethics, and of classical economics', (Sabine, 1971).

Considering the greatest happiness principle which prescribed that, 'the only rational guide both to private morals and public policy', was that of the greatest happiness of the greatest number, it is not difficult to agree with Sabine. But it is to John Rawls and his 'justice as Fairness' theory that I turn for more recent considerations of the subject.

In comparing and contrasting utilitarianism with the contract doctrine, Rawls says that, 'Utilitarianism may seem to be a more exalted ideal, but the other side of it is that it may authorise the lesser welfare and liberty of some for the sake of a greater happiness of others who may already be more fortunate', (Rawls, 1973).

We have already noticed the seeming moral weakness in the doctrine, and Rawls goes on to express his belief thus: '...however improbable the congruence of the right and the good in "Justice as Fairness" it is surely more probable than on the utilitarian view. The conditional balance of reasons favours the contract doctrine.' He maintains that classical utilitarianism fails to take seriously the distinction between persons and is thereby flawed in terms of his own theory.

The Theory of Protectionism

In his critique of 'Plato's Politics', Karl Popper unearths a theory which he calls 'Protectionism':

> *Aristotle tells us that Lycophron, (c 400BC), considered the law of the state as a 'covenant by which men assure one another of justice'. He tells us that Lycophron looked upon the state as an instrument for the protection of its citizens against acts of injustice (and for permitting them peaceful intercourse, especially exchange), demanding that the state be a 'co-operative association for the prevention of crime'.*
>
> **(Popper, 1989: pp 114–117)**

As we shall see this appears to adumbrate a theory of the state which was later to be described as a contract. The theory called 'protectionism' seems to offer much for the police leader.

Popper was of the opinion, (ibid.: pp 109–110), that in this quest for a theory of the state, we should not begin by asking 'what is the state, its nature and meaning?', or, 'how did it originate', and so on. He poses, then answers, his own rhetorical questions. 'What do we demand from a state? What do we propose to consider as the legitimate aim of state activity? Why do we prefer living in a well ordered state, to living without a state, i.e. in anarchy?' He believes this 'to be a rational way of asking this question, and that it is a question which a technologist must try to answer, for only if he knows what he wants can he decide whether a certain institution is or is not well adapted to its function'. Now this is the very question facing the high police official when seeking to discover whether a particular police

institution is well adapted to producing a well ordered society. A humanitarian, and we hope that our high police officials are humanitarian, would answer, 'what I demand from the state is protection; not only for myself but for others too. I demand protection for my own freedom and for other people's'. Now I am glad to say that this is one case where the humanitarian philosopher's theory of protection is, by happy coincidence, the same as mine was when a high police practitioner, (see Alderson, 1979).

In practice, however, it is not easy to convince police practitioners that they are to protect an abstraction such as 'freedom', or, 'liberty'. But when speaking of freedom Popper wants us to know that he is ready to have his own freedom curtailed by the state, provided the freedom which remains is protected by the state. Thus, 'the fundamental purpose of the state' should be 'the protection of that freedom which does not harm other citizens'. And furthermore, any limitations put on the freedom of citizens should be put on as equally as possible. I agree with this entirely and as a high police practitioner sought to ensure that this principle was well understood by those for whom I was responsible. It is of great help to the high police leaders when fashioning their policies to have a theory permitting a rational approach to political challenge, i.e. 'from the point of view of a fairly clear and definite aim'. The theory we are discussing is characterised by the qualities of equalitarianism, individualism and protectionism against injustice; but in one of his more combative moods, Popper, in attacking Plato's theory of justice, sums up by saying:

> *we can say that Plato's theory of justice, as present in the Republic and later works, is a conscious attempt to get the better of the equalitarian, individualistic and protectionist tendencies of his time, and to re-establish the claims of tribalism by developing a totalitarian moral theory...and...in the cause of the totalitarian class rule of a naturally superior master race.*
>
> **(Popper, 1989: p 119)**

If we are to follow Popper's analysis here, it is the high police of the totalitarian state who may have more to gain from Plato than have those of liberal democracies, for whom Lycophron's protectionist contract should be the beacon.

We noted earlier that the theory of protectionism adumbrated the subsequent development of the social contract theory; therefore in what sense, if any, might it be said that policing can be described in social contractual terms?

The social contract theory and police

In embarking upon an examination of the social contract theory and its pertinence for policing, I must make it clear at the outset that I accept without demur the adverse criticism of the historicist theory of the social contract as offered, for example, by Hume and others. That is to say, the refutation of the idea that in natural law there existed in the mists of time, beyond which the memory of man runneth not, an original agreement between ruler and ruled. However, in a politically developed and plural society political ideas, nuances, and a vocabulary, are necessary to progress. It is to the notion of an implied contract, rather than the existence of an original contract arising from some historical binding agreement, that is worthy of its place in our political thinking. It is not necessary to rehearse the arguments of those theorists who in the past had to contend with the power of myths such as the divine right of kings. It is enough to accept that 'as a legal fiction to justify government, the theory of the social contract has some measure of truth', (Russell, 1961: p 610).

In Kantian terms, the original contract is not a principle explaining either the origin of civil society or the state; but rather the principle of political government which deals with ideals of legislation and legal justice as well as administration.

The high police person facing this situation is searching for principles with which to explain the police task, or mission. Such a person is first of all faced with the need to discover a moral purpose, in order to explain such a purpose to those in his institution. The question of this moral purpose will need to be addressed in due course. What has now to be addressed is the notion that a contractual relationship of one form or another exists in most, if not in all societies between persons inter se, and between persons and those who exercise the power of government over them.

In the 1994 United States Congressional elections, the Republican Party published its manifesto called, *Republican Contract with America*, in which it promised to do many things if elected. These included 'The Taking Back Our Streets Act'; an anti-crime package including stronger truth-in-sentencing, 'good faith' exclusionary rule exemptions, effective death penalty provisions, and cuts in social spending from this summer's 'crime' bill to fund prison construction and additional law enforcement to keep people secure in their neighbourhoods and kids safe in their schools'.

The so-called *Contract with America* concluded with these words: 'Respecting the judgement of our fellow citizens, we seek their mandate for reform, we hereby pledge our names to this "Contract with America" '.

Around the same time as the US case, the various parties involved in the Algerian political crisis were meeting in Rome in order to seek a way out of the bloody impasse which agonised Algerian society. The Algerian delegates of the parties involved published the results of their findings for a pathway to peace and order in the country, which they called, 'a platform for a Peaceful Political Solution of Algeria's Crisis; or a national Contract'. This document includes sections on, 'Framework; values and principles'; 'Rejection of Violence as a means of acceding, or maintaining power'; and it deals with issues of political pluralism, universal suffrage and other political issues, (RIIA, 1995).

Though some philosophers dispute the theoretical basis for the social contract, nevertheless, acceptance of the ideas as being some form of 'legal fiction' is of political utility when discussing and carrying on government. Thus it would seem from the United States and Algerian examples quoted above, that the vocabulary of politics finds a ready use for the language and meaning of the social contract theory. In his famous work, *Ancient Law*, Sir Henry Maine referred to what philosophers called the social contract as a theory 'which, although nursed into importance by political passions, derived all its sap from speculations of lawyers', (Maine, 1917). He goes on to castigate some political philosophers, notably Rousseau, and particularly the idea that man in a state of nature had achieved the 'social compact as an historical fact'. We agree with Maine on this, and are prepared to view the theory as, 'an ingenious hypothesis, or a convenient verbal formula'.

The high police person would be aware of the nature of the law of contract and the idea that obligations are imposed upon the parties to it. More explicitly, it is one of my main concerns to stress the importance of moral obligations and liabilities arising from the social contract theory as we assess them for their relevance to policing. Maine ascribes it all to the genius of Roman Law, and believes that, 'the positive duty resulting from one man's reliance on the word of another, is amongst the slowest conquests of advancing civilisation', and 'that the movement of progressive societies has hitherto been a movement from status to contract', (ibid.: p 100). As police come to understand the Kantian doctrine of the dignity of the person, it may be to mutual advantage to accede to the notion that the people upon whom they exercise their power, or those for whom they are exercising it, stand in the kind of implied contractual relationship which calls for moral, ethical standards of behaviour, with which to characterise the exercise of their legal power.

So far, we have discovered a political theory of a contractual nature which causes the state, and we may add civil society where it exists, to be a 'co-operative association for the prevention of crime', and to regard the law of the state as a 'covenant by which men assure one another of justice'. And all this, to be characterised by dimensions of equalitarianism, and individualism. It is at this juncture that the high police have to face what is meant by the term 'justice'. But before doing so, we should not leave the social contract theory without giving Popper the opportunity to explain why he believes a social contract theory in Lycophron's terms 'is the most fitting expression of the humanitarian and equalitarian movement of the Periclean age', (Popper, 1989: p 115).

It is a contract theory which is secure from the objections to which the historicist theory is exposed, and this is because in the first place Lycophron makes no mention of the idea that a contract existed according to natural law. If Maine is right, then the concept of 'a contract' had not yet been developed by the Roman lawyers, which he believes gave politicians the notion which they later exploited.

Lycophron's protectionist theory being equalitarian and individualist, offended Plato's theory of society based on class, and according to Popper, 'we have been robbed of it'. Protectionism is not a selfish theory, since it applies to each and every person, and not to self-protection only. To protect the weak from being bullied by the strong is a moral obligation with contractual implications, and if Popper is right, as surely he must be, then principled policing has a moral obligation to the protectionist theory, and is obliged by social contractual terms to carry it out. We shall notice further revival of support for the social contract theory when we come to consider modern versions in the works of John Rawls under 'Justice as Fairness'.

Justice

I was once confronted by the ire of a Judge of the High Court of England who rejected anything to do with metaphysical notions such as 'justice'. To say that I was astonished is putting it mildly.

Perhaps he was of the school of legal positivism, which whilst having its own adherents, is not what I would imagine a high police officer in pursuit of the wider social and moral sensitivities surrounding the policing function is looking for. The idea of 'justice' has to be considered very carefully and seriously by high police officials responsible for enlightening members of their organisation concerning criminal justice. So, it is prudent to enquire what connection there may be between distributive justice and criminal justice. Would a society, or part of it, being denied distributive justice present more problems for policing? There is plenty of historical evidence that it would.

The very roots of terrorism within a state can often be traced to distributive injustices. Minority rights, denied through discrimination on racial, ethnic, or religious grounds, are the most common causes of terrorism, to combat which the high police have to develop policies and strategies which rely on force, and sometimes on Draconian legal measures. These measures have included detention without trial, criminal courts without juries, and forcible restriction and geographical confinement, and internal exile. The whole dreadful saga of the Gulag Archipelago of the Soviet Union under Stalin is so eloquently and passionately portrayed by Alexander Solzhenitsyn in his voluminous work of that name. Such extreme police measures amount to injustice rather than to justice.

But what is 'justice'? 'This question can be just as perplexing for a jurist as the well known question, "what is the truth?" is for the logician...', (Kant).

There are numerous answers (and much sophistry) to this question, which has occupied philosophers from Plato to the present time, with differing results. The policeman is not only concerned with what is called criminal justice, but also with what amounts to criminal justice. To begin with, we need to define the subject, and to do so I intend to draw on the work of John Rawls, (1973), whose modern treatment of it is comprehensive, and respected. High police should have regard to his work in which he describes justice as fairness, and the first virtue of social institutions. Much of his philosophy is sympathetic to the social contract theory of government.

Justice as Fairness

At the outset it must be made clear that John Rawls' theory of justice as fairness is the result of lengthy and voluminous exposition, and that any attempt to reduce it to short commentary cannot work. It is worthy of note however, that he throws down the gauntlet to the utilitarians in the name of justice as fairness, and this alone is an important episode in moral philosophy. Rawls insists that justice in the widest sense of the meaning of the term is the first claim on governmental institutions, and this concept conflicts at the outset with the utilitarian idea that all that matters is the greatest happiness of the greatest number. People live in society in a relationship contractual in form which insists on the moral criteria of rights and duties. But in spite of not being able to treat Rawls in a comprehensive way, it is very important to take notice here of his two principles of justice for institutions, since policing of a society requires that when social strategies and public order are under consideration, these principles of justice as fairness might be brought into use, (Rawls, 1973: p 3, *et seq*).

The First Principle is that each person shall have an equal right to the most extensive total system of equal basic liberties compatible with a system of liberty for all. An understanding of the social implications of this First Principle is required by high police, since it is not only morally correct under the equalitarian principle, but those societies which are in blatant disregard of it face problems of social unrest and potential, or actual disorder.

The Second Principle concerns social and economic inequalities, and Rawls' attempt to justify those which are inevitable, and how to deal with those which are not. It is his 'Priority Rules' which have the greatest relevance for police.

His first priority rule requires that the principles of justice are to be ranked in lexical order, and therefore liberty can be restricted only for the sake of liberty, (c.f. Kant and Popper). There are two cases:

a) a less extensive liberty shared by all:

b) a less than equal liberty must be acceptable to those with the lesser liberty.

a) would cover judicial imprisonment of the dangerous and **b)** the voluntary restrictions accepted in the private lives of those belonging to organisations such as police, military, religious order, and so on.

His second priority rule, the priority of justice over efficiency and welfare, is primarily concerned with the distribution of economic and other goods, but as a principle it can have

relevance to the policing of a society in that justice cannot be sacrificed in the cause of efficient criminal investigation and prosecution.

Finally it is worthy of note that what Rawls calls the General Conception means, 'all social primary goods—liberty and opportunity, income and wealth, and the bases of self-respect—are to be distributed equally, unless an unequal distribution of any or all of these goods is to the advantage of the least favoured'. All this seems to differ from the social morality of utilitarianism.

Rawls' formula calls for a situation in which policing policies reflect the paramountcy of liberty rather than reflecting the priority of power. Power should only be applied to enhance liberty, and the liberty of a few may have to be restricted for the freedom of the many provided that such arrangements comply with the equalisation principle.

This would apply, for example, to requirements to drive on one side of the road to avoid doing harm to others. A more controversial restriction of liberty in the United States would be to diminish the liberty to possess firearms, a right which is claimed under the Constitution, since privately held firearms damage the liberties of many innocent victims, thus denying them their freedom.

The ideal situation for police is one in which they are able to operate in a just manner in a just society. If operating in what is generally a just society it is possible, to some extent, to ameliorate a degree of injustice by using discretion, in those police systems which permit such discretion, for some do not, and not enforcing laws generally regarded as unjust, e.g. through desuetude. Care has to be taken however not to be in neglect of duty through failing to fulfil the will of the Legislature. This is a difficult line for police to tread, and it should be trodden with great care. High police officials will realise that the repeal or amendment of archaic and unjust laws is a matter for the political process. The situation presents a moral dilemma. In a liberal democracy police may not take an active role in the politics of parties. Police can only justify involvement in law reform through constitutional channels, and particularly where unjust laws are considered to be in conflict with the constitution.

Police are sometimes presented with an opportunity to exert pressure on the system of laws by putting them to the test; this is particularly the case where the law may be uncertain. Such an opportunity presented itself to me in 1981. I need not dwell on the case at length since it is fully dealt with in the law reports, and legal text books, (3 WLR, 961).

The Central Electricity Generating Board, a nationalised industry, sought to test a site within my jurisdiction for a nuclear power station. Peaceful protests ensued, and the farmers owning the land, and who had objected to this exploration, were neutralised by being served with High Court injunctions, as were many local residents. Other protesters arrived from elsewhere and obstructed the vehicles and machinery of the Board on what was private land, the owners of which did not declare them to be trespassers. The Board sought to persuade me, and my officers, as constables with power, to arrest the protesters, deeming them to be in breach of the criminal law. I refused to do this on the grounds that I was exercising my discretion not to arrest as the law was not clear. Subsequent appeals to the High Court and later to the Court of Appeal for an Order of Mandamus failed. In effect the Board were told to exercise their own powers at common law, which they declined to do. Although the entire operation lasted for six months, no persons were arrested, injured or assaulted. Had the police taken a more heavy hand to this situation, injustice and anger may have been aroused. It seems that this is a situation fitting Rawls' principle of liberty, that justice comes before efficiency.

I think it important for high police to address the question of the two justices, namely distributive and retributive justice and their relationship.

Rawls stresses, and I fully accept both the logic of his position and its relevance to my experience, that the basic structure of society and the way in which major social institutions should provide for fundamental rights and duties is the key to distributive justice, and to prospects of the peace. After all, 'in justice as fairness society is interpreted as a co-operative venture for mutual advantage', and any markedly unjust distribution of fundamental social assets would tend to the vitiation of the social contract involved. Once freed from the moral obligation of mutual co-operation, behaviour which is inimical to a well-ordered society is, from experience, predictable, and police contingency planners would be well advised to understand this, and to warn governments accordingly. The high police leader will need to consider any relationship there may be between distributive and retributive justice, since distributive injustice, if marked and obvious, may lead to

public disorder, crime, insurrection, and even to terrorism. One only has to read the daily newspapers, or listen to news reports, to find confirmation of the truth of this. Rawls says:

> *...it is true that in a reasonably well-ordered society those who are punished for violating just laws have normally done something wrong. Of course such a society, like any society, has to have a system of punishment for wrong-doing in order to uphold basic natural duties.*
>
> **(Rawls, 1973)**

The distribution of social and economic goods is another matter, 'the arrangements are not the converse so to speak, or the criminal law so that just as the one punishes certain offences the other rewards moral worth', (ibid.: pp 314–315). Criminal justice is not fully realisable since it admits of acquittal of the guilty, and from time to time conviction of the innocent, since the system can only arrive at decisions through the evidence and rules constructed for its purpose; it must always remain flawed and imperfect. This is what Rawls describes as a partial compliance theory. There is no such fundamental flaw in the theory of distributive justice which 'belongs to strict compliance theory and so to consideration of the ideal'.

Kant, Justice and Police

Kant is very helpful to the police where he addresses the questions of the use of coercion, and of justice, (Kant). Coercion is after all a central purpose, and not the only one, of the police arm of the state, or government. Now everything that is unjust is a hindrance to freedom, according to universal laws. Coercion, however, is a hindrance or opposition to freedom. Consequently, if a certain use of freedom is itself a hindrance to freedom according to universal laws (that is, is unjust) then the use of coercion to counteract it, inasmuch as it is the prevention of hindrance to freedom, is consistent with freedom according to universal laws; in other words, this use of coercion is just. It follows by the law of contradiction that justice (a right) is united with the authorisation to use coercion against anyone who violates justice (or a right). This equates with Popper's comment, that the fundamental purpose of the state, and therefore police state, should be the protection of that freedom which does not harm other citizens. When we set this test against police excesses which around the world deny freedom, we are able to talk of police as either handmaidens of justice, or of injustice. The high police have to face this: they are either just, therefore morally to be approved of, or unjust, and to be morally condemned. This point has to be taken one step further to the stage where any restrictions on freedom, which pass the preceding test of just coercion, must be applied equally, or if applied unequally, it would have passed the test of just coercion in design, only to fail as unjust in its application.

At this stage it may occur to the enquirer that freedom is dependent on the rule of law, but to answer that point we need to ask what is 'the rule of law'? since we have already noted that laws may be either unjust for various reasons, and in themselves may be unjustly enforced, e.g. with partiality.

The Rule of Law

In considering whether coercive police action is moral therefore, even when it accords with the so-called 'rule of law', we need further clarification of what might be a rule of law which is morally just. In English constitutional law, according to Dicey:

> ...it means in the first place the absolute supremacy or predominance of the regular law as opposed to the influence of arbitrary power, and excludes the existence of arbitrariness, of prerogative or even of wide discretionary authority on the part of the government.
>
> (Dicey, 1997: p 187)

This principle should motivate police to defend freedom through laws, since to do otherwise is to act unjustly and unconstitutionally.

Dicey's second point is that the rule of law 'means, again, equality before the law, or the equal subjection of all classes to the ordinary law of the land administered by the ordinary law courts'.

This ensures that police and other public officials, are not exempt from the duty of obedience to the same laws as are other citizens.

Dicey's last point is a formula for expressing that the laws of the constitution, which in some countries are part of a constitutional code, are, in Great Britain, 'are not the source but the consequence of the rights of individuals as defined and enforced by the courts', and thus the constitution is the law. But this is not enough. Dicey leaves us short of the idea of the justice and morality of laws. After all, there may be a duty of civil disobedience as a moral reflex to

unjust laws, and this places great strain on the morality of the police function.

According to Fuller, (1967), there is what he would describe as the 'inner morality of law' and he goes on to argue for the 'rule of law' to be prospective in its effect with no retrospective legislation making past actions into new crimes. Laws should be extant, comprising general rules, but not to be vague, so that people have to know what the laws are saying if they are to comply. Laws should embody constancy and not caprice; laws should be capable of compliance so as not to punish people for failing to do the impossible; lastly, police and other government officials stand in the same position as to the laws as do the general public.

The high police official in the Federal Republic of Germany would know that Article 1 of the Constitution of that Republic concerns the protection of human dignity, viz. 'the dignity of man shall be inviolable. To respect and protect it shall be the duty of all state authority.' The police leader would then have a duty to translate the idea of the rule of law, and the dignity of the individual into policies for the direction and conduct of police. But it is no longer sufficient to regard the rule of law as restricted to the domestic state. International law requires that police officials comply with certain international treaties and conventions which, in some parts of the world, notably those countries belonging to the Council of Europe, have as strong a duty to the rule of law embodying the Convention on Human Rights, as to their domestic laws. The European Convention on Human Rights and Fundamental Freedoms requires that states which are parties to the convention, shall acknowledge the jurisdiction of the Commission and Court of the Council of Europe. This body of law is designed to produce certain standards of behaviour affecting police as well as other governmental officials.

Summary

We have now reached the stage where this commentary on the science and art of policing might be assessed for its utility when setting principles, standards and goals for the organisation. In other words we have discussed some of the philosophical theories which may have relevance to the police function.

In our brush with utilitarianism, it failed to recommend itself as the guiding theory of police, due largely to moral ethical uncertainties, though police service can contribute to aspects of the doctrine.

Through Popper we have acquired the theory of protectionism based on his assessment of Lycophron's ideas: the law is a 'covenant by which men assure one another of justice'; and the state is 'a co-operative association for the prevention of crime'. Popper also posed the question for police leaders, 'only if he knows what he wants can he decide whether (his institution) is or is not well adapted to its function'. He further demands 'protection' for his own freedom (individualism) and for 'other people's freedoms' (altruism).

The freedom which is to be protected, is that which 'does not harm other citizens'; and all this is to be characterised by 'the qualities of equalitarianism, individualism, and protectionism against injustice'.

In considering the theory of the social contract, which in its particular form Popper claims the primacy for Lycophron, we accepted the criticism of the historicist theory by Hume and others. On the other hand Russell tells us that, 'the theory has some measure of truth' as 'a legal fiction to justify government'.

Justice as fairness, raised by Rawls, is of prime concern to the high police if they are to understand many of the politics surrounding their place in the order of things. Kant's explanation of just coercion, reinforced by Popper's comments, is of central importance, as is the rule of law especially when it is endowed by constitutional and moral rectitude.

So, it might be said that the primary and guiding political principles of police should be concerned with, and directed towards the theory of the common good of society.

The aim of police is not to enforce the law and coerce the people for its own sake, but to do so for the common good, and that is a good which places freedom above all other political values. Duties are important but they arise only out of freedom. As Kant insists, there can be no sacrifice of the dignity of persons for the benefit of others, even though the 'others' are powerful and influential, since if this were to be the case there is no good which is common, and the principle of equalitarianism would have been denied. When we speak of 'keeping the peace' which is an ancient and joint responsibility of government and people in the common law, an express contract, we have the common good in mind, since the peace facilitates freedom for all.

Police may also be expected to protect the common good against the actions of the more powerful, or numerous. An example might be where the common good requires that every person who wishes to go to a place of employment, should have the right to do so, which, during a trade dispute others seek to stop. It is in the common good, even of the pro tem pickets themselves, that the right to go to work be upheld.

It may also be said that freedom of speech and assembly are common goods, and should be protected, even, or especially, where the purpose is for protest, be it vehement and controversial. Thus what are called 'extremists' have a right to hold their views and to express them, though this is subject to limitations for the common good. The point at which a narrow common good becomes harmful to the wider common good of society, e.g. in the form of provocation of disorder and violence, calls for a nice sense of judgement, but police are required to have this, and to act accordingly.

Man, we know, is essentially a social animal, and therefore some notion of common good is an imperative both for happy survival, and of civilisation. Since by its nature the common good is to protect individual rights there is no conflict between the concept, and the plural society.

The police function might best be understood, and articulated through the philosophical theory of the social contract, even conceding that neither it, nor other theories of government, are likely to offer the perfect answer. At the end of the day, as Clausewitz reminds us, in the practical arts, it is 'experience which is their proper soil'.

Finally we are able to synthesise three elements we have considered which appear to support the theory of principled policing. These are the *social contract theory* as advanced by Rawls' conception of 'Justice as Fairness'; the second is *the theory of protectionism* through Popper, and the third is the *theory of policing the common good* as projected herein.

Although the theory of the social contract as an abstract idea might remain unchangeable, its terms or contents cannot do so, for they must change as societies change. Thus the terms of the social contract in the former USSR were markedly different from those which now exist in the new liberal democracies, which have emerged from the Soviet bloc. Amongst the most important of these changes would be the principles of policing, particularly in relation to freedom, and the remit and powers of the secret police. Further strengthening of the contractarian society is likely to emerge from the growing characteristics of civil society.

Even in liberal democracies, in recent times, many adjustments to the terms of the social contract have had to be made to ensure justice keeps pace with plural and multi-racial characteristics. For example, policing principles have been required to adjust to protect minorities from discrimination, and to protect the legitimate expectations of justice for women. The importance of all this, with more change ahead, is to be a constant claim on the co-operation and morality of people and government. Constant attention to the ideals of the theoretical contract is also a test for the efficiency of developing policing from principles.

Not only do the terms of the contract change, but the frontiers also. There is a constant process of expansion to bring within its moral compass the alienated, and the 'barbarians'. There is now a contract to deal with the whole human family within the terms of the Universal Declaration of Human Rights, and, for example, to prosecute war criminals through an international social contract theory.

The role of police in its widest moral sense can be conceived as advancing and facilitating contractarian purposes, not in a purely theoretical way as philosophers, or in a remote prescriptive way as legislators, but in a practical way within the actual life of society day by day. Police have to expect not simply to be called upon to exercise force, but to acquire an understanding of how to deal with people constructively in their role as trustees of the social contract, establishing co-operation and morality based on justice as fairness.

Protection of contractarian freedoms would rest on the theory of protectionism as described by Popper, the principles of which are equalitarianism, individualism and protectionism from injustice which must be central to the morality of principled policing.

The police function should be based on the notion and principle of trusteeship. Trusteeship carries with it moral obligations such as those of honourable and ethical conduct in the application of power and authority. As trustees under the social contract police are required to use their position 'constructively'.

References

Alderson, J. (1979). *Policing Freedom*. Plymouth: Macdonald and Evans.

Alderson, J. (1984). *Human Rights and Police*. Strasbourg: for the Council of Europe.

Alderson, J. (1984). *Law and Disorder*. Hamish Hamilton.

Browning, C.K. (1992). *Ordinary Men*. New York: Harper Collins.

Bullock, A. (1963). *Hitler: A Study in Tyranny*. London: Penguin.

Dicey, A.V. (1997). *An Introduction to the Law of the Constitution*, 10th edn. London: Macmillan.

Fuller, L.L. (1967). *The Morality of Law*, Revised edn. Yale University Press.

Hare, R.M. (1981). *Moral Thinking*. Oxford University Press.

Hudson, W.D. (1980). *A Century of Moral Philosophy*. London: Lutterworth Press.

Hudson, W.D. (1983). *Modern Moral Philosophy*, 2nd edn. London: Macmillan.

Maine, Sir H. (1917). *Ancient Law*. London: Dent.

Oxford University Press (1994). *Oxford Dictionary of Philosophy*. Oxford University Press.

Popper, K.R. (1989). *The Open Society and its Enemies*. London: Routledge.

Rawls, J.A. (1973). *Theory of Justice*. Oxford University Press.

Royal Institute of International Affairs (1995). *International Affairs*, Vol. 72: No. 2; April.

Russell, B. (1961). *History of Western Philosophy*. London: Unwin.

Sabine, G.H. (1971). *A History of Political Theory*. London: Harrap.

The Today Newspaper, 20 May, 1995.

Williams, B. (1972). *Morality An Introduction to Ethics*. Cambridge University Press.